I Once Knew a Guy Named Charlie

I Once Knew a Guy Named Charlie

A Memoir

JACLYN SMITH

GALLERY BOOKS

New York Amsterdam/Antwerp London
Toronto Sydney/Melbourne New Delhi

Gallery Books
An Imprint of Simon & Schuster, LLC
1230 Avenue of the Americas
New York, NY 10020

First Gallery Books hardcover edition September 2026

GALLERY BOOKS and colophon are registered trademarks of Simon & Schuster, LLC

Interior design by Jaime Putorti

Manufactured in the United States of America

10 9 8 7 6 5 4 3 2 1

Library of Congress Control Number: 2026943820

ISBN 978-1-9821-1664-4
ISBN 978-1-9821-1666-8 (ebook)

To the loves of my life, Brad, Gaston, and Spencer-Margaret

And to my granddaughters, Bea, Olivia, and Wren,

who continue to invite me to the dance

Introduction

I wasn't born the day I first put on Kelly Garrett's tiny white bikini. I came into the limelight with a grounded sense of self. As I've come to learn, in Hollywood that's a rare and precious gift for an actor. After *Charlie's Angels*, fame came quickly, but it never defined the whole of me. It was after the fanfare that life revealed its truest shape.

It's incredible to me that a show that first aired more than fifty years ago and lasted just five seasons still remains a touchstone for so many. You might not think an hour-long drama about three female detectives who yelled "Freeze!" while running down the streets of Los Angeles in wedge heels, hair flying, prop guns drawn, would have half a century's worth of cultural staying power. At the time, I knew we were doing something novel, but I didn't know just how much it would impact so many people's lives. I'll always be grateful I got to play a part in something so special. It's been a great gift to have been one of the original Angels—along with Farrah Fawcett and Kate Jackson—and the only one to appear in every episode. When we started, we were just three women doing our jobs, trusting we'd find an audience. And boy, did we.

It might seem a mystery why such a show captured the imaginations of so many viewers for so long. Certainly there are the obvious reasons: The concept was novel, the writing was fun, the fashion was phenomenal—and, of course, let's not forget the hair. But to me, the real magic of *Charlie's Angels* comes down to the core message: that when women work together, there's no stopping us.

The Angels moved through the world together, competent and fearless, bound by loyalty rather than romance, beauty rather than apology. We were a sisterhood, and when it came to the original Angels, that sisterhood was very real. It possessed a kind of permanence that kept Farrah, Kate, and me in touch over these many long years. It outlasted ratings and headlines. I've also enjoyed a lifelong friendship with Cheryl Ladd. And I think that, more than just enjoying a show about three female detectives, viewers responded to seeing women walk through the world differently, as confident allies.

I'm flattered and awed by the ongoing interest in *Charlie's Angels*. If not for its success and my part in it, my life would not have unfolded in the same way. *Charlie's* was a launchpad for my career as an actor and as a businesswoman. It's my biggest claim to fame and has certainly helped define me as an actor. But there was also a prequel to that part of my life and, fortunately for me, a very long sequel.

I was thirty years old when the pilot debuted on ABC in September 1976. I'd spent the previous years working as a professional dancer and a model. My face had been appearing in glossy magazines and on TV screens for a decade. I'd already been married and divorced and had experienced the devastating loss of my beloved grandfather.

After *Charlie's*, I went on to star in many films and TV shows. I'm truly grateful to have shared the screen with so many incredible actors and worked with some of the best writers, directors, and cinematographers in the business. And when the right part comes up, I'm still happy to step in front of the camera today.

No question, it's been an amazing journey. But beyond the fanfare, there is a simpler landscape that holds my true story. For much of my life, both professionally and personally, I've been cast as a bit of a Goody Two-shoes (somehow in spite of all those steamy sex scenes I've done). People have often looked at the persona shared in the papers—this woman who supposedly moves through life with ease—and thought, *That can't be real.* It's true that I've never gotten into drugs or alcohol, that I never ran around in my relationships or fell into any of the other traps that befall so many, especially in Hollywood. And when I talk about my idyllic childhood, my love of Texas, and the homespun values I carry with me to this day, it's easy to see a naïve girl who fell off the turnip truck and never quite woke up to the world as it really is. Until now, I've never really opened up about some of the challenges I've endured. Not because I was trying to hide them but because I've always been a private person and protective of my family.

People have long asked me to share behind-the-scenes stories, and in these pages you will find plenty. But there's another goal I had in writing this book, and that's to finally let others see the person beyond. I've always been honest about who I am—the me you've seen in the papers and interviews *is* real. Here, I wanted to go not just behind the scenes of my shows and movies, but into a deeper place: my heart.

I've often been asked how I've stayed "nice" in Hollywood, when celebrity and fame can bring you down. For sure, it hasn't always been easy. Fame complicates. It can separate you from others, and from yourself. Fame gives and it takes, often without you knowing. For me, the secret to staying grounded (or trying to, at least) is to go back to my upbringing and the values my parents gave me.

I've learned, much to my chagrin, that in this life we all experience loss. There's just no escaping it. The quest is to keep an open heart. To not let life's hurts shut you down or make you bitter, but to keep loving in spite of them. How do you do that? Well, that's something I've spent literally a lifetime learning.

And it all started in Texas. . . .

Chapter One

Before I was an actor, or a dancer, or even just a little girl with big dreams, I was a Texan. Even though I've lived in California far longer than I ever spent in the Lone Star State, I still consider Houston home. Yet it's a home I can't go back to. It's still gorgeous, still full of that same Texas shine, but in many ways it's also a ghost town to me, every street and corner whispering stories of what once was but can never be again. Every place I turn overflows with memories but is devoid of the people who made them. Growing up, I was loved so fully and so well by my family that Houston simply withers in their absence. So I visit Houston in my memories. It's like a series of Kodachrome photos in my mind. Home, I have learned, is not erased by distance. It is carried intact, incorruptible, somewhere deep inside me. When the present becomes noisy or unmanageable, I return without effort to the Houston of my childhood, a place preserved with unnatural clarity: sunlit streets, familiar corners, and the deep reassurance that, at its core, the world is kind.

My parents' first gift to me was my name: Jaclyn Ellen. Ellen was my mother's middle name, and Jack was my dad's name. So I was named after both of them. As a little girl, I didn't like Jackie, so I went by Ellen or El. My Texas friends and family still call me El. My parents were the most down-to-earth people in the world. Daddy was strong, ethical, and fair. And Mom was the goddess of love and fun. I like to think that I embody some of the best qualities of each, but it's an aspiration that, in my ninth decade of life, I'm still trying to live up to.

I always refer to my early years as enchanted, maybe because I grew up in a ranch-style house on Tartan Lane in a subdivision called Emerald Forest. I know how perfect that all sounds. People often tell me it sounds like I grew up in a fairy tale, but the truth is, no one's childhood is devoid of pain. Nor, I suppose, is any fairy tale—at least, not the original version. Innocence is lost, learning is hard-won, and happy endings come only after a series of challenges and obstacles. So it was for me. But the enchantment? That was real.

I was born in 1945, at a time before the world felt endlessly complicated. World War II had ended the month before I was born, and a sense of hope and optimism pervaded the air. Houston was a city with a small-town feeling, where men wore suits and white shirts with ties and neighborhoods had houses with big yards and paved driveways that we'd ride our bicycles up and down. I knew who lived in every house on the block. We played jacks, hopscotch, and jump rope on the street. I would cycle around the neighborhood on my blue-and-white Schwinn for hours, stopping only for the Popsicle man. When the sun started to set, I knew it was time to head home. That was the rule. Those times when we went downtown, riding on the bus seemed like we were really going somewhere. On Saturdays, we went to the Village Theatre for Fun Club, a kids' event where they'd show serials, cartoons, and some feature-length films of the swashbuckling type, or maybe the Three Stooges. At Christmas there were games where you could win a prize.

It was a time when I was discovering what I wanted from the world, inventing all kinds of scenarios. When I was a kid, my dreams were simple. I wanted a horse and a house with a winding staircase, like the one at Twelve Oaks in the movie *Gone with the Wind.* And I wanted the people I loved to be happy.

My mother, Margaret Ellen, was a devoted caregiver who always put her family first. She had a talent for happiness and boundless energy, and she gave limitlessly to my older brother, Tommy, and me. I remember how when I was a child, wherever we were, people gravitated toward her. They all wanted to be her friend. Even with her gentle demeanor, though, Mom had fire in her, and she didn't always follow social dictates. When her first husband turned out to be a crushing disappointment because of infidelity, she got out of that marriage despite the stigma of divorce at that time. Many women would have stuck it out and suffered in silence. Not Mom. She did what was best for her and her son.

Mom was stunning and stylish, with her auburn hair, riveting green eyes, and tall frame. Before I was born, a talent scout noticed her and ended up offering her a contract with Twentieth Century Fox, but she turned it down. She was a bit shy with people until she knew them, and Hollywood just wasn't her thing.

She had an innate sense of fashion and, to me, she radiated glamour. Her use of accessories was magic, and she adorned our home similarly, with warm, thoughtful touches. Her love of beauty was something we shared. As a child I was obsessed with dolls, and I spent a lot of energy and thought on arranging them on my bed and decorating my room to all "our" liking. Tastes change frequently when you're six, so every month or two, I'd set about redoing my room: rearranging my toys, moving the furniture around, and imploring my mom for new bedspreads and accent pieces. She didn't always give in—if she had, we'd have gone broke! But she understood. She recognized a kindred spirit in me, and we'd have so much fun window-shopping for new bedding, curtains, or rugs. My grandfather, whom I called Papa (pronounced *paw-paw*), would look at us and exclaim, "I declare, you and Margaret Ellen can trade *anywhere*!" He was right—we could treat a five-and-dime like it was Bergdorf Goodman.

Like Mom, I was inspired by whatever I was exposed to. After we visited Mount Vernon, George Washington's home in Virginia, I became fixated on a four-poster canopy bed I had seen there. I talked about that bed constantly, to the amazement of every adult I came into contact with. But my mother understood. She asked, "Are you sure you want it?"

"Yes!" I exclaimed.

She laughed and nodded. "Well, maybe for your birthday or Christmas." I nearly exploded with joy when they finally bought a four-poster for me. Mom and I went shopping for fabric and found a beautiful old pale-blue bedspread with champagne-colored lace insets, which we turned into a canopy for the bed. We carefully took off the lace and sewed it back on around the edges of the canopy, and we did some ruching across the spread with other fabric we'd found. We delighted in the details and the fact that we'd done it all ourselves. My mother encouraged any kind of creativity; we spent countless hours doing projects together.

When I was seven or eight, Mom took me to see *Gone with the Wind.* As we exited the theater, I said to my mother, "Remember that rug at the bottom of the grand staircase at Twelve Oaks? What kind of rug was that?"

Mom turned to me, eyebrows raised. "You just watched that whole movie and the one thing you zeroed in on was the *rug*?"

It was a really beautiful rug. An Aubusson. I had also noticed the gowns. I became captivated with *Gone with the Wind* and believed that I *was* Scarlett O'Hara. I must have seen it twenty times in the span of a few years. I remember daydreaming about Scarlett's gowns while running errands with Mom. She'd ask, "What are you thinking about?"

"The dress that Scarlett wore to the picnic at Twelve Oaks," I replied. It had a ruffled off-the-shoulder neckline, a voluminous skirt in white toile with a hunter-green floral print, and a dark-green ribbon sash around her eighteen-inch waist.

A short time later, Mom took me to the fabric store and we found a close-enough match to the garden party toile. Then we went home and designed a dress pattern for me, and Mom got a local dressmaker, Mrs. Rascal, to put it all together. I wore that dress like I was the Queen of the South, even if it was just around my own house.

But Mom was the true queen of our home. Whatever she chose to wear, she stood out. I think she really wanted to be a dress designer, but instead she built her life around her family. I was in awe of her, proud of her popularity with others, while knowing that her family was what she cared about the most.

My mother delighted in her children. We tend to assume that *mother* means devotion, but my experience—having a mother who was so deeply engaged—was rare. (Like her, I've done my best to arrange my life around my children.) There was a genius about my mother, and it was in how she gave love. She had a presence and a way of talking to you that made you feel more important than anyone else in the room. Even if she was only making my breakfast, which she continued to do for me for forty years every time I visited home, she did it with the utmost care and joy. She not only made dinner, but she sat down and talked with us about what was going on with our school friends. She reveled in making sweet gestures, constantly thinking up ways to delight us. Even as an adult, when I came home for visits, there'd be a little surprise under my pillow or a new nightgown waiting on my bed. Our home was filled with all our favorite delicious treats, and my school lunches were things of legend. Sometimes I'd find a love note tucked under my sandwich. On Valentine's Day, long before Pinterest, when no one else was watching, she'd make heart-shaped sandwiches on pink bread. Mom made you feel loved without ever announcing her effort.

When I was growing up, Mom would always have candy all over the house, a box of chocolates by her bed, gumdrops in dishes. Access to sweet treats was a hallmark of our house—just one more way that Mom, with her talent for happiness, added sparkle and magic to our daily existence.

We were a family who celebrated, thanks largely to Mom. She could make a celebration out of a flower. On special days, she really went crazy. Birthdays were filled with balloons, party favors, and the most gorgeous cakes. At Halloween, we carved pumpkins and made costumes by hand. Our Christmases were marvels to behold. We made our own ornaments by taking Styrofoam balls and pinning sequins, beads, and pieces of jewelry onto them. I still have some of the ornaments I made as a little girl, and they go on our tree each year. Christmas carols played throughout the house, garlands were hung from every ceiling, and there was a wreath on every door.

We opened presents on Christmas morning, then hosted a holiday lunch for family and friends, the table buckling with roast turkey, ham, sweet potatoes with marshmallows, ambrosia, freshly made cranberry sauce, brussels sprouts, spinach soufflé, parsnips, and, most importantly, Mom's homemade corn bread dressing. Even after I left home in my twenties and even when my career took off, I always went home for the holidays. December is still my favorite month of the year.

Our Easter tradition was to make "Easter trees." We'd go outside, pick a nice, sturdy branch, and spray-paint it white. Then we'd cover eggshells with fabric and put little sewn chicks inside. We made pink felt bunnies and other beautiful, intricate things and glued them onto the white branches along with Easter candies. One year, we were sitting in the living room and I realized something was suddenly different about the Easter tree. Every branch was inexplicably bare. I said, "Mom, where is the candy?" She looked at it, and then we both turned to glare down at Mimi, our black standard poodle, who just sat there wagging her tail at us as if to say, "Thanks for the gumdrops!"

Mom made commonplace happiness come alive. Even today, her absence incorporates a presence. I sense her energy that never goes away. When I think of her and the home she created for us, the tears come fast, like I've saved them and can't hold them in anymore.

The very best thing about Mom was her gentle Southern drawl and how her words had the power to comfort me. When she said, "Everything's going to be all right," I believed her, for all my life.

My father's name was Jack but I called him Daddy, all the way until he died. He was a dentist, born in Pittsburgh, but you'd have been a fool to try to tell him that he wasn't Texan through and through. He thought it was the best place in the world, and of course that rubbed off on me. Maybe his unabashed love for the state of my birth was because that's where he met my mother. When their paths crossed and she looked on him favorably, it was like he won the lottery. It was a real love match, and he wooed her for the rest of his life.

Daddy's early life had been hard. When his father, Benjamin Kupferschmidt, arrived at Ellis Island from Germany in 1901, he didn't speak a word of English. He taught himself by reading a dictionary, learning a few new words each day. Like many immigrants, his family changed their name. It was for simplicity's sake, but also from an awareness of the prejudices that existed against Jewish people at the time (and that, sadly, continue among some today). And so it was that the Kupferschmidts became the Smiths.

Benjamin married a woman named Ann Feldman, and they brought six children into the world, including Daddy. But at some point Benjamin departed, leaving my grandmother to care for their three girls and three boys all on her own. Daddy used to tell me how hard it was to watch his mother struggle, and so, starting at age ten, he began selling newspapers to help out. I think that's one of the reasons he was such a present parent, not wanting to walk in the footsteps of his own father. Meanwhile, after his hard beginning assimilating in a new country, Benjamin went on to great success. In 1920 he founded Big Three Industries, a natural gas and machinery company that would eventually trade on the New York Stock Exchange and provide the nitrogen fuel to NASA for the first trip to the moon in 1969.

Unlike Daddy's brothers, who would join their father at BTI when they came of age, Daddy struck out on his own. At sixteen, he enrolled at Baylor College of Medicine in Houston and became a dentist. Though Daddy differentiated himself, he did share something in common with his father, and that was his work ethic. Whatever the task, Daddy always showed up and did the very best job he could, whether anyone was watching or not. It was just who he was, and it was something I wanted to emulate.

From the time I was a little girl, I wanted to contribute. I'd ask if I could sweep the driveway or clean the garage. My mother would ask me, "Honey, why do you want to work so much?" It was just in me. Still, I regret not taking my mother up on her encouragement to learn how to cook. To this day that's a skill set I have yet to master.

In my generation girls were raised to be wives and mothers, and without a doubt I wanted both of those things. But I also wanted something many of my friends didn't seem to be thinking about, and that was a career. I wanted to make my own way in the world. To have my own work. Maybe it was an unconscious desire to experience some of my mother's own unlived legacy—an opportunity to do some of the things she'd chosen not to. But without a doubt, I also wanted to be like Daddy.

Daddy was a thinker, brave, genuine, an honest-to-goodness pretension-free man. He was totally unbiased and willing to see the best in anyone. At the same time, if he had an opinion, he didn't hold back. Daddy was never cruel, and his intention was never to hurt anyone. He simply didn't mince words. Without a doubt, Daddy loved me like crazy, and I think his unfettered honesty was in some ways a form of love. He had a strong point of view and never tempered what he said. It was part of his integrity, and I admired him for his honesty and consistency.

My mother, by contrast, was rarely critical. I was raised by parents who loved me in different ways—one always took my side and the other told it to me straight. My mom smoothed the rough edges and Daddy provided plenty of backbone. Between them, they taught me how to navigate a world that would ask more of me than I ever imagined.

Whereas Mom was chic, Daddy was immaculate. Every morning, he'd head to his dental office in a crisp suit and tie. At the end of the day, he'd come home, take off his office wear, and put on a sport shirt—still very proper. Maybe some of his fastidiousness came from his time in the military. During World War II, he served in the navy. I have many photos of my dad in his uniform, tall and handsome with his dark hair and blue eyes.

To this day, I have a soft spot for dentists. Just the smell of a dentist's office makes me emotional, and not in the negative way most people feel about dentists! Not long after my father passed, I had to get some work done on my teeth. That dentist looked in my mouth and said, "Gold fillings. You don't see work like this anymore. Who did this for you?"

I paused and said, "Well, my dad." Then I burst into tears.

I've always been sensitive, and as a kid it wasn't a quality I was necessarily proud of. Being quick to cry was embarrassing, and I sometimes wished things wouldn't affect me so deeply. (They still do, but now I'm a bit less apologetic about my tears.) If I hurt someone else's feelings, even inadvertently, I felt *awful.* Back in one of my early ballet classes there was a girl who'd gotten ringworm, and it was so bad that her hair had to be shaved off. She wore a scarf on her head secured by a bobby pin. At one point while she was doing an arabesque, her carefully pinned scarf fell off, and everyone started laughing at her. My immediate reaction was to laugh along with them, but when I realized what I was doing, participating in her humiliation, I stopped immediately. I felt sick to my stomach, and after that the guilt just would not let me go. I kept seeing her face in my mind, thinking, *How could I have laughed at her?*

My mother didn't understand why I got so upset, but she assured me that everything would be okay. She had an uncomplicated view of the world. When I expressed embarrassment at my overactive conscience, Daddy would try to bolster me. "Don't be ashamed of an open heart," he'd say. "It's the most beautiful part of you."

I always say that Mom was the heart of the family, but Daddy had lots of it. He cut quite a figure in my young life, as did another man—my grandfather.

My mother was born in San Antonio and spent much of her childhood moving from one small Texas town to another, going wherever her father, Gaston Hartsfield, a Methodist minister, was called to serve. He was born in Alabama in 1877 but spent most of his lifetime—over a hundred years—in Texas. He lived on a farm, picked cotton, married a woman named Ethel Elise, and had two children, Mom and my uncle Warren. In that time he watched the world go from candlelight to electric light, from radio to TV, from the very first propeller plane to spaceships. He'd seen it all, and, as a great Southern orator and preacher, he had stories upon stories to tell, and I wanted to hear every one.

I was a child with a lot of questions. I wanted to know what was what and I didn't like to leave things to chance. Answers felt comforting, and I asked for them in abundance. My grandfather was always there to satisfy my curiosity. And I went straight for the biggies, asking things like "Papa, what's heaven like?" He said we were all going there someday, so I wanted to know what to expect! He'd always take his time to give me the clearest answer he could, and he never condescended to me.

Papa was also the one who helped me with my homework—when I did it. School wasn't my strongest subject. I'm only half joking when I say that—across the board it didn't hold much appeal for me, and I didn't see much of a point in homework. Papa tried to keep me on track. If I was struggling with something, he'd lean over, slide my book toward himself, and say, "Here, let me take a look at it." Back then adults didn't get as involved in kids' schoolwork, so the outcome was on us. But Papa didn't see the harm in helping me out, as he often did.

Papa was my very best friend, and he doted on me shamelessly. To me, he represented all that was good and right in this world, and I think others saw him similarly. As a minister, he walked the talk. He was generous and giving almost to a fault. (That "to a fault" part is something my daughter, Spencer-Margaret, accuses me of—

maybe I got it from Papa.) Papa's life was never about himself, and his faith never wavered. Instead, he stayed vigilant for ways he might be of service to others. Even after he broke his hip, I caught him rolling around in his wheelchair, trying to help clear the dinner table. "Papa," I'd tell him, "you're so good you make Jesus look bad!"

It wasn't just his behavior that stood out; Papa made a real visual impression as well. I loved the way he looked, with his sky-blue eyes and snow-white hair that always seemed perfectly in place. In the summer, he wore light-colored pinstripe suits with long-sleeved shirts and a straw hat, which he switched for a felt one in the winter. He was old-school in every way, elegant without trying, with those seersucker suits, a tie, and a hat angled just so. He'd always tip those hats to people in an old-fashioned gesture of acknowledgment.

Papa's laugh would make me want to follow him down whatever road he was going. We were constant partners in small adventures. He formed the basis of my first understanding of what love truly is: It's living beyond yourself. I spent a lifetime admiring him for his kindness. Papa was my pilot light. His default setting was open delight. He made you feel you were on your game.

My grandfather's kindness was not born out of naïveté or a pampered life. My grandmother, Ethel Elise, the love of his life, died of a cerebral hemorrhage when she was only fifty. Her sudden death was a shock to the whole family. I don't believe my mother ever completely got over it. A new widower, Papa appeared strong on the outside. He had a small family to hold together. But no matter how much self-control he mustered to contain the stress, anxiety, and depression, on the inside it overwhelmed him. He dealt with it in his way, though, not wanting to burden anyone.

Try as he might to convey a stable presence, my grandfather was understandably not himself, leaving my mom, at sixteen, and her brother, Warren, in his early twenties, to contend with a frightening new reality. They'd lost their mother, and their father was grief-stricken. They had no idea if he'd recover.

My mother's step-grandmother, whom everyone called Mamie, moved in to help my grandfather during this rocky time, and she became like a second mother to Mom and Uncle Warren. My mom took it upon herself to encourage Papa to get back to preaching, which he eventually did. Although my grandfather was in the prime of life when his wife died, he never remarried.

Still, for the rest of his life he was surrounded with love; I took it upon myself to provide much of it. I was the apple of Papa's eye, and he was the same for me.

Chapter Two

When Daddy returned to Houston after serving as a dentist in the navy at ports all over the world (including Hawaii and Ventura, California), he struck gold when he met my mother, Margaret Ellen, by then a divorcée with a young son, my brother, Tommy. He found something better than any horizon he had crossed. As he told her, "M.E., you've ruined a good war for me." They married in 1943 and in October 1945 had me. My mother already knew that if I was a girl, she'd name me after my father, and so it was that I became Jaclyn Ellen Smith.

Not all siblings welcome a new arrival, but six-year-old Tommy couldn't have been happier. From the moment I was born, he always looked after me, and I looked up to him. He was my model of loyalty. When I think of Tommy, I remember most clearly his hand extended toward me, steady, confident, as I climbed into tree houses, or onto bicycles, or into any situation I might otherwise have feared. That gesture—hand outstretched—was an element of how I understood love. It was protective. It was unwavering. It was our special language.

Tommy hung the moon. In my eyes, he could do absolutely anything. He amazed me with magic tricks and how he could fly his kite higher than anyone. After Christmas, when the trees came down, he would collect the discarded ones and build the most magical Christmas-tree fort. I can still smell that scent of pine. He also built a tree house that was the envy of every kid on the block, as high as the sky. Mom told me I wasn't allowed up there. I remember Tommy calling down to me to climb up to him. "But Mom said I couldn't," I answered, peering up the makeshift ladder he'd made by nailing small slats of wood into the side of the tree.

He smiled. "You can if I'm here," he said. "I'll protect you." And there was that hand reaching down to help me. I believed him.

Tommy's friendliness and talent made him well-liked by everyone, including kids his age and my mom's friends. Wherever we went as a family, people were drawn to Tommy, saying, "Isn't he the sweetest? Isn't he just the best?" I'll be honest: Sometimes that adoration was so intense, I felt like I was in Tommy's shadow. Not that he didn't deserve it, but it seemed like everyone, even my mom, favored Tommy. In her case, I think it was because she was trying to make up for the early abandonment he'd experienced from his biological father. Plus, my mother knew that from day one, I was Daddy's everything, so while they both loved each of us, it all evened out. After *Charlie's Angels*, Tommy joked that if I was in his shadow in childhood, in adulthood he was certainly in mine.

Tommy's biological father had disappeared when he was little, taking no role or interest in his son's life. Tommy grew up very much seeing Daddy as his father, which in all ways but biology was true. At some point, however, a cousin made an unkind announcement to Tommy, declaring, "That's not your real dad!" It was confusing for Tommy, but not nearly as confusing as when his biological father showed up out of nowhere when Tommy was thirteen, declaring he wanted a relationship with my brother. I remember my parents agonizing over whether it was all right to let Tommy's birth father see him. It was hard on Daddy to have this man want to come in and take over his role, and my mother worried over whether it was the best thing for Tommy. In the end, they decided to allow it. Just the fact of those conversations introduced me to the idea that love is sometimes thorny and difficult. Then it got even harder.

This man showed up like it was Christmas and tried to give Tommy the world, including a motor scooter! At some point, Tommy even took his last name, changing it from Smith to Beville. But then, just as suddenly, a few months later he disappeared again. We had no idea what had happened to him. Several more months passed, during which Tommy had left for military school. Then a notice arrived for him there in the mail saying that his biological father, who'd been a pilot, had died in a plane crash. It was shocking—but the worst part was, it wasn't even true. His birth father was alive. He'd simply made up the story because . . . well, who knows what he was thinking? I was confused and heartbroken for Tommy. Years later, when his birth father was dying, he reached back out to Tommy for help. Tommy took care of him until he passed away—a reflection of Tommy's character more than his father's. Tommy always walked on the side of the good guys. We may have had different fathers, but with us there was no "half." We were siblings through and through. Whatever divided us by blood was eclipsed by something stronger.

Tommy and I shared a lot growing up, including delightful summers on our family's farm in Luling. The farmhouse and two hundred acres had originally belonged to my great-grandfather on my mother's side, Thomas Moore. When he died, he left the land to Mamie, Mom's step-grandmother. When Thomas bequeathed the farm to Mamie, he told her, "If I leave you land, you will always be all right." He couldn't have known just how right he was. Soon after she took ownership of the property, Mamie struck oil! Texas tea, as it's been called. When Mamie died, the farm passed to Papa and then on to my mother. When Mom died, it passed to my brother and me.

After school ended for the year, my mom, my brother, and I would get up at five in the morning and go on a road trip to the farm. While I slept in the car, Tommy would peel Texas peaches, my favorite fruit, and put the sweet, slippery slices into a bowl for me to have when I woke up. The flat country highways ran straight to the horizon. We passed acres of crops, and I loved the pops of color that eventually turned into fields of bluebonnets, the Texas state flower. Part of our road trip ritual was to stop and wander into one particular pasture to pick bluebonnets. We'd fill our arms until it seemed we carried the entire landscape with us.

As we reached the last stretch of the three-hour drive, we'd look for the windmill at my cousins' house. Tommy would always see it first. It loomed large and marked the beginning of summer fun with my cousins Maggie, Mollie, and Carrie Webb.

At the farm, the days would start with a serene beauty, unbroken by the sound of a car or the sight of another person. With its endless acres of placid green, it would be so quiet your ears would ring. We'd walk to the San Marcos River, which ran through the farm, and there was not a slab of cement in sight. Mom, Tommy, and I would have lavish picnics on the riverbank. We'd put our drinks in the water to make them cold. I loved swimming in the rapids. Everything felt so free and easy, running around in cutoff jean shorts and T-shirts. Tommy loved fishing. Sometimes he would catch catfish and Mom would fry them in cornmeal for dinner.

Maggie, Mollie, and Carrie were my comrades in arms. We'd pretend we were cowgirls defending something vast and unnamed. I'd sit astride an old oil barrel and pretend it was my horse. We were wild and free, in what felt like the best place in the entire world.

Those were the moments and memories I'd lean on later, when life got harder and things became more complicated.

These summers were the kind of life every kid would dream of. Carefree and spontaneous. The sound of the river. The gentle, old-fashioned ways of a small town, so different from Houston. The summer days stretched out without deadlines or distractions, and the future felt not urgent but inevitable. Those are memories I treasure. It was life at its best. The summers at the farm in Luling exist in my memory with a kind of suspended clarity, as though untouched by time.

Another place I treasured was the ballet studio. The first time I went to a ballet class I was about four years old. It was my mother's idea. I was pleased enough that I got to wear a checked one-piece ruffled uniform with my name on it. Beyond that, I didn't think much of dance. As time passed, my teacher tried to encourage me, telling me I had a natural turnout, natural elevation, and the body of a dancer. That didn't mean much to me at first, but one day when I was ten years old, something shifted.

My teacher used to set up three lines after our barre work—front, middle, and back. Which line you were placed in was a reflection of how well you were doing in the class. The best students were in the front. I was all the way in the back. I was a big daydreamer and didn't always pay close attention to the combinations. A girl from my neighborhood named Desma had just joined the class, and as I stood there and looked at her, I noticed she was studying the teacher, hanging on her every word. It was as if some part of me that had been asleep suddenly woke up. *I want to do this!* I thought. *I don't want to be in the back line; I want to be in the front line!* Suddenly I saw the difference between drifting and choosing to be present, and I chose the latter. So I started trying harder. And I progressed. Dance became engaging, and the effort I put into it had an easefulness about it. Before long, I was in that front line, and once I got there, I determined that I was never going to leave. The first time the teacher called on me to demonstrate a move, I knew I was where I belonged. Dance offered satisfaction in mastering the alignment of the body. It also offered something less definable—a sense of rightness.

Dance gave me a place to apply my work ethic and inborn love of precision; it also provided an outlet for my frenetic energy. The discipline and detail required to perfect my technique suited me. My teacher was right—I was a natural—and I was happy to build on my talent with lots of hard work. From that point on I loved every minute of it. I was driven to dance.

By junior high, my grade school ballerina fantasies had matured into an obsession. I could not stop doing pliés and arabesques. Even when I was out shopping with my mom, I did grand jetés down the aisles of stores. When I was standing still, it was in first or second position. If I was sitting, I was flexing my feet. Every moment of my waking life was focused on ballet. It wasn't just a perfectionist's need to get things right; there was a glorious connection between music and movement that exhilarated me.

After dance recitals, my family had a tradition of going to Bluebonnet Gardens. We'd sit at wooden picnic tables shaded by beautiful tall trees and eat sliced watermelon from big silver trays. I probably decided under those trees that I wanted to be a dancer when I grew up—maybe a principal dancer in the Ballets Russes. I started to nurture a dream that would take me far, well beyond the warm streets of Houston. Dance also gave me a solid base to spring from.

I often say that it was through my grandfather that I first learned what love really is. Not just love's gentleness or boundless capacity, but its fierceness. I also saw the challenging parts of truly caring for someone. As a kid in a kind home, you tend to think of love as a fait accompli. It's simply what happens between parents and children. But with Papa and his son, my uncle Warren, I also saw the pain that love can cause.

Over the years, my uncle developed a problem with alcohol. Again and again I witnessed my grandfather's love and his faith tested as he continued to be there for my uncle in spite of all the tricks and the treachery that addiction foments. Warren would do his best to recover, but then the steely clutches of addiction would reach for him once more. He'd relapse and try to hide his drinking from Papa. I wasn't fully aware of what was happening at the time and I didn't know Warren all that well, but I know he was a brilliant man. A gifted violinist who spoke multiple languages, he seemed to travel in a rarefied world of intellectuals.

A couple of times, Warren went away for an extended period to rest and "get well." Over time I came to understand that my uncle was an alcoholic, and that all his health issues and stints in treatment centers were related to his drinking. Papa did whatever he could to try to cure his son, but nothing worked. As a child, I did not fully understand the relapses, or the endurance of a father who refused to give up on his son, no matter how often his hope was dashed. With an adult's perspective, I can see how my grandfather blamed himself for Warren's illness and death, although he had no reason to. He'd done all he could, yet Warren continued to drink no matter how much love and support he was given. Although pneumonia eventually killed him, my uncle's body had been weakened by a lifetime of heavy drinking, and that was the real cause of his death.

It was heart-wrenching to watch, and was the reason why, at twelve years of age, I swore that I'd never drink alcohol. It was tearing my grandfather apart and making a tragedy of my uncle's life. My beloved grandfather had done absolutely everything he could for his son. It's hard to describe that loss. It changed me. For the first time I realized that when it comes to love, there's no such thing as a safe heart, only a willing one.

Warren was fifty-four years old when he died, and it was hard for the family to lose him so young—a heartbreaking echo of his and my mom's own mother, Ethel Elise, dying in her early fifties. Mom mourned for her brother, and we were all sad about it. But for Papa, in his mid-eighties by then, losing his only son was a loss beyond comprehension. We began to worry about him. I recalled my mother telling me that after Ethel Elise's death he was overcome with grief to the point of affecting his health and she'd feared they'd never get him back. Between my burgeoning propensity to worry and my adoration of my grandfather, I became frightened.

All throughout Warren's funeral I fixated on Papa, trying to discern how he was doing. I'd watch him greet people with so much strength, holding all that grief in. I feared he wouldn't be able to withstand it and at some point his heart would simply burst.

Tommy and his girlfriend (later his wife), Charlotte, drove me home from church. Mom stayed behind to talk to the mourners. Our poodle, Mimi, was in the back seat with me, and I hugged her tightly, thinking, *How is Papa going to get through this? Why has such sadness come to such a good man?* And then, *I can't lose him. He's my best friend!*

That was when I would start what was called *magical thinking*—a belief that one's thoughts, actions, and even rituals can influence events. This is common in young children and is a normal part of development. Yet as I would come to learn years later in college, it can develop into OCD. In my case, I invoked magical thinking to try to prevent a feared outcome. From that day on, in times of stress, it was something I turned to. My OCD, which was based in religion, was about prayer and sacrifices to God, always for the benefit of a loved one—in this case, my grandfather.

During that ride, holding my dog, I felt desperate and powerless. But then a notion came over me. Maybe there *was* something I could do. I remembered hearing Papa say in sermons how God helps us through prayer. Maybe if I prayed hard enough, I could save Papa. I'd never felt such an intense longing for another person's safety and wellness before. I would have done anything in the world to take away Papa's pain. What Papa must have felt for Warren for all those years, I felt for him now—an aching to save him.

I took it upon myself to get Papa through his grief and glued myself to his side. This longing to help him wouldn't leave me. I would stand there while he was sleeping, watching intently for the reassuring rise and fall of his chest. Each exhalation brought a fresh wave of worry. And so I'd pray even harder. I'd do anything to keep him safe. It was not rational, even for a twelve-year-old; some part of me understood that. But fear has its own logic and, once accepted, it's difficult to stop. That fear of loss settled into me, shaping my thoughts in ways I could not fully articulate at the time. I became fixated on him. On his survival, his grief, and what this would do to him. I watched him closely, searching for signs. When the fear became too great, I turned to something else. Prayer at first, then rituals. They began simply, almost innocently, but grew into something more consuming: a belief that took hold of my actions.

I thought that my sacrifices could somehow protect the people I loved. I'd heard that God liked it when we sacrificed for him. I guess from going to Sunday school at a young age that was ingrained in me. Maybe I could please God even more by giving up things that I wanted. Mostly, my sacrifices were small, like choosing not to have a piece of candy. I'd think, *If I don't eat this, then Papa will be okay for one more day*. Then my worry and praying started to extend beyond Papa. Sometimes I'd spend an hour praying, making sure I covered every single tiny blessing for my entire family. There were times when I'd run up to my room to get dressed before going out, and my mother would call up an hour later and ask, "What's going on, El? When are you coming down?" Not only was I praying, but I'd also created a series of rituals whereby I had to do all my tasks in a specific order. In habit lies safety. I had to cover all the bases or none of it would "work." I also became increasingly convinced that if I didn't pray, those I loved might get sick or hurt and it would be all my fault.

During this time, the only person I told about my sacrifices and rituals was Mom. She looked at me with that loving smile and said, "Honey, that's ridiculous. Just stop doing it." She had no idea what a hold it had come to have on me, and that I couldn't just stop. That was the last time I brought it up.

As the weeks and months went on, the stress I felt started to show itself in physical symptoms, including a missed period. Mom insisted I go to a doctor, even though my period started again the day before the appointment. The doctor examined me and ordered a blood test. After reviewing the results he announced, "Your hormones are all messed up. You might not be able to have a child." I was shocked. How could he or anyone make such a dire diagnosis about a twelve-year-old after a single blood test? Granted, it was the 1950s, and human physiology wasn't as well understood as it is now. But on a purely human level, it felt cruel to tell an anxious, grieving adolescent girl that she could be infertile. He was the doctor, so I believed him, and my anxiety doubled instantly. I'd always dreamed of being a mother, and now that dream was gone.

Lifted by his faith, Papa did eventually overcome his sadness. I'm certain his grief over Warren never left him, but as time went on, he seemed like himself again. Yet while Papa returned to his normal behavior, I didn't. In times of stress I'd return to my worry, invoking rituals and prayer to try to protect the people I loved.

Chapter Three

At home, I always felt I belonged—a sense difficult to name, but unmistakable. But as I reached early adolescence, school became another matter. I attended Lamar High School in Houston's River Oaks neighborhood, which sat on one end of the main road, with the River Oaks Country Club at the other. Kids from other high schools referred to us as the Lamar Teasippers. They weren't wrong. It was a chichi area, and since busing had not yet come to Houston, most students were upper-class and white. Instead of a sweet sixteen, many families threw debutante balls for their daughters. But the girls I knew who "came out" weren't looking to find a husband; they just wanted to have a big party and wear a lavish gown. For my part, I wasn't interested in a debut. At least, not that kind. By that point my life revolved around ballet, and my world shrank to the size of a dance studio.

Ballet gave me a place where I belonged, a soft place to land when I suddenly and inexplicably fell out of the in crowd when I entered Lamar. Through middle school I'd been popular. I'd been voted Best Citizen. In eighth grade I was Most Popular Panda. (Our mascot was the Persian Panda—don't ask me why.) When I crossed to high school, though, I lost some of that sense of fitting in.

I went along with the popular girls to football games and made an attempt to be one of the gang, yet the truth was that I felt increasingly out of step. I didn't actually care about football or the social scene around the games. I didn't want to wear shirtwaist dresses, circle dresses, or a bubble hairdo. Instead, I kept my hair long, often wrapped in a tight, shiny ballerina bun. I also had no interest in adorning my chest with giant mums—a custom at Texas football games—to reflect how much my boyfriend cared for me. If you were going steady with someone, the boy would give you a mum. One was plenty, but some girls, like the cheerleaders, got two. To me it was ridiculous—you could barely move! But that's how it was.

My new status, or lack thereof, was confusing and painful in the way that trying to navigate schoolgirl politics so often is. Eventually it didn't much matter to me that I didn't have a place within the football crowd; I preferred to be at the ballet studio. I could spend hours pretending I was dancing *Swan Lake*, and that suited me fine. I loved everything about dance. I loved the leotards, the toe shoes, the energy of the class, the smell of the rosin box, how dancers always stood in first position, the tight ballerina buns that identified us immediately.

Houston felt like a small town in many respects, but it was also a cultural center, and I was fortunate to have access to some talented, inspirational teachers. My first serious mentor was Florrie Olenbush, the doyenne of her own dance school, where I got advanced training in classical ballet in the Russian style. Florrie was my first mentor in dance who made a real difference in my life. She represented the right kind of authority. She demanded excellence from every student lined up at the barre, and I had a strong desire to prove myself. Eventually I started to win her over.

Every moment of my waking life became focused on ballet. It became my number one topic of conversation at home and with my friends. They wanted to talk about what to wear to a big Saturday night party, which didn't interest me. If I could make any excuse not to go to the party, I would, and then I'd spend the whole night in my room, practicing fouetté turns. Florrie encouraged my obsession. She said, "Ellen, you were meant to dance." She was saying exactly what I wanted to hear, and it only made me practice even harder to live up to her faith in me.

My parents were a bit concerned with how laser-focused I was on dance, often at the expense of my studies and my friendships. But they also saw how good it was for me—for my confidence and self-esteem. They applauded at every recital but didn't push me. I loved dance, and they loved that I loved it. When it came to Papa, though, forget it. If I did anything at all, he said it was the greatest. He was my cheerleader.

When I was dancing, I felt exhilarated. Nothing could compare—certainly not school, boys, or parties. I attended school events with reluctance, and at parties I became a bit of a wallflower. It wasn't just that I was more interested in dance; as I grew older those parties sometimes included alcohol. With my uncle Warren, I'd seen enough to know that I wanted nothing to do with drinking. That didn't do anything to boost my popularity. The result was that at school I felt like a loner. Fortunately, that didn't last.

Everything changed when I discovered the Drama Shack. That was our nickname for our acting class, which was overseen by the remarkable Ruth Denney. Ruth became a legend in theater instruction and would go on to found the Houston High School for the Performing and Visual Arts in 1971. As a teacher, Ruth was ahead of her time. She knew how to talk to kids and give us the necessary confidence to get onstage and develop a character. She gave us every reason to be the best we could be.

Our artsy little gang put on shoestring yet inventive productions of *Bye Bye Birdie*, *Bells Are Ringing*, *Wish You Were Here*, and *West Side Story*, to name a few. Another Drama Shack regular, a tall, slim boy named Tommy Tune, choreographed some of these productions. Tommy went on to fame as a Broadway choreographer and director who won ten Tony Awards, including a special award for Lifetime Achievement in the Theatre. Many Drama Shack alums—such as Robert Foxworth, Paula Prentiss, Tommy Sands, and Lisa Hartman Black—wound up having successful entertainment careers.

The Drama Shack became my new home at school; it was where I met my people and already included my two best friends, Claire Dishongh and Irene Fox. Claire had a lightness of spirit that made her stand out. She exuded fun, and everyone loved her. She was a natural beauty who never had a shortage of boyfriends. Irene was curious and engaged in the world. Amusing and funny, with a quick wit and pale-blue eyes with a lot of light in them, she was always true to herself. I'm still close with both of them today. It's a blessing to have found, so early in life, two such special friends to ride through the years with. Even though we now live in different states—Claire in Oklahoma and Irene in New York—we are still deeply connected.

The three of us formed the nucleus of a crew that included future Broadway star Candy Tovar and future Joffrey Ballet dancer/choreographer Margo Sappington. Our group was small, with Texas-sized talent. We delighted in one another's personalities and our shared dedication to drama—and we encouraged and inspired each other.

I loved drama, but I still had my sights set on dancing. Ballet was my foundation, but I knew that if I wanted to become a professional, I'd need to expand my repertoire. I started taking classes in jazz, tap, and musical comedy at the Swayze School of Dance. I worked directly with Patsy Swayze herself, and she was a marvel. She could do anything, in movement and life. Patsy eventually went to Hollywood and choreographed a number of hit movies, including *Urban Cowboy* in 1980.

Patsy and her husband, Jesse, had three kids at the time, and she continued teaching throughout each of her pregnancies. I remember her children running around the studio, all of them gorgeous. Her son Buddy, known later as Patrick, was a standout among them and an absolute doll. He was seven or eight when I was taking classes with Patsy, but he made a real impression on me. Even then he was a natural dancer. As he got older, he became a star athlete as well. And after that, well, you know the story: *Dirty Dancing*, *Road House*, *Ghost*, *Point Break*, and so many memorable movies.

I got to Los Angeles prior to Patrick. Before he got into acting, he and his wife, Lisa Niemi (the two had met at his mom's dance studio as kids), had a contracting business. When they first came to LA, Patsy told them, "Please call Ellen." I'd bought a house that needed some renovations, and I hired them to do the work. Patrick and Lisa were Ken and Barbie—they were that cute. It was a hoot to see the two of them, stunning as models, in their shorts and tank tops, hammering and sawing away in my yard. No wonder there was a sudden uptick in traffic accidents on the street out front!

But their contracting company didn't last long. The very next year, Patrick was cast in a movie called *Skatetown, U.S.A.*, which is largely forgettable except for the fact that it launched his incredible career. Whenever I ran into Patrick in LA or Houston, I was thrilled for him and his success. He was a hometown boy who'd made it big. Sadly, he passed away in 2009 after a long battle with cancer. He was just fifty-seven years old. Whenever I happen to catch one of Patrick's films on TV, I always take a few minutes to watch. Each time, I'm overcome with awe, thinking of that talented young boy running around Patsy's studio. It's truly rare to see a dancer with the body and stretch of an athlete who can turn around and dance a pas de deux with such grace. Patrick's every movement took your breath away. I'll never forget his positive energy, even with his cancer diagnosis; he performed like a whirlwind. When he danced, it was like fly-fishing, smooth, exact, and flowing. I'm so grateful to have known him.

With Patsy, I had access not only to top-quality dance instruction but also to her extensive network. She connected me with a local drama company called Theater Inc., where I danced in professional-level productions of *Gentlemen Prefer Blondes* and *West Side Story.* Onstage I wasn't a wallflower. Patsy watched me doing *Gentlemen Prefer Blondes* and said, "You're more alive than I've ever seen you. This is your place." Being onstage to sing and dance for live audiences seemed like the most fun I could have in life. I was hooked. After those experiences, it was simply unthinkable that dance and theater wouldn't be central in my life forever.

My goal, of course, was to be onstage. But, ever practical, I resolved that if things didn't work out for me as a performer, I could open my own school and teach dance. I looked at what Patsy had created, with her big happy family and her own studio, and it excited me. In those days, when I daydreamed, one version of my life looked very much like Patsy's.

I never feared rejection because I knew I would learn something from it. Daddy always told me to have a Plan B (advice I still follow today), and that became it: I could live in Houston, open a dance studio, and still be a suburban mom . . . But something else kept calling my name.

Chapter Four

The assassination of President John F. Kennedy was what they call a flashbulb memory—an event so emotionally charged and impactful that you recall exactly where you were when it happened. I was in drama class. It was 1963, my senior year at Lamar. The announcement came over the loudspeaker: "Our president has been shot."

The room exploded in gasps and wails. Mrs. Denney tried to restore calm, but without much success. Everyone was crying. It was like one minute everything was peaceful and safe, and the very next the world tilted on its axis. Nothing made sense, and with little information immediately available, we didn't know what it meant. Who had done it? Was our nation safe? Our alarm was underscored by the fact that the shooting happened in Dallas, a mere three-and-a-half-hour drive from Houston. I just kept thinking, *It can't be true!* Our new president, Lyndon Johnson, was also a Texan. As the weeks and months wore on, it felt like the eyes of the nation rested on my home state.

But I was looking beyond our borders. I had already decided that my next steps would take me beyond Texas. All of senior year, my best friend Irene and I talked about going to New York to study with the very finest teachers. My parents had other plans. As supportive as they had always been about my dancing and acting, they balked at the idea of me not going to college. More school? The idea made my stomach churn. Not only did I dread the thought of more classes and homework, but I wanted to dance.

My parents, however, were not hearing it. And so, with a sense of loyalty and dread, I applied to and was accepted to Trinity University. Trinity was about three hours west of Houston, in my mother's hometown of San Antonio. She was excited to visit so she could show me off to her many old friends who still lived there. My reluctance was no reflection on the school—I simply had my sights set on New York.

Trinity did have a drama program, headed by Paul Baker, who was also the director at the Dallas Theater Center. He had a wonderful reputation, so I managed to work up some enthusiasm about college. But almost from the moment I stepped foot on campus, it was evident that Trinity didn't suit me. My overwhelming unhappiness opened the door to extreme homesickness. I arrived at college oblivious to the difficulties of being away from my family. It was like stepping onstage at my first ballet recital and realizing I'd never learned the choreography. As strange as it might seem, I'd never stopped to think what life might be like without unfettered access to my family. When you leave home your world changes, but you have to adjust—to learn the dance. At Trinity, I never got the steps. I was among my classmates, but I was not one of them. It was like when I'd started at Lamar, only this time I didn't have my family support system around me.

To make matters worse, I was disappointed by the drama program. Paul Baker might have been a genius, but he was never on campus; he was always in Dallas. Maybe I'd been spoiled by Florrie Olenbush and Patsy Swayze, but the teachers in college paled in comparison to my previous mentors. I was not thrilled with my classes either, and I toiled away in the library on reading and homework that left me feeling disengaged and uninspired. Socially, I didn't fit in. Parties were wild and soaked in oceans of beer, which was a total turnoff for me.

Meanwhile, Irene's parents had let her go to New York. She was studying with Matt Mattox and taking classes at June Taylor's dance school. She would write me colorful letters about going to dance classes. I read those letters with mixed feelings—delighted for her and heartbroken for myself. Instead of focusing on my studies, I would daydream about Irene's life in New York, wondering what my own would have been like if my parents had allowed me to move east with her. I lamented all our lost adventures taking in the brilliant sights and sounds of the big city, especially New York's rich arts culture. Every day at college felt like wasted time.

Papa did his best to cheer me up. Every few weeks he'd make the drive to San Antonio in his two-door, two-tone Ford, cream with turquoise. He would take me out for Mexican food. It says a lot that the only bright spot in my life as a college freshman was having dinner with my grandfather!

As alone and frustrated as I felt in San Antonio, I knew I needed to figure out how to get by. My parents had paid a lot of money for me to go to college, and they wouldn't get the money back just because I hated it. As each day dragged slowly by, my sadness and stress increased. At some point, the idea popped into my mind that perhaps if I studied more, things would get better. Quickly I spiraled back into my old behavior, invoking prayer, rituals, and sacrifice to try to manage my emotions. My mind would turn inward, looping and searching for control where none existed. I didn't have language for it then; I only knew that anxiety would take over in times of worry. I carried it silently.

I began to believe that if I studied and was disciplined with my work, I might begin to like it at Trinity. I'd force myself to sit at my desk for hours without interruption, to stretch my willpower in a kind of demonstration of my dedication to making things at Trinity work. Instead, they got worse.

When my intense study sessions failed to work, I thought of something else I could give up: my looks. Instead of taking care with my hair and the way I dressed, I tried to diminish my appearance. I abandoned stylish clothes completely, instead choosing dresses that were drab and dowdy. When Mom came to visit, I disguised myself in plainness. I chose a cotton patchwork dress with a white collar and cuffs that looked like it came from Amish country. I erased every trace of color. I tied my hair back with a black ribbon into a messy bun, with no makeup or accessories. It was a strange form of penance, as if beauty itself became something I no longer deserved.

My mother had spread the word to her San Antonio friends: "Wait until you meet my daughter. She's so beautiful and so sweet!" Then I showed up for tea with the ladies looking like a novice at a convent. When my mother saw me, her eyebrows shot up, then settled into a deep crinkle, her forehead creased with concern. Whenever Mom looked at me, it was never through me but deep into me. Her concern was unmistakable. Afterward, when she asked me what was going on, I downplayed the situation. "I'm just not feeling well today, that's all," I said. Mom nodded. She didn't press the matter, but she knew I wasn't telling her the whole story.

I had always cared about what people thought; I grew up seeking approval. I didn't tell Mom what was going on because I didn't think she'd understand. Plus, I really didn't understand what was happening myself.

Fortuitously, among my courses that semester was psychology. At one point when I was doing the assigned textbook reading, I came across a collection of behaviors that caught my attention. *Persistent unwanted thoughts, repetitive behaviors, or mental rituals the person feels compelled to perform . . . That sounds like me!* I read on and discovered the condition was called obsessive-compulsive disorder.

It's not fun being diagnosed (or self-diagnosing) with a psychiatric disorder, but at the same time I felt relieved. There was a name for it, and I wasn't alone! I remember feeling fascinated at the many different ways our brains can work. At the time, the science around mental health and the brain was rudimentary at best. Certainly, medications like SSRIs didn't exist back then, and I don't know if I'd have taken them if they did. I just accepted my anxiety and sacrifices as my secret burden.

I knew my habits weren't common, but I didn't think I needed help. After all, I knew what caused them: stress. With Papa, I was terrified that he would die. At Trinity, I was somewhere I did not want to be. Both of these circumstances felt beyond my control, and that was a trigger.

I knew my behavior disturbed my mother, so after her visit, I willfully, painfully forced myself to stop, knowing in my heart of hearts that I couldn't control anyone's destiny; it was just a way to relieve my stress. Every time rumination threatened to take over or I felt compelled to do a ritual or to pray, I clamped down on the urge, refusing to acknowledge it. As the weeks passed, I found that I was able to control my behavior. The stressful thoughts persisted, but I managed to keep myself from acting on them.

After what seemed like forever, my freshman year finally came to a close and I returned to Houston for the summer. I couldn't bear the thought of going back. "Daddy, I'm not happy at Trinity. I don't know if I'm going to make it there."

He said, "You want to leave college? After one year?"

"It's not for me. I think I should go to New York and live with Irene."

Daddy shook his head. "Now, honey, why would you want to leave Texas? New York is so far away."

That would be a challenge, of course. But I was aching with unrealized ambition, and I wanted to make my own way. I needed to do *something*. I had all this frenetic energy, and in the past year of college, it had had nowhere to go. The way Irene described New York, with all its energy and vibrancy, I was convinced it was the place for me. If I wanted to dance professionally, it seemed obvious that New York had to be an eventual stop. I also wasn't getting any younger. In the world of dance you have only a brief window to make your mark.

As a traditionalist who was highly protective of his only daughter, Daddy didn't like the idea. But he saw how unhappy I was and knew how desperate I was to make a real go of dancing. He looked into the logistics of where I might live in New York and how I'd get around. He and Mom settled on a plan. They wanted me to enroll in the Finch School, a small cultural finishing "college" with a protected atmosphere on the Upper East Side of Manhattan. Alongside a handful of other girls, I'd read classic literature and poetry, train in etiquette, and do a bit of acting and dance. No doubt I'd also be introduced to a carefully selected cadre of worthy husband candidates. It sounded painfully old-fashioned, even to me, and I chafed at the idea of their one-year commitment requirement.

I had read about the famous Barbizon Hotel for Women on Lexington Avenue, where Grace Kelly, Eileen Ford, Joan Didion, Sylvia Plath, and Joan Crawford had once lived. At the time, Irene was living with her grandmother in New Jersey, and I pitched the idea that she and I could live at the Barbizon together. Daddy priced things out. In the end, my parents grudgingly agreed that, with certain rules, I could rent a room at the Barbizon. In return, I vowed to be careful, to never walk alone at night, and to never take the subway (I still haven't to this day).

Still, in an attempt to dissuade me, Daddy would show me articles he'd read about violent crimes. "Look at this, El—a woman was mugged on Fifth Avenue in the middle of the day, and everyone stood around and watched her get beaten up. No one helped! This is where you want to live?"

In hindsight, it's truly remarkable that they let me go. But they trusted me to be sensible, trusted that the values they'd instilled in me would see me through. I'm sure they hoped that once I got to New York and saw the gritty reality of big-city life, the wanderlust would evaporate and I'd come right back home. If we are wise, we enlarge our minds and hearts rather than discard that which gave us our first base of understanding. I was nervous about making such a big move, but I knew that the road to everything I wanted in life ran through New York. It was worth facing my fear. I had my parents' uncomplicated love to take with me. I knew the immensity of their gift in letting me go, and I was determined to make the most of it.

Chapter Five

As I stood on the sidewalk in front of the Warwick Hotel, watching my parents' cab pull away, emotion welled up behind my eyes. That was it. They were gone. It was October 1965. I was about to turn twenty years old, and I was on my own in New York. Fortunately, not completely on my own, since I had Irene. Once again without my family, and this time they wouldn't be just a three-hour drive away but across the country.

My throat tightened. You know the feeling, when you think you are going to choke and die on the spot, emotion bunching up behind your eyes. I started to cry. "El, why are you crying?" Irene asked. "This is what you wanted!" She was right, of course, but no amount of excitement or anticipation would ever stop me from missing my family. They were the net beneath the high wire.

Irene put an arm around my shoulders, I wiped my tears, and we turned and walked off toward my new home, the Barbizon Hotel for Women. The Barbizon was also known by another name: the Dollhouse. I met young girls there from all over the country, many of them aspiring dancers, actresses, or models. Others were students, and some simply dreamed of meeting a rich man who'd marry them and sweep them away to a penthouse on Park Avenue.

Daddy was covering my rent and giving me a monthly allowance, paid in American Express Travelers Cheques. It wasn't lavish by any means, but it spared me the pressure of having to figure out where my next meal would come from. I met girls at the Barbizon and at auditions who didn't have that security. I felt extremely grateful and, I'll confess, a little guilty. Yet even with that safety net, I'm still amazed at how much courage it took for me to move to New York and how much confidence my parents had in me to let me do it. The deal was that I'd stay until December 1, then head home for Christmas.

From the start, New York overwhelmed me. Not in a bad way; it was just *a lot* to take in. It was fast and noisy and a less patient place than Houston. All around me were things I'd never seen before: people jaywalking, garbage spilling out of cans onto the sidewalk, people living in makeshift shelters constructed out of cardboard. Cabdrivers had an approach to driving all their own, flooring the gas before hitting the brakes so hard at red lights that you'd have to brace yourself to keep from sliding clean off the seat. There were wonders and delights as well. Charming city parks, delectable restaurants, and fashionable boutiques abounded. Strolling through the city, it seemed like every block held some new treasure.

My room at the Barbizon was on the sixth floor, and from my window I could see Sixty-Third Street. The view was spectacular, looking out over an assortment of beautiful town houses. Some were brick or stucco, while others were painted—each had its own unique style. I was fascinated by the architecture. Every door had brightly polished brass fixtures. The front of each home was adorned with topiaries. Some were in Versailles boxes, others in stone urns, always with flowers of the season around the trees. They didn't have houses like that in Texas! I bought a window box and planted beautiful artificial flowers outside my window to brighten things up and give the illusion of real flowers.

That view offered an expansive feeling to an otherwise tiny room. It was like everything was in miniature. The desk looked like it belonged in a dollhouse, and the bed wasn't a full twin, more like a large crib minus the rails. The single small closet wasn't big enough to hold all my clothes, so I had to hang a wire over the back of the door for my coats. The wall-to-wall carpet was celadon, and the bedspread was a chintz fabric dotted with tiny pink flowers, with curtains to match. The furniture was a pale, distressed wood. I made it my own with pictures from home.

I wrote to my parents every single day. I'd sit there crammed at my little desk, so tiny there was just enough room for the phone and a piece of paper. I narrated my everyday life in exacting detail, dutifully providing dispatches about which dance class I'd taken, how much it had cost, and whether I'd arrived by bus or cab. I described every observation I had made about the city and told them what I'd had for breakfast, lunch, and dinner. In hindsight, I'm sure they laughed at how thorough those letters were. They wrote me, too, though not every day, and certainly not about the minuscule details of their lives. They'd give me updates here and there and, most important to them, ask if I needed anything. Sometimes I'd get a letter from Papa, filled only with good things, whether news, humor, or comfort. I lived on those letters as if they were oxygen.

Even though she'd come from Houston as well, Irene loved the frenetic energy of New York. She became my guide. Irene had a wide-open smile and an extra lilt in her Texas accent that became more pronounced when she'd been talking to family. She was independent and unafraid to be on her own. She had a quick wit (still does), and she could always make me laugh. I don't think Irene has ever said a curse word in her entire life. We were both old-fashioned girls, which was why we got on so well and why she made a great companion in such a bustling, foreign place. But whereas I was more emotional, Irene kept her feelings close. She once told me, "El, you cry on the outside. I cry on the inside." Without a doubt, I was a romantic. In addition to dancing, I loved the idea of meeting someone and falling in love.

By the time I showed up, Irene had already been in New York for a year. She'd been taking dance classes and going to NYU. I was excited to jump in. I had barely unpacked my suitcases before I was eager to start classes and learn the ropes. But there was so much to learn. I asked Irene, "How do we find out about auditions?"

"What?" she exclaimed. "We're here to study! We're here to go to the New York City Ballet, to City Center. We're supposed to have *fun*." For Irene, being in New York wasn't just about auditioning. That would come. First she wanted to soak in every last ounce of New York's arts culture.

I wanted to have fun, but I also needed to prove myself. Sensing my anxiety, Irene said, "Let's go to Bloomingdale's." So we walked to the massive shopping mecca on Lexington Avenue and Fifty-Ninth Street, just a few blocks from the Barbizon, and looked at the gorgeous window displays featuring mannequins in miniskirts and go-go boots and mod geometric dresses the color of sherbet. Houston was home to NASA, but at the time, the new space-age style was pretty far-out for me. I'd never seen the like. After an hour browsing at Bloomingdale's, Irene and I walked to Rockefeller Center and gazed up at the iconic bronze statue of Atlas, the Greek god, shouldering the heavens. From there, we strolled through Central Park, with its riding paths and footpaths, its old trees and green expanses, and its lively collage of people (and dogs).

Irene moved freely through the streets of New York. With her vigorous excitement, she wanted to show me everything. We went to the World's Fair in Flushing Meadows and saw the Unisphere. She shepherded me to City Center to see concerts and to sign up for classes. She was unfazed by the people crowding the streets, the bellowing buses and speeding taxis, and the collective cacophony of it all. Every bit of it was new to me. For the first few weeks in New York, I existed in a perpetual state of amazement. It was hard at first, but Irene made it manageable.

It might seem odd, given what a fish out of water I was, but in those early days in New York, my compulsive behaviors never really surfaced. Sure, I was stressed at times, but I was where I wanted to be. Ironically, the novelty of New York calmed me down. My mind was going a million miles a minute, but so was everything else. The pace and energy of New York matched my own, and I relaxed into a sense of belonging that I'd never felt at college. New York has always uplifted me.

Everyone I loved, my entire family, was well. I didn't have to worry about them. Instead, I was free to focus on making my way.

Before my mom returned to Houston, she wrote the directions to the American Ballet Theatre on a piece of paper and handed it to me. Soaking in the city was fun, but my priority was to sign up for dance classes. It was my first experience at a professional school. Being in that class took a level of confidence because everyone there was *so good.*

During my first class, each student was asked to do a series of grand jetés across the floor. Standing there awaiting my turn, I watched as the other dancers stepped out, then gracefully raised their arms overhead in fifth position as they leaped, legs outstretched. It all looked so effortless. *You can do this,* I told myself. *You've done it a million times.* When my turn came, technically I was fine, but I felt relieved when that class was over. Still, I'd done it. I'd taken my first ballet class in New York, and I'd held my own.

In dance classes I was surrounded by talent. Raw, disciplined, and hungry. I watched and learned, absorbing the language of movement, the unspoken hierarchies. It took courage simply to stand at the barre and be seen. I could always spot the dancers who'd already done Broadway shows. You might see someone like Ann Reinking or Donna McKechnie in your class. As you'd imagine, it was intimidating.

When I went to New York, I was a little old, for a dancer at least. I realize that sounds silly to say about a twenty-year-old, but most of the other dancers had gotten there earlier, or they were from New York. I had to work hard to close the gap. But I was accustomed to that. Dance is all about hard work. With dance, when you're onstage, you have to be able to hit it every time, every day. It taught me a lot about my body, which later translated to acting. Dance helped me to be confident in my presence just standing there. It paved the way. Dance studios became my proving grounds.

My job was to hold steady, to find my place in this challenging city. Every day I was gaining ground. In dance class, whatever deficits I arrived with I knew I could make up for by putting in extra time. I learned to pour all my energy, mental and physical, into microscopic adjustments to the way I moved. I would make my tendu look like melting ice cream or my frappés like beating eggs. It made it impossible for me to worry about anything while I was in class. I loved that when I entered the studio I didn't think about anything except the placement of my body. I learned to pace myself and not procrastinate. If there was something I didn't understand or a combination I was struggling with, I asked for help. Dance taught me discipline and helped me to gain self-esteem and confidence. I learned to take chances. Today, I always tell my kids, "Go out on that limb—that's where the fruit is!" Though I've adhered to that advice in many settings, dance was where I first discovered its truth.

My parents weren't the only ones who had rules for me in New York. The Barbizon came with a full set of them. But I was a rule-follower, so, for the most part, they suited me fine. For one, you couldn't wear slacks in the lobby. Back then, pants were considered unladylike, and it was forbidden to linger in public view dressed in them. Just standing around and having a pleasant conversation *in pants*? Absolutely not! That felt a little outdated to me, but it was no big deal to go along. Every day I wore heels, hose, a top that didn't dip too low, and a skirt that didn't rise too high. Girls who dared to wear jeans knew to hustle from the elevator to the front door.

Another unbreakable rule: One could not entertain a gentleman past the mezzanine level of the building. The mezzanine had some common rooms where you could sit and talk (without touching). But where there's a will, there's a way. Some of my fellow residents managed to sneak men up to the higher floors—the bedrooms—via a back "servants'" stairwell that led all the way up from the basement.

Over my years in New York, I would make friends with plenty of people who walked on the wild side, but Irene was not among them. She represented home. If Irene hadn't been there, as much as I wanted to be in New York, I don't think I would have stayed. She helped me acclimate. In later years, whenever I've said as much to Irene, she's shaken her head and said, "No, El, you were meant to have a career. If it hadn't been in New York, then it would have happened somewhere else." I'm not so convinced. I continued to feel the pull of the past and the absence of faces I wanted to see. It was hard, but with each day, time pushed me forward, and as it did my excitement grew. Still, when December came, I flew home as planned.

When I got to the arrivals gate and saw Mom and Daddy waiting to pick me up, my heart exploded. Driving home, I soaked in the familiarity and ease of Houston. It was like falling into a familiar dream. At the same time, as Christmas ended, I couldn't wait to go back to New York. Living in New York for just a few months had opened a window on the world I didn't want to close. Seeing all that it had to offer awakened a fresh sense of ambition. Something inside me was insisting, unequivocally, that I had to make my own way and define myself as an individual. I sensed that my life would require new territory, more than my hometown could give me.

I was simply a girl trying to understand who I'd become, without leaving my family behind. I'd miss my parents, but I knew they'd visit. I knew distance couldn't separate us. What I'd begun in New York had its own momentum, and it was pulling me back. I had such anticipation, knowing in my heart that I was at the beginning of something.

On January 2, 1966, with one foot in my childhood home and the other boarding a plane for New York City, I turned toward my future. My new life and my career were about to begin.

New York was the perfect place to begin my career. It gave me a connected community respectful of shared ambitions, and it was a place to learn and experiment. It was the home to everything I loved beyond my family—dance, theater, museums, and all else. And it was there that I nurtured a newfound love of architecture.

There are so many things about the city that I still love all these years later. When I first arrived, the foliage was breathtaking. New York took on a golden glow, leaves fluttering everywhere. When the sun would peek through the buildings, it was like a bright light had been switched on. Then there was the novelty of snow. Even when it turned to slush, I adored it. Just the simple change of seasons was something I'd never experienced in Texas.

In spring there were the tulips—thousands of them, all up and down Park Avenue. They're planted in the winter months before the spring bloom, with the train lines sending up warmth from underground and helping the tulips survive the winter. I remember seeing those red tulips stretched out before me and thinking of the scene in *The Wizard of Oz* with the field of red poppies. The colorful blooms lent a welcome calm to the teeming heart of the lively city.

New York was fun in the summer as well. Cafés with tables on the sidewalks, everyone eating outside. Gentler than the harsh Texas heat, the warm night air was like breathing in silk. The city gets quieter in the summer. Buildings empty as it seems like half of town heads to the Hamptons or other vacation destinations.

The city provided me with endless distractions and opportunities. I loved to climb aboard a city bus and ride it for blocks and blocks, looking out the window at the street scenes. Passing through the glass doors of Bloomingdale's was like going on a mini-holiday. I'd wander among the racks and explore the design rooms. No one knew where I was or how to reach me. Even though I was surrounded by people, I felt blissfully at peace in my anonymity.

My time in New York wasn't all dance classes and décor. I was on a mission. I was determined to find paying work and went on countless auditions for dance jobs. Irene and I scoured the listings in *Backstage*, *Broadway*, and *Equity News* magazines for casting calls. We'd pack up our leotards and head out at a moment's notice to dance for current and future luminaries such as Michael Bennett. He was just starting out then, too, and would go on to fame and fortune choreographing shows like *Company*, *Follies*, and *Dreamgirls*. He was best known for directing the Tony Award–winning *A Chorus Line*, based on dancers' experiences at Broadway auditions just like the ones we were doing. Irene and I tried out for Bennett's *A Joyful Noise*, which featured a fiddle-friendly country clog dance. The show was not a hit but nonetheless won him his first Tony nomination. (We didn't get cast in it, unfortunately.)

Onna White was one of the only female Broadway choreographers at the time and without a doubt the most accomplished. Her choreography credits are staggering: *Bye Bye Birdie*, *The Music Man*, *Oliver!*, *Mame*, *Carmen Jones*. If memory serves, Irene and I auditioned for White's new show, *1776*. I didn't get that job either, but it was an honor just to audition for an exceptional female choreographer.

My weak point in auditions was picking up combinations quickly. The seasoned dancers we were up against all seemed to get it right on the spot. Sometimes I did, but more often I didn't. However, I excelled in technique. As the months went on, I auditioned constantly and found myself in enough choruses to stay hopeful.

In 1964, Peter Gennaro was coming off a hit with *Fiorello!* and staged a revival of *West Side Story*, which he'd co-choreographed in the fifties. In 1967, they were casting for a touring company. Richard Chamberlain was selected to play Tony. When I read about it in *Backstage*, I got excited, thinking, *This is the one*. Surprisingly, Tony Mordente—a choreographer, director, and actor who starred as Action in the 1961 film adaptation and who originated the role of A-Rab in the original Broadway production—wanted me to audition for Maria. But I turned it down. I was always sensible about what I was capable of, and I knew Maria was out of my reach, at least at that time. I didn't have the voice to carry that part.

Tony then offered me the part of Velma, Riff's girlfriend, who was a lead dancer for the Jets. That appealed to me, but at the same time another opportunity arose. I was offered a role in a summer stock production called *Peg*, a musical starring Eartha Kitt and choreographed by Katherine Dunham. The producers of the show hoped to take it to Broadway. Unfortunately, the production closed out of town after Eartha hurt her back. In retrospect, of course, I wish I'd taken *West Side Story*. Also, how crazy was I to turn down an opportunity to work with Richard Chamberlain? Like countless others, I had a huge crush on Dr. Kildare. Fortunately for me, the opportunity to work with Richard would come around again.

It was an incredible compliment that Tony Mordente paid me, wanting to cast me as Maria. Peter Gennaro planted a little seed of prediction as well. At one point he pulled me aside and said, "You're on the wrong coast. You should be in movies." At the time I was in a whirlwind of experimenting and seeing what might happen next, and I was convinced that New York was where I belonged. I wanted to dance, so in the moment, his advice was almost lost on me. I appreciate it now, though.

The next big thing Irene and I read about in *Backstage* was an audition for a new musical called *Hair*. If you know anything about the show, you're already laughing at the idea of two prim Texas girls thinking we should audition. The show focused on themes central to American hippie counterculture in late 1960s—peace, love, and freedom—and it cast a critical eye toward the Vietnam War, racism, and societal conformity. They were looking for a diverse and vibrant ensemble with raw energy and a natural, expressive movement style—a far cry from our classical training. There I was in a pale-blue leotard with pink tights, white jazz shoes, and my hair in a bun, singing "How Are Things in Glocca Morra?" from *Finian's Rainbow*, a song made popular by Julie Andrews. Imagine Julie Andrews in *Hair*, and you'll get a sense of just how out of place I was. I looked like I'd just stepped off a flying saucer. Needless to say, I wasn't chosen for the ensemble. That was okay. As I said, I always welcomed a learning experience. Rejection carried instruction. Every no taught me something about where I belonged and where I did not. I had that deeply held certainty that I would get along fine, that as long as I stuck with it, things would work out. I did go see the play and loved it. I appreciated that the show broke new ground with its rock music score and racially integrated cast.

If it reads like opportunities fell from the trees like apples in October, you're getting a clear picture of what it was like to be a pretty young dancer in New York in the late sixties—not only for me, but for the many other attractive women who crowded New York's dance studios and theater houses. I'd walk down the street and men would stop me to ask, "Are you a model? I run an agency . . ." or "Are you an actress? I can get you a screen test. . . ." Back then it wasn't just a line. Well, most of the time. I'm sure many of those "Take my card!" men simply wanted to get a date, but it appeared more gentlemanly to have a pretense. I learned quickly that attention is not opportunity, and beauty is not a guarantee of success.

I never followed up with anyone who gave me their card on the street. I didn't have to. I enjoyed a freedom back then that young dancers, actors, and models don't have today. If I heard or read about a casting call for a new show, I could just show up at the audition and dance. Now it seems like you need an agent and a manager, a lengthy résumé, and a large social media following to get your foot in the door. There are a dozen layers and hoops to jump through just to get in the same room with casting directors. But back then, access was easy. It wasn't about keeping people out but about discovering new talent, anywhere and everywhere.

During one of my parents' visits, we went to see the Broadway show *Hallelujah, Baby!* starring Leslie Uggams. At intermission, a couple who'd been sitting in the audience approached me. "My name is Andrea Eastman," the woman said. "I'm a casting director at

Paramount Pictures. I'd really like a meeting with you." Andrea was one of the only female executives at Paramount. When we met that night, she was casting *Goodbye, Columbus*. In the following few years, she worked on *Love Story*, the 1970 tearjerker starring Ali MacGraw and Ryan O'Neal (the future companion of my *Charlie's Angels* costar Farrah Fawcett), and 1972's *The Godfather*. As an agent, later in her career she represented Sylvester Stallone, Barbra Streisand, Richard Gere, Billy Crystal, and Dustin Hoffman.

Then the man reached out to shake my hand. "I'm her husband, Bruce Becker, a talent manager," he said. "I'd really like to work with you too." At the time, he was managing the careers of Charlotte Rampling and Sam Waterston.

Just like that, I had a manager and a test-option contract, meaning they could send me out for any Paramount film and TV audition. Along with my contract, the studio paid for dialect training at the Herbert Berghof Studio, an acting school and a New York institution where Jack Lemmon, Anne Bancroft, Liza Minnelli, Al Pacino, and Robert De Niro got their training. I also took acting lessons with guru Robert Modica in his small classes at Carnegie Hall.

Bruce also made another big mark on my career. In one of our early conversations he said, "You know, Ellen Smith doesn't *make*. It doesn't pack a punch." At the time, managers and agents had everyone changing their name—Tab Hunter, Rock Hudson . . . Bruce gave me a list of potential names, but none of them sounded right. They all felt a bit contrived.

"I'm not going to change my name," I told him, and then I offered a simple solution. "We could use my first name. It's Jaclyn."

"Hmm," he said. "Jaclyn Smith . . . That's *good*!"

I worked with vocal coach Sue Seton (the coach of Bette Midler, Lainie Kazan, and Shirley MacLaine). During one of our sessions, Katharine Hepburn walked in for her voice lesson. She wore pleated pants and a khaki-colored safari jacket with a black turtleneck, and even in that she looked undeniably feminine, her hair done up in a Gibson girl bun. And her cheekbones! She was eye-catching, even in her sixties. She was training for her Broadway show *Coco*. I couldn't believe my luck. She was one of my favorites! Needless to say, I was in awe. She had such gravitas that even if you'd never seen her before, you knew you were talking to someone important. But she was friendly, too, with a kind curiosity—both engaged and engaging.

Sue introduced us, and Katharine looked at me in that very direct way she had and said, "I like your bag. Where did you get it?"

"Henri Bendel's," I said, with the emphasis on the second syllable.

"My dear," she replied, "it's *Ben*-dels. He's a Jewish merchant."

I didn't mind at all that she'd corrected me because she had said it with such charm. And she was Katharine Hepburn!

In just a few years, I went from being a college dropout and Broadway hopeful to studying with the best of the best. That was, and still is, the magic of New York. With all my expert help, I polished and perfected a five-minute monologue that I performed at countless auditions. It was a scene from *Gypsy*—what's known by actors as "Louise's monologue." It comes at the very end of the show when Louise, burlesque dancer Gypsy Rose Lee, finally confronts her overbearing stage mother, Mama Rose. After years of being dominated, Louise demands to be taken seriously and given her well-deserved independence. It's a powerhouse scene with intense emotion, passion, and some funny lines. ("If you want an ulcer, get your own. You can't have mine.") I performed it for Universal Pictures casting director Renée Valente and was offered a deal with them as a "contract player." The catch was that I'd have to move to Los Angeles.

I turned it down. There was no way I was going to leave New York. Not yet. Our romance had just begun, and I sensed the city still had much to offer me. I knew with a clarity that surprised me that staying in New York was necessary, that these were meaningful times artistically, personally, and professionally. There was a spirit of support from my classes and teachers, and I wouldn't give any of that up easily.

Chapter Six

New York in 1968 felt tumultuous. The throbbing heart of a nation in crisis. The city was always bustling, but that year also brought the roiling of political turbulence. With the tragic assassinations of Dr. Martin Luther King Jr. and Robert Kennedy, along with widespread protests over the Vietnam War, New York felt like a pot that was about to boil over. Yet at the same time as the country was tearing itself apart, my own life was starting to come together.

I'd been in New York for a few years and, bit by bit, was beginning to see the fruits of my labors. Andrea Eastman considered me for the part of Brenda, the brash Radcliffe student who seduces and betrays Richard Benjamin (the husband of my Drama Shack friend Paula Prentiss) in *Goodbye, Columbus.* She gave it to her discovery Ali MacGraw instead. The director, Larry Peerce, said about me, "I really like her. She is the perfect stew; she just needed a little garlic added to that stew." In his eyes I was still too young and innocent, with not enough life under my belt to play a convincing seductress. It was a fair evaluation. But Larry did offer me a small part in the film. And I mean small, as in blink and you'll miss me, which my parents did! I was a model posing in a fur hat with a Great Dane in front of the Plaza Hotel. My parents were so excited to see me, but even though I told them when I'd appear they still didn't manage to catch me.

I was going out for dozens of parts, and as I discovered, auditioning was its own art. I studied it meticulously like I studied dance, always thinking about what I could do better next time. I didn't have an agent, so I went to a lot of open calls, including one for a Listerine commercial. For some reason I always felt more confident when it came to commercial auditions. I never had the same jitters as I did for dance auditions and cold readings. I walked into the ad agency and read the lines, they thanked me for my time, and I walked back out again. Around the same time, I auditioned for a dance role in a Las Vegas revue starring Tony Bennett and was told I'd gotten it. But, of course, that meant I'd have to move to Vegas. Still, the pay was great: $325 a week, which seemed like a million dollars back then.

It was summer, and while I considered the offer, I flew home to Houston to visit my parents. While I was there, I got a call. I'd booked the Listerine job! It felt like pennies from heaven, and I knew that if it ran, I would have money coming in on residuals. I was already on the fence about Vegas. My parents, however, were clear. They hated the idea! They would have warmed to it if I'd really wanted to go, just as they had with New York, but they never had to. I decided to go back to New York and do the commercial.

Before I headed back, I went out to LA to visit Tommy and his wife, Charlotte. On a whim, Charlotte and I decided to drive to Las Vegas to catch the show and see what I'd missed. We sat in the front row. Little did Tony Bennett know that this girl staring up at him, enthralled, had almost been next to him onstage. It was a sweet moment of serendipity. The show was wonderful, but I felt good about my decision.

As often happens in this business, just when you feel like things are heating up, they cool off again. After Listerine, things quieted down. I told Irene, "If I don't get a regular job soon, I'm going to apply at Bloomingdale's." I wouldn't be the first aspiring dancer/singer/actor to work in retail, and why not do it at one of my favorite places in the city? I went to the store, sat for an interview, left my résumé, and waited for the phone to ring.

It did, but it wasn't Bloomingdale's calling. I had auditioned for a part singing and dancing in a musical revue in Central Park. It starred *Star Trek*'s leading man, William Shatner, and crooner Andy Williams. It was going to run for a couple of weeks and felt like it would be a fun summer job. It was! I even had a little crush on Captain Kirk.

Things settled down again after the summer, but I knew that if I just kept at it, eventually something would happen. And it did, but not in the way I'd planned. At a casting call for a commercial, I met a square-jawed, blue-eyed actor named Roger Davis. At the time, he was one of the stars on the ABC daytime vampire-themed soap opera *Dark Shadows*. (Yes, vampire themed. Somehow it worked.) Owing to his down-home, mellifluous voice, Roger had a lucrative side income doing voice-overs for commercials. He was incredibly charming and very sought-after. *Dark Shadows* had debuted in 1966 and gotten off to a rocky start, but by that time the show had picked up considerable steam. Roger was on a roll of popularity and enjoying every moment of it.

I didn't get the commercial, but I did get a boyfriend. Roger and I hit it off, and he asked me out. Our first dinner was at V&T Pizza, one of his regular spots near his alma mater, Columbia University. As we chatted, we discovered that we were undeniably compatible. Neither of us drank. We were both Southerners (he hailed from Louisville, Kentucky). And we both grew up in the same provincial way, with a focus on family and traditional values. (Little did I know at that time, his idea of traditional values differed immensely from mine.) We also shared an aesthetic, including a love for eighteenth-century design. What were the chances? We seemed so well suited—it felt fated that we'd fall in love.

We'd been dating for a month or so when Roger called me one day, sounding excited. "Alexandra Moltke is leaving *Dark Shadows* and they're looking for a replacement. You're perfect for the part! I got you an audition." A newlywed, Alexandra was pregnant and had decided to leave the show to focus on being a mother.

I agreed to audition and was offered the part of Victoria Winters, Roger's character's wife, but I turned it down. I didn't like the idea of being Roger's love interest both on- and off-screen. I didn't even like the idea of working on the same show—it was just too much overlap, and I worried that it would have a negative impact on our relationship.

It was a big role on a popular show, so Roger saw my decision as a huge sacrifice on my part. Even though we'd been dating only a short while—two months, to be exact—he proposed, and I said yes. I was twenty-two years old; Roger was twenty-eight. That might seem young today and it probably is, but back then it was commonplace. Growing up, marriage and a family were always part of my plan, and with Roger it seemed like that plan was coming together.

When Roger arrived on the scene, my letters home tapered off to a few times a week, then less. My mother was not used to what amounted to radio silence from me. Ten days without a letter? Mom also corresponded regularly with Irene and expressed her dismay, writing, "Ellen acts like she's fallen out of a tree!" And that's how I felt. The disorientation of infatuation hit me hard.

I couldn't wait to tell Mom and Daddy that I was engaged. This couldn't wait for a letter. I dashed to the phone booth down in the lobby of the Barbizon.

"Hello?" my mother said.

"Mom, it's me. I'm engaged!" Just like that, with no preamble.

"Well, goodness, honey!" she said. I could tell I'd knocked the breath out of her with my sudden announcement, but she made a quick recovery. "Well, here, let me put Daddy on."

Daddy said, "Well, of course you must bring him home to meet your family." I'm sure they were shocked, but even though my father was plainspoken, he loved me dearly and heard how excited I was. They wouldn't have dreamed of tamping down my enthusiasm with a word of caution, but they certainly wanted to meet him.

Soon after that, I brought Roger home. A consummate performer, Roger understood his audience and made a great impression on Mom, Dad, Papa, and Tommy. He was intelligent, an Ivy League graduate, a student of English and design. He'd even worked as an adjunct professor, teaching classes in English literature at UCLA. On top of all that, he was a well-known actor starring in a hit TV show that aired every day. When he came to Houston that first time, he dazzled.

When we arrived back in New York I started planning the wedding. It would be in Houston. Mom was involved in the organizing. She wasn't such a fan of big weddings, and during one conversation she said, "Why don't you take the money and travel instead? Or take the money and redecorate your apartment?"

I was firm. "No, I want a wedding," I said. I'd dreamed of a wedding since I was a little girl. It wasn't just the romance, though that was part of it. I wanted the chance to indulge in all that beauty. The dresses, the flowers . . . I wanted it all. It didn't have to be lavish; I just wanted the full experience. And with Roger's passion for design, he was on board.

In keeping with the rushed pace of our relationship, Roger and I had a short engagement. In just a few months we pulled together a two-hundred-person wedding, and it was glorious: a puffy white gown, a ten-piece orchestra, and a seven-tiered cake. I had six bridesmaids. Irene was my maid of honor and Claire, my other best friend from the Drama Shack, was also in the party. The bridesmaids wore silk dresses in cornflower blue, with little Juliet caps with streamers. They carried Victoria nosegays, a kind of small decorative bouquet popularized by Queen Victoria and frequently carried in the Victorian era as a fashion accessory. My dress was a high-necked lace gown, reminiscent of Grace Kelly's when she married Prince Rainier. It had a traditional veil, and I wore my hair pulled back off my face. It really was like a fairy tale.

Roger's family came to Texas from Kentucky, and Papa officiated, though he was long retired by then. I don't know if he really wanted to take on that important job, but he would have done anything for me. When I look back at that day, I still get tearful picturing him at the pulpit, smiling at me, his heart brimming with love.

The next day Roger and I returned to New York and had a one-night honeymoon at the Plaza Hotel. Then we resumed our lives, already in progress. We started searching for an apartment together and found one on East Ninety-Second Street and Park Avenue. We fell in love with the architecture. It was bursting with old-world charm, with beautiful high ceilings and ornate molding, high baseboards, and wide windows that let in loads of light. It just needed some tender loving care.

Roger was a perfectionist about architecture and décor and immediately fixated on things like which rugs we'd buy—Savonnerie or Aubusson? As much as I loved decorating as a kid, and still do, it became consuming. We spent hours refinishing furniture. We did most of the work on the apartment ourselves, including scoring the molding white, painting the walls a subtle off-white, and adding wainscoting. I started to notice that making a home was not the same thing as building a life. The thing was, Roger was an elitist, and it felt like there was a superficial edge to his interests. I began to see that, for him, it wasn't so much about feathering our love nest as creating a space that would impress others.

Even though Roger was doing well financially, his bank account wasn't as extravagant as his tastes. And, of course, my own career had yet to take off, so we had to be at least somewhat judicious with our purchases. But there were exceptions. On one shopping mission at Lord & Taylor's antiques department, I saw a brass bed with a domed canopy that made my heart sing with every schoolgirl fantasy I'd ever had. I needed that bed. (I know, me and canopy beds!) It was priced at $5,000, far more than I could afford. But I had to have it. I bought it anyway and paid for it month by month. It took me years to pay it off, but it was worth it. It's still in my home today. Where there's a will, there's a way!

Even if we struggled at times to make our vision (or at least Roger's vision) for the apartment into a reality, it was fun, and I loved that we were in it together. I was young, in love, and in New York. Everything was wonderful . . . for a while.

Chapter Seven

Meeting Roger at an audition for a commercial seemed somewhere between providence and a happy accident. But it wasn't the only stroke of good fortune I experienced at that time in my life. One afternoon, while I was on a lunch break from the summer musical revue I was in, a ball came bouncing toward me from the nearby playground. I picked up the ball, brought it back to the two beautiful children who'd lost it, and started chatting with them. "Thanks for your help," their dad said, flashing a smile. "My name is Harry Abrams. I'm a commercial agent, booking models for TV ads. I'd love to represent you." Just like that, another chance encounter altered my life.

Meeting Harry truly was life-changing. After I signed on with him, a deluge of offers from Madison Avenue flooded in. In the late 1960s and early '70s, the ad business was on the cutting edge of culture. Madison Avenue was reinventing itself, placing actors in small, scripted moments of ordinary life. Before then, TV commercials were usually just an announcer reading a cue card while holding the product. In their new iteration, they'd become mini-entertainments in and of themselves. The work was lucrative, and it demanded sincerity. I fit the moment—wholesome yet suggestive, innocent with edge. I wanted Broadway, but I understood opportunity when it arrived wearing another costume.

I never anticipated that commercials would become a big part of my career. If you'd told me back then that I'd appear in more than a hundred of them, including a decades-long relationship with Max Factor, I'd have thought you were putting me on. But unlike my hesitation over the role of Maria, in the world of commercials I felt right at home, and I guess that came through. I wasn't self-conscious or shy; it was an area where I was comfortable. I liked it so much more than modeling, where I was just standing there wearing clothes or smiling and holding a product. And as happy as I was to enter the world of TV acting, I was equally happy to enter the world of residuals! Sure, some part of me wanted to be acting on Broadway, but I knew that ads could lead to films or more serious TV work.

Plus, it was a chance to hone my skills. Doing commercials, I learned how to put across a fully formed idea in thirty seconds. I would take the script and make a little movie of it in my head. I learned so much watching myself on film—the way my face looked and how my body moved. The camera sees absolutely everything. And when the camera is "in a choker," you have to get it right or it'll show. Today, with people's limited attention spans, everything is bigger and louder. There's little to no subtlety. But back then, it needed to look natural. I loved the challenge.

And it all started with Harry. When someone sees more in you than you see in yourself at that moment, it gives you an inkling of who you could become, like when Peter Gennaro told me I should be in movies. People who care enough to encourage you, people who put thought into your career, can make all the difference. Harry Abrams did that for me.

Harry had a good eye for talent. He saw something in me, and casting agents agreed. The first ad Harry got for me was for Camay soap. I had three changes of costume: a white day dress with cutouts and a bubble hat, then a towel, and finally a slinky black evening dress, also with cutouts. My lines were: "Today, you want to look more than clean. You want to look clean and creamy, all over." I had to splash my face with water (and avoid getting any in my mouth) while rhapsodizing earnestly about my creamy complexion.

Camay was the beginning of a hot streak for me. I turned out to be the perfect pitchwoman for beauty and health-care brands: wholesome, yet sexy. I could look like the girl next door while delivering provocative lines.

For a Dial antiperspirant ad, I stayed dry no matter how strenuous the activity.

For Palmolive, I sat on a table in nothing but a towel while a fully dressed man talked about how delectably soft my skin was, and how using the soap was like "a facial for your whole body." All I had to do was sit there and smile coyly.

In a Ben-Gay ad, I rubbed ointment into a man's shoulders and back while he moaned.

For English Leather cologne ads, I said, "I make sure all my men wear English Leather. Or they wear nothing at all."

And then there was Breck. As a Breck Girl, I appeared in countless print and TV ads selling Gold Formula Breck shampoo. I swung my tresses, ran my fingers through my long, shiny strands, and made sure viewers knew that Breck "has far less detergent than any other leading brand." For one ad, I wrapped my head with a shirt instead of a towel and said, "You might wash your blouse with detergent, but not your hair."

The camera, I learned quickly, was merciless. It captured everything: every hesitation, every doubt. Even the smallest flicker of insecurity. The reason I can still recite so much commercial copy is that we often had to do so many takes to get it all just right. There's a kind of endurance required with this type of repetition; you've got to make it sound like it's never been spoken before. My work ethic and dancer's diligence helped me during those shoots. It takes a lot of stamina to look and sound like you really mean what you're saying after three or four hours of doing it. I wore swimsuits on a beach in February and heavy wool clothing on the street in August. People were constantly dabbing my face with powder to cover up goose bumps when I was freezing or take the glow off my forehead when I was sweltering.

It was an incredible time for me. I was having a blast and enjoying a huge sense of accomplishment. My family got a kick out of it too. Every time one of my commercials came on, Daddy would call out to Papa to come see. Papa was losing his vision at the time, so he'd get up close to the TV to try to catch a glimpse of me. They were proud of me, and I was proud of myself. My parents would have been happy to keep pitching in to support me, but I wanted to make my own way. I was finally realizing my little-girl dream of having my own career.

Unfortunately, not everything in my life was going so well.

I've often felt like I belonged in another time and place. That was certainly true for me in early-seventies New York, when people my age were tuning in and turning on, shedding their crochet vests and bell-bottoms to swim naked in the fountain in Washington Square Park. We were rewriting the rules of love, loyalty, and allegiance, as if history itself was a rough draft. As a generation, that is. I don't know how many rules I was rewriting personally at that time. While my contemporaries were swapping bed partners, tripping on acid, and marching in protest of the Vietnam War, I was living in a nineteenth-century building, surrounded by eighteenth-century treasures, in an early-twentieth-century marriage. Like our new apartment, that marriage ended up creating more work than I'd bargained for. I found myself inhabiting a version of marriage that was older and more rigid. Roger and I looked perfect on the surface, but appearances, I would learn, are often the most fragile constructions of all.

One day in 1970, I met Irene for lunch at the Hickory Inn on the Upper East Side. It was one of Roger's and my favorites. I'd never outgrown my childhood love of hamburgers, and the ones they had there were fantastic. The restaurant was on the ground floor of a town house, and Roger and I were on the verge of renting an apartment across the street. I described the place to Irene during our meal, and after we settled the bill, I said, "Let's go up. I'll show it to you."

We went outside and bumped right into Warren Beatty. He was *the* leading man at the time. Gorgeous. Tall and thin. You couldn't take your eyes off him. His presence just pervaded the moment. He'd starred opposite Faye Dunaway in the Arthur Penn–directed smash hit film *Bonnie and Clyde* and was starting to direct and produce his own projects. Imagine my surprise when he looked at me and said, "Hey, I know you."

I was floored. "How do you know me?"

"You were in *The Adventurers*. I stayed through the end credits to learn your name, and I remembered it because of the unusual spelling: J-A-C-L-Y-N."

Warren Beatty was spelling out my name right there on the city sidewalk in the middle of the afternoon. Was this really happening?

He was right. I'd had a small part in *The Adventurers*, a thriller featuring Candice Bergen. The cast was star-studded: Olivia de Havilland, Charles Aznavour, Anna Moffo . . . But my part was nothing to get excited about. I played a reporter from *Teen* magazine in a single scene. My big line of dialogue was to ask the playboy son of a South American politician, "Is it true you've slept with every woman in this room?" He leered at me and said, "Not yet." I'd have gotten a bigger part if I'd agreed to a nude scene, but I wasn't interested.

More memorable than my role in the movie was how I fainted on set. My character was in the front row, standing there holding a glass of champagne while watching Anna Moffo, the legendary opera singer, onstage performing. Suddenly I felt nauseated. *Oh no!* I thought. *I'm going to throw up in front of all these people!* There was a sofa on set and I tried to sidestep over to it without drawing attention to myself. I made it, but the moment the camera dollied past me, I slid straight down onto the couch and passed out, right in someone's lap. When I came to, everyone was standing over me, asking if I was okay. It turned out I was fine; I'd just had a drop in blood pressure due to jet lag. Roger was flying to Rome to see me, and he arrived right after that. His visit was enough to perk me right back up. I finished filming, and Roger and I had a glorious time—our own Roman holiday.

Thank goodness Warren didn't know that little piece of movie trivia. He said, "You know, I'd like you to come in for an interview. I'm doing a new film and might have a part for you." For all I know, he wanted to interview me for his movie *Shampoo*, which would have been only a bit ironic, given my experience as a Breck Girl. But before I could say, "I'd love to!" Roger appeared as if from nowhere and approached our little group.

"Oh, Roger!" I said. "This is my husband, Roger Davis."

He and Warren shook hands. Warren said, "I was just telling your wife I saw her in *The Adventurers*, and I'd like to interview her for my new film."

Roger smiled. "No," he said, "she only does commercials."

We all just looked at him for a moment. Then Warren smiled at me, offered a genial goodbye, and went on his way.

Irene looked at me but didn't say a word. I just stood there, not sure how to react. I wasn't angry, more like confused. I was still a bit shy, but I also felt that if there was a conversation to be had, I didn't want to have it right there on the street in front of everyone. I didn't like Roger speaking for me, but I also figured, *Hey, I have an agent. If Warren actually does want to find me, he knows how. If it's meant to be, it's meant to be.*

So I let it slide. Irene begged off on looking at the apartment, and Roger and I went home. I never brought it up.

I ran into Warren many times after that in a variety of circumstances. At one point, I had the opportunity to play Vivien Leigh in a made-for-TV biopic. While trying to decide whether I should take the job, I found myself sitting next to Warren on a plane and thought he was the perfect person to discuss my dilemma with. We talked about the script. I was concerned about certain aspects of her personality, including unexplained strong sexual behavior. Vivien had some mental health challenges that probably today would be characterized as bipolar disorder. At that time, people just labeled her a nymphomaniac. As I read the script, it felt like an unfair label, and I wanted to run the whole thing past someone who might get it. So I asked Warren, "Should I do it? They described her as a nymphomaniac without giving any indication of her disorder or what she was dealing with."

He smiled suggestively and said, "There's no such thing as a nymphomaniac."

I laughed. "Not in your eyes!" I said.

In the end, I didn't take the offer—the job or Warren's.

At the time we'd run into Warren on the street, Roger had been working with a real estate agent named Laura. I had gotten to know

Laura and her husband, Bill, an actor, while Roger and I were dating and thought of them as good friends.

Bill would sometimes ask me for advice about dance, and at one point I brought him with me to a movement class I was taking. When the class was over, we shared a taxi uptown. We'd gone all of two blocks when he turned to me and said, "Jaclyn, you know I'm very attracted to you."

"What?" I blurted. "This is crazy. Bill, you're married. Laura is my *good friend*. I don't get why you're saying this to me."

Instead of looking chagrined, he seemed confused. "Well . . . you know about Laura and Roger," he said.

"What are you talking about?"

"They're having an affair. It's been going on for a while."

I stared at him, incredulous. The idea of Roger betraying me, let alone with someone I trusted, had never crossed my mind. I loved Roger. Bill was only saying that so I'd go to bed with him. If there was any truth to the accusation, I'd need to hear it from Laura herself.

"I need to talk to Laura," I said.

"Fine," he replied. "Let's go."

We took the cab straight to Bill and Laura's apartment, where I asked her point-blank: "Are you sleeping with my husband?"

She just looked at me. "Yes," she said, her tone so matter-of-fact you'd have thought I'd asked her if she had change for a dollar. She delivered that yes without apology.

She's lying, I thought. "How long?"

"It started before you got married. While you were planning your wedding, we were together."

I couldn't imagine how two people I trusted could have betrayed me, and for so long. Laura was telling me to my face what she'd done, but I still couldn't believe it.

"Remember the day you ran into Warren Beatty outside the apartment, and Roger suddenly appeared on the street out front?"

"Yes," I said, my heart racing.

"He'd been upstairs in the apartment having sex with me."

"No," I said, shaking my head. "I don't believe it."

Overwhelmed, I ran out of their apartment and stumbled home. On the way, my mind flooded with things Roger had said to me over the course of our relationship.

"You know, you would really be something if your eyes were blue."

"You shouldn't wear skirts. You have dancer's legs; they're too muscular for skirts."

"I don't like your fragrance. I want you to change it."

A realization was starting to crystallize. Roger was controlling in ways that disguised themselves as taste. Dogmatic in ways that masqueraded as principle. His own certainty about how things should be done crowded out my own. Each remark he'd made had erased a little more of me, but the effect had been so gradual I hadn't even realized it. Laura's revelation had thrown back the curtains, and I was seeing things about my husband for the first time.

When I finally got home, unlike in the incident with Warren, I confronted Roger immediately. "Are you sleeping with Laura?"

He looked at me and tilted his head, shoulders sagging as if I'd wounded him. "How could you accuse me of that?" he said. I told him what had happened. "No," he said. "Laura's just jealous. She's always coming on to me, but of course I'm not sleeping with her. You know, Bill probably wanted to sleep with you, and this is their game."

Denial, I discovered, can be seductive. At that moment, blind belief was easier than truth. And some truths must be seen to be believed. My options were to leave Roger then, after only two years of marriage, and feel humiliated by my own naïveté, or to give the man I loved the benefit of the doubt and hope I'd made the right decision. I chose the latter.

I don't know how I moved on from that day, but I did, slowly and cautiously. But I became a suspicious wife. I hated myself for not trusting Roger, but I also knew I had good reason not to. He always had plausible excuses for being unaccountably unreachable. A meeting ran late. There was traffic . . .

One day I went to our jeweler to drop off some pieces I wanted to have cleaned. "Oh, hi, Mrs. Davis," the jeweler said. "A girl just dropped off your husband's watch for repair yesterday." I didn't have the courage to ask Roger about it. I didn't yet have the life skills to handle it.

Another time we went to dinner at a restaurant we liked called Gallagher's. When the waiter saw Roger, he said, "Back so soon, Mr. Davis? Didn't get enough at lunch?" The look on Roger's face said it all: He'd been there with a woman for lunch and was now there with me for dinner. I was dumbfounded.

Each moment was a bitter dose of reality. Roger had his excuses, and I had mine for how I could overlook his barely hidden transgressions. I talked myself into sticking it out for one more day, one more month, one more year. I convinced myself that he and his new costar, or a chatty saleswoman, or a flirty stewardess, were just being friendly, just doing their jobs. *He really was in a long meeting,* I told myself, over and over. Our marriage lingered, hollowed out by lies. Then I saw the truth with my own eyes.

A year or so had passed since Laura's horrifying admission. Roger and I had both started commuting between the coasts regularly, so we'd rented an apartment in Los Angeles. I would go west at least once a month for TV and movie auditions and for various commercials. Ever the real estate magnate, Roger bought an apartment building on La Brea Avenue to renovate and flip. Before long, we were both traveling so much and on such erratic schedules that we didn't see each other that much. I tried not to imagine what Roger might be doing on all our nights apart.

For our fourth anniversary, I had all of Roger's TV scripts bound in leather, each labeled with the script's title and date. It was such a special gift, I decided to surprise him by flying to LA to give it to him in person. He wasn't at our apartment, so I drove over to the La Brea building. As I was walking up the path to the front door, I saw Roger through a window. He was standing there talking intimately with a girl in a stewardess outfit. I don't know what made him look up, but he turned and saw me standing frozen by the window, watching them, *and waved at me.*

I turned around and drove straight back to our apartment. For so long I'd wanted someone, anyone, to seize the wheel and steer me away from disaster, but no one had come. In that moment, I realized it was up to me.

When Roger showed up an hour later, he saw my present with its big red ribbon sitting there on the table. "Hey, is this for me?" he said, as if nothing had happened. He picked it up and unwrapped it. "Oh, El," he said, "what a beautiful gift. Thank you."

"Do you like them?" I said.

"I love them." He smiled.

"Okay," I said, standing up. "Well, pack them up with the rest of your stuff and leave."

It was the simplest sentence I'd ever spoken.

The next day, I called a lawyer.

Something had awakened in me, yet at the same time, something else had shut down forever. The tragedy of a first marriage ending in divorce is not in the loss of the marriage itself, but in the loss of innocence.

When I finally called home to let my parents know that the marriage was not going to work, my mom said simply, "Come home." She always gave me safe passage, and she understood. I was too humiliated to tell her all the details, but she knew what was going on, as mothers always do. She felt my pain but was powerless to change Roger, and she just wanted me to be free. Now that I'm a mother, I understand the special agony she must have felt, watching her daughter suffer but unable to fix it. Still, as I learned, motherhood is not about control; it is about presence. About standing steady. About loving your children fiercely enough that they know without question where home is.

The end of my marriage was clean in a way the middle never was. Though I felt a sense of failure, there was also an exhilarating sense of clarity.

And I still had my family to lean on for support, and my career to carry me forward.

Chapter Eight

In 1974, Richard Nixon resigned the presidency after our long national nightmare, and there was a great sense of relief. I felt the same way about being free of Roger.

I was in no rush to start dating again, but I did see a few people casually here and there. After the emotional turmoil, I was grateful to focus on my career and not dwell on the daily blame and shame of being in an unfaithful marriage. My professional life took center stage.

My first appearance on a TV series had been in an episode of *The Partridge Family* in 1970. It was there that I got my first real sense of what it might be like if my career took me in that direction. The episode was called "When Mother Gets Married." I'd been a fan of Shirley Jones since I was a kid and saw her in *Carousel* in 1956, and later in 1962's *The Music Man*. She played the matriarch of the Partridge family and their band. In the episode, Shirley's character met up with an old friend, played by John McMartin, and the two started dating. David Cassidy and Susan Dey, the two eldest children, happened to see McMartin in a jewelry store buying a ring for a pretty girl: me. In typical sitcom fashion, they immediately leaped to the wrong conclusion about the relationship. It was later revealed that I was McMartin's niece, not his girlfriend.

I had three lines and one minute of screen time wearing an Emilio Pucci dress, which I believe was my own (and that I wish I still had!). Susan Dey (who'd later star in *L.A. Law*) and I had the same hairstyle—middle part, long and straight. It was a look that would be featured in dozens of shampoo ads to come. One of the most memorable parts of the experience was getting to meet David Cassidy. At the time, every teenage girl in America was in love with him, and scores of them were lined up outside the soundstage just hoping to catch a glimpse.

The entire cast was unbelievably nice. They truly seemed like a family just having fun together. Behind the scenes, there was an easy, relaxed feeling, and I thought, *If this is what it's like to work on a series, I'm all for it!*

Thanks to my ads, important people started calling me. One of them was Glen A. Larson, TV writer of *The Fugitive* and, at the time, the producer of *McCloud* and *The Virginian*, as well as a composer. Later in his career, he would work on *The Six Million Dollar Man*; *Battlestar Galactica*; *Knight Rider*; *Quincy, M.E.*; *The Fall Guy*; and *Magnum, P.I.*; among other hits.

As the story goes, Glen was watching TV and happened to see one of my Breck ads. He asked his assistant, "Who's that girl?"

"That's Jaclyn Smith, Roger Davis's wife." We were separated at that point, but Roger was working on one of Glen's TV shows, *Alias Smith and Jones*, a reimagined TV Western written by the late, great William Goldman.

Glen said, "I want to put her on *McCloud*. It'll be the love story of the season!"

McCloud was one of the biggest shows on TV at the time. It starred Dennis Weaver as a cowboy cop in a sheepskin jacket and a ten-gallon hat, catching bad guys in New York City while oozing down-home charm.

The love story of the season? I'd have more than three lines of dialogue and one minute of screen time, that was for sure. It seemed like more than I was ready for. But I agreed to play a model who got mixed up with the wrong people and was forced to be a drug mule in an episode called "Showdown at the End of the World." The first step was to meet Dennis Weaver. He was in New York shooting on location. I met him in a hotel room to rehearse our scenes.

I was not good at cold readings. Dennis was generous and patient with me, but after a few tries, I said, "You know what? You deserve the best. I think you need another girl." After all, this wasn't a commercial or a quick stint on a sitcom. I knew they needed someone with more experience.

I don't believe anyone had ever said no to Dennis Weaver before; he was that charming and irresistible. Dennis was tall and quick to laugh. Focused. A normal guy. The human inside that public figure couldn't have been nicer. Underneath the celebrity, he was just a good old boy.

Dennis wasn't giving up that easily. "We can take care of that," he said. "I'm going to bring in a director who'll make all the difference. You'll see. He'll get rid of the nerves and make you want to do this." If Dennis Weaver trusted this person and really wanted me in this part, I would certainly give it a try.

"Who is it?" I asked.

"Lou Antonio," he said.

Lou was, and is, an actor's director. An actor himself, he had a résumé a mile long that included *Cool Hand Luke*, *Star Trek*, *The Rockford Files*, and *McMillan & Wife*, among many others. Most TV directors work by one rule: Get the take and move on. Lou not only went for the shot—he went for the heart of the shot. He was a charming man with a facility for giving directions succinctly, clearly, and in a nonjudgmental tone. He would talk directly to an actor intimately, his words just for them.

Lou really worked with me. He had studied at the Actors Studio under the direction of Lee Strasberg and later taught there himself. His work with me was like a crash course in acting. He always started with a relaxation exercise. He'd pick up my arms and shake them, feel my shoulders, pull my jaw open and closed. He was seeing if I was holding any rigidity, which he said would block emotion.

Then we would *create* the character, getting a sense of her backstory, motivations, and so on. Where was she from? Did she have a big family or was she a single child? Was she close to her family? What were her likes and dislikes? It was about the subtext, and seeing the character beyond what was written on the page. Lou opened up the world of acting to me in a different way. In my theater experience, I'd taken on well-established characters like Gypsy Rose Lee, whom everyone knew and understood. But on *McCloud*, I had a role that no one knew, including me. I had to understand her and give her a history. That wasn't in the script, but was crucial to how I interpreted her reactions and dialogue. Once we had the character, we rehearsed my lines in different settings, doing different things, like having dinner or running in the park. (Picture me jogging through the park with Lou, practicing the whole time!)

During this process, I got an education in acting from a master, and I made one of the best friends I've ever had. Lou is a person who will give a great toast with no notice, crack the perfect joke in a tense moment, and make everyone feel at ease. He is still one of my best friends today.

Lou and I worked together many times over the years: again on *McCloud*, in an episode where I played a ballerina, and when he directed some of my movies and miniseries in the eighties and nineties. I owe my life as an artist to Lou. I will never forget the debt or dismiss his teaching. I thank him with my whole heart for his wisdom. Dennis couldn't have been more right about Lou.

Through *McCloud*, I also found another great friend in producer Glen Larson. Glen had a steady calm about work. He approached it with a balance of duty, fun, and humor. The long hours, difficulties on set, network politics—nothing seemed to affect him.

I credit Glen with giving me my start in TV. Everyone needs a Glen Larson in their career. He was always protective of me and determined to find roles I was right for, even if he had to write them himself, like that ballerina part in *McCloud*. The thrill of that role, aside from making a second appearance on a hit show, was that I got to dance with the San Francisco Ballet. It was a dream come true.

After *McCloud*, Glen cast me in a pilot called *Fools, Females and Fun*, a concept show that took each of the seven deadly sins and built an episode around it. I represented lust opposite Barry Nelson. He was a married man driven mad by desire for me. Other cast members included Dick Sargent, one of the two Darrens on *Bewitched* (and a future *Charlie's Angels* guest star); the legendary Catwoman, Julie Newmar; and a teen idol of mine, Barbara Rush. The pilot for the show didn't get picked up, so in the end they cobbled together a few of the scripts and turned it into a four-part TV movie.

From there, I worked steadily in TV movies and guest-starring in roles on shows like *Get Christie Love!* and *The Rookies*, usually as a model or a hapless drug smuggler, or both. *The Rookies* was produced by Aaron Spelling, who'd also made *The Mod Squad* and *S.W.A.T.* and was launching *Starsky & Hutch* and *Family*. Even though *The Rookies* was a cop show, the most popular character was a young nurse played by breakout star Kate Jackson. I didn't have any scenes with Kate, but I remembered her as very talented and serious about her work.

Actors are always looking for their one big break. My path was more a matter of accumulating a lot of small and medium-sized breaks that eventually led to the big one. I was stacking bricks, building a solid foundation. Another brick came via Glen for his new show, *Switch*. It was about a retired cop played by Eddie Albert whose partner-in-crime-solving was a reformed con man portrayed by Robert Wagner. My role was Ally McGuinness, a freelance con artist who was called in every so often to help out with that week's caper. The pilot was set in Las Vegas, and a local news station came to film us shooting the show at a casino. I was in the scene and, to my surprise, I made the evening news.

The next day Robert (called R.J. by his friends) told me that he'd gotten a late-night phone call from Dean Martin, who'd caught the news segment. "Dean would like to meet you," Robert said, giving me his signature lopsided grin.

I passed on Dean's invitation, but our paths would cross later. In the second season of *Charlie's Angels*, we filmed in Vegas, and Dean ended up being our guest star. His love interest on the show was Kate. Dean was full of mischief, but he was also generous, with a comic charm and likability.

Switch was a turning point for me because it was the first time I was a series regular. I also got to work with some incredible actors, including Richard Kiel, who became world-famous as the character Jaws in the James Bond movies. Then there was Sharon Gless, who'd go on to star in *Cagney & Lacey*. She played Eddie and Robert's secretary.

R.J. was one of my favorite costars of all time. He was, and still is, remarkably handsome. He has a face you might linger on. A perfect nose. Thick hair. Defined cheekbones. A smile that would make you fall in love. And he is one of the kindest men I have ever met.

I was now meeting and working with people who had influence and could open doors for me, including R.J. I had started to contemplate my next move when, one day on the set of *Switch*, R.J. announced, "By the way, Jaclyn, I recommended you for a new show that some producer friends of mine are developing."

"Who?" I asked.

"Aaron Spelling and Leonard Goldberg."

"What's the show?"

"It's about three female detectives in Los Angeles."

Chapter Nine

Aaron and Leonard had been thinking about a show that could be a cross between *The Avengers* and *Honey West*, with an irresistible combination of eye-catching style, action, and beautiful women. Creatives Ivan Goff and Ben Roberts joined forces with Aaron and Len. Their take on the original idea was a show called *The Alley Cats*, about female detectives who lived together off an alley, wore a lot of black leather, and carried whips.

In the immortal words of screenwriter and author William Goldman, "Nobody knows anything. Not one person in the entire motion picture field knows for a certainty what's going to work. Every time out it's a guess and, if you're lucky, an educated one." The same can be said about television. Putting together a show is a risk, no matter how experienced you are and how much testing you do. It's expensive, and reputations are always on the line. You are only as good as your last hit or flop, which Aaron and Len knew as well as anyone.

Now we can look back at their creative partnership and at their individual careers and say that they were hitmakers supreme, producing shows such as *The Rookies*, *S.W.A.T.*, *Starsky & Hutch*, *Family*, *Charlie's Angels*, *Fantasy Island*, *Hart to Hart*, and *T. J. Hooker*. Aaron went on to produce iconic shows such as *The Love Boat*, *Dynasty*, *Beverly Hills 90210*, *Melrose Place*, *Hotel*, and *Charmed*, to mention a few, as well as movies for the big and small screens. Yet their track record wasn't perfect. (Does anyone remember *Chopper One*?)

Still, their instincts about what would appeal to the American public were as bankable as you could get at the time. Aaron had been an actor and a writer. Len had experience behind the scenes as a network executive. They were veterans of the business and had learned to trust their gut, especially when it came to casting.

Aaron and Len went immediately to Kate Jackson, who'd played Nurse Danko on *The Rookies*. Hiring the breakout star of an already popular series to lead the cast would smooth the way when they sold the show to a network. The producers invited Kate to Aaron's office and laid out the basic premise of the show.

Aaron's office at Warner Hollywood Studios was as big as a basketball court and opulently decorated by his wife, Candy. It had every trapping of success: silver trays laden with food and drink, a huge fireplace, art and sculptures everywhere. Aaron was not modest when it came to luxury. A fellow Texan, he had grown up in Dallas and hadn't had an easy childhood. For one, he'd been the target of antisemitic bullying. I also remember him telling me about a time when his local kids' theater—a lot like the Fun Club I'd had in Houston—ran a story-writing contest. The first prize was a bicycle, and Aaron was determined to get it. He worked so hard on his piece and was certain he was going to win, but he came in second. The second prize was a basketball, and Aaron wasn't into sports. He was so crushed that he ended up in bed for a year. Between the stress of the harassment and his sadness over the loss, he literally lost the ability to walk. It was a psychosomatic illness, and Aaron eventually recovered, but during that time, he dove into reading and further developed his writing skills, which would become legendary. When it came to Aaron's love of luxury, I think he compensated for his childhood by living as extravagantly as possible. Sometimes living well is the best revenge.

"The show is called *The Alley Cats*," Aaron told Kate. "It's about three female private detectives who are strong, independent women, but sexy."

Kate bristled at the title. Cats? Really? It had been twelve years since Gloria Steinem's groundbreaking *Show* magazine article "A Bunny's Tale" that exposed the life of a cocktail waitress at New York's Playboy Club. Yet sexualized women were still being compared to soft, furry animals. As a feminist, Kate rejected the title immediately. While trying to come up with a new one, her eyes drifted to the wall behind Aaron's desk, to a painting of three angels. A lightbulb switched on. Cats were out, angels were in. Since the owner of the fictional detective agency was a man named Harry Townsend, the show would be called *Harry's Angels*.

Never reluctant to share her input, Kate also thought it would add a layer of intrigue if the Angels never actually met their boss but took direction from him via a Western Electric speakerphone, cutting-edge technology at the time. It was a clever idea, and Aaron went for it right away.

Then a new problem with the title emerged. There was another show on TV at the time called *Harry O* (which, as it happened, counted Farrah Fawcett among its cast). So, Harry was out. They had to come up with another name and picked Charles more or less out of a hat. Thus *Charlie's Angels* was born.

Once the script and the characters' profiles took shape, Kate was given the part of Kelly Garrett, the orphanage-raised, motorcycle-riding, "streetwise" Angel. The second casting decision was to hire Farrah Fawcett-Majors as bubbly, athletic, all-American beach blonde Jill Munroe. Farrah got the part without an audition. Aaron had seen enough of her acting as a regular on *Harry O* and on her husband Lee Majors's juggernaut *The Six Million Dollar Man*. Aaron and Candy were friendly with the Majorses and played them in doubles tennis matches.

Like me, Farrah had two careers: acting and modeling. She had Noxzema, I had Max Factor. I had Breck, she had Fabergé. We'd met briefly on a Max Factor commercial. It was shot in wintertime by a pool, and the two of us would have to warm up in a sauna between takes. That's why I often told reporters that Farrah and I originally met in a sauna. Farrah was an eight-by-ten glossy come to life, with a beautiful smile and a natural warmth that I loved immediately. Both Texas girls (she was from Corpus Christi), we just clicked.

When Aaron tapped Farrah for *Charlie's Angels*, she was on a roll. Earlier that year, she'd posed for photographer Bruce McBroom at her own pool, in her own red one-piece bathing suit. The resulting image of Farrah—all big hair, smile, and prominent nipples—became the best-selling poster in history. (At more than twelve million copies worldwide, it still is!) It led to her landing a part in *Logan's Run*, a prestige sci-fi movie with Michael York that is now a cult favorite. Lee Majors was all for his wife working on his friend Aaron's new show. He reasoned it would be something to keep Farrah busy while he was filming his own series.

With the brunette and blonde boxes checked, the creative team went in search of a redhead to play Sabrina Duncan, the fashionable, "smart" Angel. As legend has it, Aaron, Len, Ivan, and Ben interviewed a thousand redheads and weren't happy with any of them. Because R.J. had suggested me to Aaron, I got to read for the part. When I went in for my audition, there were a dozen people in the room—all the creatives and a handful of network executives. I had no idea I'd be performing for a packed house, and my nerves really kicked in. My reading wasn't very good and I didn't expect a callback.

If they'd judged me on my audition alone (and my hair color), that would have been it. But Ivan and Ben were big fans of my work on *Switch*, and they lobbied for me. One of my *Switch* scenes was a daring jewel heist that predated Tom Cruise's *Mission: Impossible* feat of dangling from wires over a weight-triggered alarmed floor. It was just like that, but I wore a black leotard and ballet slippers. The *Charlie's* team knew that I wasn't afraid to do action sequences—one place my dance training came in handy!

R.J. was in one ear telling Aaron, "Jaclyn is fantastic. You have to go with her." In his other, Ben and Ivan were saying, "We love Jaclyn. We want her!" My fan club! Thanks to them, despite my poor audition and having the wrong hair color, I got the part.

I was standing in the kitchen of my house on Lindacrest Drive, a place that Roger and I had bought for $89,000 and that I got in the divorce (I sold it for $1.2 million a few years later; it was the best thing I got out of the marriage!), when I got the phone call that changed my life. But the offer was one thing. We still had to work out the details.

My agent at the time, Jim Jacobson, said, "Kate will be making ten thousand per episode. They're offering Farrah five, and you three." Three thousand dollars per episode was a lot of money, but I had to look at the big picture. Farrah and I had both done some TV, a few movies, and plenty of modeling. As far as I was concerned, we were on equal footing and I deserved equal pay.

I said, "Unless I get favored-nation status with Farrah, I will walk away." And I meant it. I was excited, but not desperate. The show had a lot of promise, but it was still just a pilot.

"You're sure about that?" Jim said, worried I might miss out on the opportunity.

I stuck to my guns and, after some back-and-forth, I got what I wanted. I remember feeling proud of myself about my negotiating skills, and also a bit stunned that this was really happening. Ten years after I arrived in New York to become a dancer, I was living in Los Angeles and starring in a TV pilot for Aaron Spelling, one of the best producers in the business.

We had a powerhouse team, and at its heart was Aaron. He wasn't just talented; he had his hand on what the audience wanted to see. He loved actors. He wanted their point of view. He understood the psyche of an actor since he had started out as one himself. You felt you were on equal professional footing with him. In my years of working with Aaron, I knew he was on my side without condition.

Aaron had an incredibly sharp wit and the calm assurance of a man who trusted his instincts. He understood something elemental about television. He knew that beauty alone was never enough; it needed narrative, mystery, and just enough danger to keep the audience leaning forward. Under his watch, *Charlie's Angels* took shape not merely as a show, but as a fantasy that Americans could step into once a week and forget their own worries for an hour.

Then there were the Angels. Before we ever shot a scene, I appreciated how different the three of us were.

I knew from *The Rookies* that Kate's acting was natural, like she wasn't even working at it. She vibrated with energy and managed to be spontaneous while also paying close attention to every detail. Unlike many stars, Kate had no qualms about playing unlikable characters and loved being goofy both on- and off-screen. Because Kate had the most acting experience, she immediately became our leader. But it wasn't just that. She was a born leader—perceptive, outspoken, reflective, cerebral, observant, quick-witted, uncompromising, and strong. Just like when she'd challenged Aaron on the title, Kate never hesitated to let her decisive opinions be known. Similarly, she often challenged the writers and showrunners on the scripts and shooting decisions, which only made our show better.

Kate fought for us to recognize the power we had to advocate for the betterment of the show. From the outside, you might look at Kate and only see confidence, but on the inside, there was an unexpected element of shyness about her. Yet when it came to love, she wasn't bashful! Kate had more boyfriends than you could count, including (the ever-present) Warren Beatty, Dustin Hoffman, Sam Elliott, Chevy Chase, and Edward Albert Jr.

And then there was Farrah. Just mentioning my friend's name conjures up her golden look, including her magnificent million-dollar smile. She possessed an unnameable quality. At one moment she was the Girl Next Door, and the next she was the Pin-Up Goddess whose poster hung in every college boy's dorm room. She was catnip to men. To me, she was a true girlfriend.

As for me, I was determined to nail the part of Sabrina Duncan and bring her to life. But after thinking about it for a bit, Kate changed her mind about being Kelly Garrett. She thought it would be more of a departure for her if she took the part of Sabrina, the skirt-wearing upper-crust Angel, and I took over as Kelly, the daredevil from unfortunate circumstances. I had absolutely no problem with the change. To me, the character of Kelly had more texture and dimension in the pilot, which made her more compelling. Minute by minute, we all had equal screen time in that first episode, but Kelly's scenes were riskier, like having to play a character within a character, and I couldn't wait to dive in.

Another last-minute switch was to the voice of Charlie. Gig Young, a sixty-two-year-old Oscar-winning star from Hollywood's golden age and a friend of Aaron's, had been cast as the voice of

Charlie. But when they were recording his voice-overs, Gig was too drunk to read his lines and literally passed out in the booth. (Sadly, a year later Gig committed suicide after murdering his wife.)

Aaron ran through his mental Rolodex, thinking, *Who has a great voice who might come down to the studio right now and record the lines?* He called his tennis buddy John Forsythe and begged. John came to the rescue, rolling out of bed and arriving in the studio in his pajamas and slippers in the middle of the night. Aaron and John would work together many times over the years, most famously on *Dynasty*, the blockbuster evening soap that defined the eighties as deeply as *Charlie's* reflected the seventies.

But who would Charlie be without his Angels? As a group, the three of us had each other's backs from the start. Kate was already successful, but Farrah and I were never desperate actresses clawing to make our mark. We were just having fun. We were professionals who did our best, but even from the beginning, *Charlie's* never felt make-or-break, and I think that opened things up for us as a cast, and as friends. We were never competitive; we were a team. A sisterhood. And audiences saw that magic.

Chapter Ten

What I love about TV production—especially having worked on *Charlie's Angels*—is that it's an act of faith. You show up on the set not always knowing what's going to happen, and if the circumstances aren't what you anticipated, you have to make the best of them. When we started filming the pilot, I had no idea what to expect. Would the show be a hit? Would we get along? None of us could have predicted that *Charlie's Angels* would become a cultural phenomenon that defined an era.

It was July 1975 and a hot summer day was dawning when I arrived at the soundstage. I was directed to a set of three chairs at a makeshift makeup station. Farrah and Kate arrived at the same time and we all sat down together, each of us with our own makeup artist and hairstylist. Our characters weren't supposed to look fully glammed, so they used a light touch. We were young detectives who solved crimes. It was the seventies, so the "natural look" was in. Unlike with many actors today, what you saw on TV was how we appeared in person, and we each had our own look.

There was definitely a buzz in the air that first day on set. Kate, Farrah, and I didn't know each other well, but it was easy to fall into a rhythm together. Everyone was so happy to be there, the conversation came easily. In no time we were fast friends, but we were also excited to get down to business. The Angels were ready for action.

Nolan Miller, our costume designer, had been hard at work pulling together just the right outfits for our characters. Once hair and makeup were done, we were each given a rack of clothes. One of the hangers on my rack held the famous white string bikini that I wore in my very first scene in the series. I was in a pool wearing the bikini along with a white bathing cap, then climbed out to pick up a ringing telephone. After taking off the cap and shaking out my hair, I sat down on a lounge and answered, "Yes, Charlie?" I wore that bikini a few more times that season. I thought that they should have put Farrah, the red-swimsuit poster girl, in it, but she was self-conscious about her appendectomy scar. So the dancer with the muscular legs got to wear it instead.

Another of my costumes for the pilot was a black-leather-jacket-and-pants combo with a motorcycle helmet. In that scene, the camera follows a motorcycle rider going up a long, winding road through the woods, then up the driveway to a mansion on a vineyard. The bike slows to a stop in front of the mansion and two goons come out. "Hey, help you, mister?" one of them calls out. Then the rider removes the helmet and does a saucy hair flip. I had to do the helmet reveal several times to get the hair flip just right. But it was worth it. The moment turned out so well, it was used in the show's opening credits for the next five years.

When you film a TV pilot, you have no idea if anyone other than network executives is ever going to see it. It might never air, like the vast majority of pilots. It might air and get such low ratings that it dies that night. Or it might air and get decent enough ratings for the network to order more episodes. Once you get that green light, the show's future depends on weekly ratings. We constantly felt the pressure of ratings. We wanted to be in the top ten, but the reality was that we didn't have the time or energy to track it closely—we were too busy shooting. The network execs sure were watching, though, especially in those early days.

Back then, there were only three networks, so if a show failed on one channel, it wasn't going to have a second life elsewhere. We only had one shot. As Charlie told the Angels at our first briefing, we had to be "letter perfect," and I felt the weight of my responsibility.

My storyline in the pilot was tricky. I was playing Kelly, who was impersonating another woman—an heiress to a winery. I'd done some multilayered work before on *Switch*, but in much smaller parts. In a nutshell, the actual heiress had run off when her father, the owner of the business, mysteriously disappeared. He'd been missing for seven years, the point at which he could be declared legally dead. Unless the prodigal daughter returned in time to claim her inheritance, the winery, mansion, and vineyards would all go to his second wife, whom the daughter suspected of foul play in her father's disappearance.

Kelly's undercover job was to impersonate the heiress, infiltrate the mansion, and convince everyone there—the stepmother, her lover, his henchmen, and their lawyer—that she really was who she said she was. Her arrival was intended to shake them up so they'd reveal the location of the missing father's body.

Our costars were stellar. Diana Muldaur, an actress I admired, played the duplicitous stepmother. Bo Hopkins was her murderous lover. Tommy Lee Jones played the heiress's childhood friend, all grown up and ruggedly handsome. When the cameras started rolling, my nerves faded and I got comfortable with the character and my part, but Tommy was still plenty nervous. It was so early in his career. Eventually he got into the swing of things, of course, and went on to win an Oscar for his role in *The Fugitive*.

In that first episode, along with the three Angels, the Charles Townsend Agency had two administrators. David Doyle played John Bosley, as he would for the entire run of the series. In the pilot, he played an exaggerated, bumbling version of the character. David Ogden Stiers, who would later join the cast of *M*A*S*H*, contrasted Bosley's buffoonery with an uptight, stiff character named Scott Woodville. Woodville was the one who actually connected us to Charlie. When the series got picked up, the producers decided to cut the dry Woodville. They kept Bosley for comic relief and boosted his IQ by about thirty points.

Another change from the pilot to the series was allowing the Angels to pack heat. For the pilot, they thought it'd be a stretch for the audience to accept three women solving crimes at all, let alone carrying their own firearms. We could use disguises, our wits, and some karate chops, but no weapons. For the actual series, the writers nailed down our characters' origin stories. As the opening goes, "Once upon a time, there were three little girls who went to the police academy . . ." If we were trained police officers, surely we could carry weapons. In the new opening credits, Kate as Sabrina Duncan was shown at a firing range. So, from the second episode onward, we were given prop guns that we would whip out of our handbags and point at the bad guys. The guns were usually the only things in there.

The producers brought in a technical advisor to teach us the right way to handle a gun—how to plant our feet before aiming, how to load and unload it, the two-fisted grip, when to pull it out, and how to point it when you came through a door. Farrah and I tried to take it seriously, but we would look at each other acting tough with our firearms and just start laughing. It wasn't a natural movement for us to palm a pistol and yell, "Freeze!" And no matter how many times the technical advisor told us, "Don't wave it around when you're running down the street!" we couldn't help it. We'd have shot ten pedestrians on the sidewalk if those guns had been real.

Kate, on the other hand, might as well have been born a cop, she handled her gun with such expertise and precision. She was confident about everything—any stunt or prop—as if she'd done it all a million times. And she was strong. Looking at how slim she was, you'd think a stiff breeze could knock her over, but Kate could run, jump, and throw a punch. With all that power and skill, it's no wonder she was our fearless leader.

Many actors have tricks for loosening up before a scene, but Kate's was legendary. Right before shooting would start, she'd shout every four-letter word in the book (including some I'd never heard before) at the top of her lungs. Just a long, bellowed string of expletives that made even the cameramen and lighting guys blush.

The first time it happened, Farrah and I just looked at each other, blinking. "What on earth is she doing?" Farrah whispered to me.

"I'm warming myself up!" Kate declared. "I can't embarrass myself on-camera after doing that! I'm free now."

I came from a house where if you said "Damn it to hell," eyebrows would go up. Listening to Kate warm up was one of many moments in life when I realized just how far I was from Houston.

The pilot aired on March 21, 1976, eight months after we'd wrapped shooting. It was frustrating, waiting so long to see the light of prime time. We had no clue how it would go over or if we'd ever make another episode. During this limbo, I took some small parts and continued to model. I didn't need *Charlie's Angels* to be picked up by the network, but I wanted it to be. Having a regular job would be nice after a decade of commercials and guest-starring roles. But the show's future was completely out of my control. I believed I'd done good work on the pilot, but I had to be okay with any outcome, whatever it might be.

During that long hiatus, the ABC network execs tested the pilot with focus groups. The test audiences' reactions were through-the-roof positive, but the execs were still convinced that the show would be a flop. Network president Fred Silverman refused to believe his own data. It simply wasn't possible that audiences could relate to a show about three women who were not damsels in distress. He would need more convincing.

At seventy-two minutes, the pilot was too long to be an hour-long drama. The producers decided to stretch it out to a two-hour Movie of the Week with commercials. I watched the show at my home on Lindacrest by myself. It was pure entertainment, with classic Spelling-Goldberg touches like the bright lighting, multiple locations, and constant costume changes. Their approach was to make well-crafted shows and to give their cast and crew the best of everything, from top-of-the-line cameras to beautiful clothes and locations, to make it look fabulous. Aaron Spelling once described the show as "eye candy," a phrase he's credited with popularizing. The finished pilot of *Charlie's Angels* wasn't just eye candy; it was the whole candy store.

The very next morning, the principal cast was called to the enormous Stage 8 on the Twentieth Century Fox studio lot. As Kate, Farrah, David Doyle, and I sat on the set where we'd filmed the interiors of Charlie's office, Aaron announced, "The ratings are in, and they are huge!" The pilot got a 54 share, which means that over half the televisions in the country were tuned in to our show, making it number one for the night. The network execs didn't believe it. They aired the pilot again the next night to confirm the miracle! Lo and behold, our ratings could not be denied. Even then, the ABC executives hesitated to order a full series of episodes of *Charlie's Angels*. Apparently, there was a hung jury. Some were on board and ready to move forward; others were still hemming and hawing. The weeks rolled on with no news from Spelling-Goldberg.

Yet while the waiting was hard, it wasn't nearly as agonizing as what happened in the meantime.

Chapter Eleven

While we awaited news from the network, I got a call from home. At age 101, Papa had been admitted to the hospital. He'd been in and out over the previous years for one thing or another, minor infections and a broken hip, yet he'd come out of it all just fine. But this time was different.

When Mom called, I went straight to Houston. There was nowhere else I wanted to be. We were with Papa around the clock. I sat by him, hour after hour, measuring time by the rhythm of his breathing. When I asked him how he felt, he always answered in the same way. "Fine," he would say, never wanting me to worry. He never complained. I was always caught up in the calm of his voice, something that had comforted me since I was a little girl.

Papa had been blessed with more than a century of life, yet I clung with everything in me to the belief that he would come home again. I laid my hands on his back and silently sent all the strength I had into him, trying to manifest a positive outcome. Suddenly I was that twelve-year-old girl again, convinced that love could alter fate.

A few days into our vigil, while I was sitting there holding Papa's hand, he turned to me and said, "I'm tired. Why don't you and your mom go home and have dinner?"

"Sure, Papa," I said. "We'll go and you can have a nap." I gave him a kiss and a hug, just like always.

Mom and I had barely walked through the door back home when the phone rang. My mother answered, and the look on her face told me everything. In that instant, I knew the best part of my childhood was gone. I went to my room, closed the door, and stayed there, unwilling to face a world without him in it.

It was Palm Sunday, April 11, the same date on which his wife, Ethel Elise, had passed away years earlier.

I have since learned that the good and gentle often know when it is time to let go, and they make their own decision about how and when to do that. When I think back, after I had time to collect my thoughts, I realized what he was doing. He sent me away so I wouldn't be there when he passed away. He knew how it would affect me. As always, being unselfish was second nature to him.

He loved me with a completeness that asked for nothing in return. He was going to miss the whole rest of my life, and each day he would only be further away. It was hard for me to comprehend a world that continued in his absence. Yet it does. A great silence opened up where his voice had always been, and I have learned ever since how to live with its echo.

He was the soft cushion between me and whatever might hurt me. His even temper was like shelter to me.

The hard thing about being loved well is the immense chasm left behind when those dearest to you depart. When you bury someone you don't think you can live without, part of you feels as if you are falling away with them. Grief settled into my body, uninvited and relentless, bringing with it a hormonal imbalance that affected my health.

After Papa's death I was so sad that I don't even remember getting the call that *Charlie's* had been picked up for production. In some ways, *Charlie's* was like a lighthouse, beckoning me to the next part of my life. As Papa taught me so clearly from the time I was a little girl, *onward and upward.*

Chapter Twelve

In the end, I'm not sure what made the network execs finally come around. Maybe Aaron used some of his Texas charm to make them see the light. Regardless, the waiting was over. For better or worse, starting production on the show was like one of our stunts, jumping into a car that was already moving.

The network didn't just greenlight the show; they asked each of us to sign a five-year contract. Unfortunately for Kate, her contract did nothing to acknowledge her considerable contributions to the show beyond acting—how she'd come up with the title and the idea of Charlie being off-camera, along with the strong feminist tone that made the show unique. As the show became successful, this caused a lot of resentment for Kate. She felt that she was owed both an acknowledgment and a piece of the profit as a creator. The producers disagreed. I can see both sides, but it was certainly a lesson learned. If there's a question about intellectual property, get it all spelled out up front.

The first season of *Charlie's Angels* was an unparalleled experience, and it changed our lives forever. In our Ferragamos, we trod the crossroads between the past and the present, personally and professionally. What made it extra special was that we bonded off-screen too. How could we not? Kate, Farrah, and I were the only three people who understood how it felt to be at the center of this massive whirlwind. Forged in heat, our kinship solidified and became unbreakable. On-screen, our bond was the heartbeat of the show.

The three of us kept one another grounded. We held space for one another as we dealt with the demands of becoming astonishingly famous almost overnight. Fame can be a seductive feeling, and you need a healthy level of reality around you. I don't remember any complications or ego among the three of us. There was just togetherness. It was a kinship that time couldn't break, and it was that way from the start.

Looking back, I understand how rare that time was. Not just the success but the innocence that preceded it. We didn't yet know how swiftly the story would complicate itself. We only knew that we were standing at the beginning of something vast, luminous, and unknowable, and that once we stepped fully into it, there would be no turning back.

I was pleasantly surprised when, on our first day of shooting, a chauffeured limo picked me up and brought me to the Fox lot, to the door of a brand-new $25,000 Pace Arrow motor home. The trailer was fully stocked with beverages, snacks, and fresh flowers. I probably spent more time in that Pace Arrow over the next few years than I did at my home on Lindacrest, and I made it my own. It was my escape pod, my napping chamber, my dressing room. Not every star on every show, even other Spelling-Goldberg productions, was given such an extravagant gift. The newness intimated another world that was limitless and free. An open road to a career I had been dreaming about. It was about beginnings and possibilities.

As a rule, Aaron didn't skimp on his stars' comfort. He wanted to give us the world, and he did. That said, he also knew that if we didn't have our private sanctuaries, we might go a little bit crazy. Our shooting days started at 5 a.m. and ended at 7 p.m. at the earliest—and then only because Farrah had it in her contract that she could get home in time to cook her husband Lee's dinner every night. When we objected to the early call, Aaron said, "You come out of the house in your pajamas, get in a limo, stretch out, and sleep until we get to location." Some of the locations were hours away, so I learned to use that sleep time well.

Once, Aaron and I attended a charity auction together, and I mentioned liking a pair of earrings that were on the docket. He didn't miss a beat. "You want them?" he asked. I had to hold him back, or he would have bought them for me. When Aaron was launching another show, *The Love Boat*, he asked me to guest-star on the second episode. I wasn't too keen on it—after all, my *Charlie's* schedule was brutal. But, of course, I did the show. Anything for Aaron! To thank me, he could have written me a note or sent flowers. Instead, he sent a cream-colored Mercedes, a cute little two-seater that I loved and drove for years.

Although Aaron let Ivan and Ben run their show, he was a presence on set and became the de facto diplomat whenever there was any kind of dispute. "If you're not happy," he'd say with his Texas accent, putting an arm around your shoulders, "we'll just have to do something about that." Anything he could do to help us or pamper us, he would. He knew that being an Angel was hard work. He knew the hours on the show were difficult. And many times we would have commercial shoots on the weekend, like I did for Max Factor.

Our first episode, "Hellride," defined the action and humor to come. Sabrina went undercover as a race car driver, while Bosley and Jill disguised themselves as a grifter preacher and his card-shark daughter. We were off to the races, literally. In episode three, "Night of the Strangler," I took center stage as a model (break out the white bikini again) and the bait for a mysterious killer who was strangling mannequins with a rag doll. (Yes, a rag doll.)

Episode four, "Angels in Chains," was one of our favorites, and an audience favorite as well. The Angels went undercover at a women's prison where inmates were disappearing. As we discovered, the warden was forcing some prisoners to dress up in fancy evening gowns and go to sexy parties at night. That episode had it all: sadistic guards, a terrorizing prison mama, a gorgeous and vulnerable victim. The victim was played by Kim Basinger, in one of the first roles in her career. Kim had an innocent Southern charm. She was bubbly and open, a true natural beauty. Throw in a car chase, a group shower, and a chain gang, and you've got TV gold. As strange as it sounds, we loved being chained together. When it was time to break for lunch, the crew asked if we could stay that way. It was just easier than undoing the chains, letting us trek back to our motor homes to eat or take a nap, and then having to redo them. So we stayed and ate there on set. It was fun having lunch while we were shackled together. Through it all we grew quite "attached" to each other. The episode itself was high camp at its best, totally tongue-in-cheek. And it was provocative for its time. Plus, thanks to the group shower, we got to wear our hair wet minus our layered feathery dos, which otherwise would not have been allowed.

Another episode that season, called "Lady Killer," was controversial, and the reason critics began to describe the show as "jiggle TV." Jill disguised herself as a potential centerfold for *Feline* magazine to find out why other models were being bumped off. As a Feline Club cocktail waitress, she wore a skimpy costume with ears and a tail, while I kept an eye on things as the club's lounge singer in a beaded evening gown. I even got to do my own singing. It was a moment that took me back to my Broadway dreams.

I thought the criticism of the episode, and of the show, was unfounded. Critics called us "exploited" without recognizing that our characters were chaste, competent, loyal, and strong. Sure, the Angels might have to flirt or wear some skimpy clothes here and there to get the job done, but we never compromised our principles. You might actually say that the men were the ones who were exploited, since we were always using our sex appeal to distract and outsmart them, and they fell for it pretty much every time. On the show and in life, the Angels were stronger than anyone gave us credit for. We learned early how to navigate rooms that underestimated us. How to show authority without apology or excuse. And how to turn scrutiny into fuel. We carried ourselves with composure, understanding what we were worth, and that we didn't need permission to claim it.

Charlie's was an adventure for all of us. It gave us a place to take a chance and to lose ourselves in so many different characters. In subsequent episodes, we went undercover as army recruits, Vegas showgirls, Roller Derby skaters, art smugglers, student nurses, and basketball coaches. We busted up blackmailers, a political assassin, a mad arsonist, pornographers, extortion racketeers, a prostitution ring, and a massage parlor drug dealer. You name a nefarious criminal or deed, and the Angels (and our sidekick Bosley) took them down.

Aaron Spelling's productions had certain common elements. For one, they were usually very much of the moment. Even the high-concept shows like *Fantasy Island* reflected the attitudes of the time.

Beyond that, they had broad appeal and a mass-market sensibility. They also had a certain look. The style of our show could be described as ultra-contemporary. Whatever was the mode in fashion, décor, and design during that era, you would find it on our show. We drove the sexiest new cars: Kelly's was a beige Mustang II Ghia; Bosley drove a hunter-green Ford Thunderbird; Jill had a Mustang Cobra; and Sabrina's was a bright-orange Ford Pinto. The set design was classic seventies, from chrome and Lucite fixtures to Naugahyde, suede, and leather furniture to shag carpets; the color scheme was beiges, creams, and tans mixed with emerald, ruby, amethyst, and sapphire tones. Our lighting guys knew how to make those fabrics, materials, and colors pop so it looked like we were detecting our way through Technicolor. They even made a prison, a hospital, and army barracks look glamorous!

As the season progressed, our characters became more distinct. Farrah's Jill was a smiley, openhearted risk-taker who would chase a bad guy through a public park on her skateboard or speed down a dirt road in her Cobra. Kate's Sabrina was smart, but she was also a jokester with her crazy disguises and wacky accents. In season two's "Circus of Terror," the Angels were hired by guest star and *Gidget* actor James Darren, whom I will always think of as Moondoggie. I had a big crush on him after seeing the movie. Darren's character had to investigate a series of mysterious mishaps under the big top. Sabrina went undercover as a clown, which I thought was hilariously fitting.

As written, Kelly was both hardened by life (she was raised in an orphanage by a sadistic proctor) and up for anything dangerous, yet also softhearted, especially when it came to children. She was the kind of woman who could take down a two-hundred-pound man with two punches and then babysit a kid with special needs—and take a bullet for him.

Our off-camera characters were distinct as well. Kate was serious, with intensity and unflagging energy. She was perceptive, observant, and intelligent, and in many ways, Sabrina was an organic extension of Kate's personality.

Farrah was very much what-you-see-is-what-you-get. When she smiled, it was because she was happy. If she seemed stressed-out, it was because she felt the strain of working for fifteen hours straight, day after day.

As for me, others tended to see me as a bit of a people pleaser, and I can't argue with that. I led with my heart, and those I loved, I really loved. I was clear-eyed and focused, with a solid work ethic.

Underneath it all, I think we each had self-awareness about what and who we were, and that carried through to our characters. I think it gave the Angels an authenticity that viewers really connected with.

When it came to clothes, though, we diverged. Farrah and I loved the clothes with a capital *L*. Each of us had eight costume changes per episode, and it was heaven for the two of us. Because we had to run and move, we typically weren't dressed in evening gowns and stilettos. But we had the most gorgeous selection of designer peasant blouses, bell-bottom jeans, velvet pants, and cashmere sweaters, along with a wide array of platform wedges. On the weekends, Farrah and I would go shopping to see all the latest trends, then come back on Monday and report to the costumer, telling them exactly where to go and what to buy. Nolan Miller, our costume designer, had things well in hand, and we weren't trying to step on his toes (or his clothes). But he was totally open to our input, and Farrah and I were happy to share it. I don't think I rejected a single outfit they wanted me to wear; they were all beautiful.

Nolan once explained the show's popularity by saying, "Men watch the girls, women watch the clothes." Although Farrah was thought of as the sex kitten of the show, she only wore a bathing suit once. (It was the second episode, "The Mexican Connection.") Her signature outfit was a T-shirt and tennis shorts, which fit her athleticism and personality perfectly. She was sporty and could make anything look like a million bucks.

Yet another fellow Texan, Nolan was one of Aaron's go-to people and worked on many of his shows, most famously *Dynasty*. Nolan, Aaron, and Candy Spelling—Aaron's wife—were all close friends. If you didn't love clothes and like wearing them, Nolan didn't have much time for you. Needless to say, I adored clothes, and he and I got along fabulously!

Kate rejected glamour and wouldn't show any skin at all. The first year, she wore A-line maxi skirts with knee-high boots, tailored blazers, and high-necked blouses. Her outfit for the opening sequence was jodhpurs and riding boots. By the second and third seasons, she more or less stuck to her standard uniform of a small assortment of wide-legged trousers and turtlenecks. Keen-eyed fans might have noticed that when we gathered in the Townsend Agency office at the beginning and end of every episode, Kate was usually standing behind the bar the entire time. That served two purposes. First, she came off like she was in charge. But also, you couldn't see what she was wearing from the waist down. Kate hated to stand for trouser fittings.

Kate tried to get into fashion here and there, but it just wasn't her personality. After she left *Charlie's Angels*, she'd call me up and ask for fashion advice. I remember taking her on a shopping spree on Rodeo Drive, and she spent a fortune in one day. But when I went by her house a while later, all those new things were still in boxes with the price tags on. Her functional wardrobe consisted of jeans, turtlenecks, and tennis shoes.

Our fashion influenced the generation at the time, but years later it also inspired talented designer and future fashion star Tom

Ford. He launched his first collection with velvet hip-hugger pants and jewel-toned silk shirts, inspired by our characters.

Along with guns and cars, our hair was our most important accessory. I've often joked that Farrah's hair was the fourth Angel and needed its own phone line. Her legendary wings were originally styled by José Eber, now my dear friend and business partner, whom Farrah really preferred to keep to herself during the run of the show, wanting each of us to have our own unique look. Later, in the second season, José gave Kate a more stylized version of her classic bob by putting in a few layers. And when our fifth season wrapped, I happily went to José and have been going to him ever since.

For the show, my own voluminous, long layers were created by New York–based stylist John Sahag and maintained by me. We all had such great cuts and good hair to begin with that we didn't have to do much to get our tresses camera-ready. We rolled and dried our dos in the morning and were essentially good for the day. I thought we were low-maintenance, but David Doyle had another opinion. He once told a reporter, "The time I spent waiting for the girls' hair to dry probably put one of my girls through a year of college." Fair enough.

Volume and bounce were important to the show's hair aesthetic, so we fluffed at every opportunity. During breaks between takes, Farrah and I would bend at the waist, flip our hair forward to shake it out, and then snap back up. Once, when the crew was grumbling under their breath about having to wait for us to fluff, Kate said, "Hey, guys, let the money do their thing!" She was right. Our hair practically had its own fan club.

Our makeup artists did not skimp on the glitter either. While they stayed away from things like false eyelashes, which would have been too much for our more natural looks, they made our eyes, cheeks, and lips pop! Aaron made sure that our faces were brightly lit and that the camera caught the shimmer of every glossy smile. Kate thought that Farrah and I should meet the show's glamour quotient, and she'd be the tailored, understated one. She had her own process that made her cheeks look richly rosy. But she didn't need makeup anyway. She had a special quality in her look.

The popularity of the show was immediate. The public response arrived like a tidal wave: magazine stories, crowds, the shock of being recognized in places where no one had known our names before. It was intoxicating and disorienting all at once. You begin to understand how quickly the world can take possession of you.

Overnight we were on the cover of every magazine, every tabloid. We were offered six-figure endorsement deals. *Hustler* magazine offered us a million dollars each to pose nude (we declined). When I took my nephews to Disneyland, we didn't have to stand in line. When I visited Martha's Vineyard, the hotel owner insisted we take out his yacht, no charge. If we wanted to eat at any restaurant, we could just walk in and get the best table. In one episode of the show, Farrah wore a pair of Nike sneakers while skateboarding. The next day, we were each sent boxes and boxes of sneakers. If I wore a hat or a pair of sunglasses, we'd be inundated with samples from designers. Farrah was offered a deal to launch a jewelry line of faucet-shaped charms.

I'd been close to extreme fame while working with stars like R.J. and Dennis Weaver. But this was something else. It was fantasyland. Everything was thrown at our feet, all because of the characters we played on TV. While I enjoyed it, I also wondered, *Can this really be happening? Do we deserve this? Is it going to last?* It was all a bit shocking for a girl from Houston who had thought that she was going to end up opening a ballet school for kids. But I guess some things are just meant to be.

From the outside, people see the glamour and riches of fame, and there was plenty of that. But when you're on the inside, you feel a strange disconnect. You're still the same person you were before you became a household name. You have the same feelings, the same stresses, the same ups and downs. As a celebrity, you're constantly judged. You try to fulfill everyone's expectations, and there is a lot of pressure to that.

Success extracts its price. Fame doesn't erase vulnerability—it magnifies it. It teaches you how visible your vulnerability truly is. Fame is a bubble that takes away your privacy. But it's only a trap if you believe that you can't survive once that bubble pops. To me, fame doesn't change who you are; it reveals who you are.

Behind the scenes, in the refuge of our motor homes, we leaned on one another. The set was our sanctuary, the place where friendship took root under the hot lights and long hours. We laughed easily; we worked hard; we trusted each other with our exhaustion, our fears, our private doubts. That trust mattered. It kept us steady when the outside world grew too loud. We were all on the same wild ride, so we each understood what the others were going through.

Many of the things that were written about me in the tabloids were outlandish lies, and they bothered me. There were rumors about my social life, like how I was a bigamist with two husbands. According to one rag, I was hiding my out-of-wedlock newborn in my motor home on the set, a particularly upsetting lie to read about myself, considering my deep desire to have children.

Some tabloids tried to drum up conflict among the three of us. For example, they liked to perpetuate this idea that we were jealous of each other. Not true. Another rumor was that we fought each other for more screen time. It was just too predictable to try to pit women against each other. The truth was, we fought for each other to have *less* screen time. One of Aaron's tenets was that his stars appeared on-screen in every scene. The more popular we became, the more power we had, and we started to demand that one or the other of us not have to be in a given scene. And then that lucky person could go take a nap. We made our decisions by committee, and we stood by one another.

Our shoots turned into mob scenes, and security became an issue. Aaron hired guards to keep the crowds under control, but occasionally they got unruly. One man climbed over the gate and insisted to the guards that he was my husband. When confronted with the facts—I was no one's wife—he said that we'd gotten married via telepathy. This same man showed up at my house one day, so I filed a restraining order against him. It wouldn't be the last.

Kate and Farrah had their share of stalkers too. Whenever we got a piece of fan mail that seemed unhinged, we put it into our "nut file." One of our nuts had also written a threatening letter to President Jimmy Carter, and in it mentioned his obsession with me. The Secret Service came to the *Charlie's* production office and asked for the letter he'd written me so they could analyze it. They also gave me a terrifying warning: "You should be aware that this guy is mentally unstable. You might be in danger." *Thanks for the heads-up.*

After that, we had on-set security guards around the clock. Men with real guns were posted outside our motor homes. When we traveled for the show, we were each assigned our own bodyguards. Kate didn't love the invasion of privacy. Once, when we were on location in Hawaii, she gave her security guards the slip by diving into the ocean.

When you watch an actor on TV each week, it's only natural to think you're getting to know that person, that you're somehow intimately, emotionally connected. The reason actors become so popular is that fans believe that if they ever met the actor, they would become friends. To be honest, I have met fans at events and struck up long friendships with them. It does happen. But in the early days of *Charlie's Angels*, it would have been hard to befriend someone who ran up to me on the street and tried to grab me.

Fortunately, the vast majority of our fans were simply people who loved the show, and they continue to embrace us all these years later. Whenever I do public events, to this day nearly every fan I meet tells me what *Charlie's Angels* meant to them. I think the show made for entertainment, and for many young women, it was a first glimpse of possibility. Crime stories had always belonged to men. Here, for the first time, women stepped into that territory. Not as ornaments, but as agents, watchful, clever, and unapologetically central. Women were at the center of the story, chasing danger instead of being rescued from it. Our characters had exciting lives and took risks, and their friendship was nourishing and sustaining—something young women didn't see elsewhere on TV. I'm proud to represent that for so many.

My biggest fans and supporters were, of course, my parents, who watched every episode. When magazines started to do profiles about me, word got out that my father was a dentist in Houston. People would track down his office number and call to ask him about me and the show. He would inform them that it was a dental office, not a fan club. He also received a lot of mail. With some of the letters, if there was a negative comment, he would reseal the envelope and write on it, "Trash not received at this address," then send it back. No one was going to say anything negative about his daughter.

We knew we'd really made it when, in November 1976, *Time* magazine wanted to put us on the cover. It was a very big deal, to share the same newsstand real estate as world leaders. But there was a problem. The day of the cover shoot we had a tight filming schedule, and the showrunners didn't want to lose a minute of it. It was decided that we would sit for the *Time* photographer during our lunch hour.

It wasn't ideal. I preferred to use lunchtime to rest and take a nap. I was okay with sacrificing it that day, though. It was *Time* magazine! My first cover. Farrah was okay with the plan, too, but Kate was not having it. "I don't care if it's the cover of *Time* magazine! They can't make us give up our lunch hour!" she said. She marched Farrah and me into her motor home and locked the door. When people started knocking and demanding that we come out, she said, "Something's wrong with the door. It's jammed! I can't get it open."

Farrah and I glanced at each other. "Really?" Farrah said to Kate. "Do you want to do this?"

Kate was adamant. "They can't push us around!"

"Let's just do it and get it over with," I said. Kate was sticking up for our rights, which I applauded, but her tactics seemed a bit excessive. Besides that, it was creating more problems for us than it was solving. We still had to do a certain number of scenes that day, along with the photo shoot, and her protest was using up valuable time. I figured we could just do it and get back to work.

The second assistant kept trying the door, to no avail. Kate yelled, "Sorry, it won't open. We can't get out." Then she yelled to the crowd gathered outside the motor home, "Maybe if we took off the top vent, you could drop a wrench in here and I can use it to open the door." She had the crew searching for tools and scrambling up the sides of the trailer while we were all in there laughing.

Farrah and I always went along with Kate, though we didn't always agree. The three of us stood together, and that all-for-one-and-one-for-all spirit turned into pure chemistry on-camera.

Later, *Time* finally got their photo shoot. The cover read "TV's Super Women," and we were dressed in matching sequined gowns in pink and platinum—the same dress I wore as a lounge singer in "Lady Killer." It was the first of many covers to come. Along with appearances on *People*, *TV Guide*, and various entertainment magazines, we were spoofed by *Mad* magazine. I was photographed by Richard Avedon for *Vogue*, and Helmut Newton for *Harper's Bazaar*. Bill King, Matthew Rolston, and Charles Bush were talented and creative photographers I would be lucky enough to work with over and over. I got to wear the most glorious clothes on the pages of those fashion magazines.

It was hard to believe that, in just a few months, I'd gone from selling products in magazines to appearing on the covers. And as I'd soon find out, that was just the beginning.

Chapter Thirteen

It's rare to have a successful show, and rarer still for that show to become a bona fide national obsession. For a historical perspective, the first season of the original *Charlie's* began airing in 1976, only four years after the *Roe v. Wade* decision, when less than 8 percent of adult women were in the workforce. By and large, women on TV had been relegated to a standard set of supporting roles: the nurse, the secretary, the June Cleaver–type housewife, the sexy girlfriend, the nurturing grandma, the victim. *Charlie's* changed all that.

Today, it's common to look back at pretty much everything in history and criticize it in light of the present. I understand that, and there's validity to it. Back when they were casting *Charlie's*, diversity looked like having a brunette, a blonde, and a redhead all on the same show. Still, our writers and producers made a concerted effort not to present a totally whitewashed show, casting with an eye to inclusiveness. Unlike other cop or detective series, in which most actors of color portrayed drug dealers, nannies, or janitors, those who appeared on our show were doctors, lawyers, nurses, models, students, and teachers. Behind the camera, we had female writers and directors. Georg Stanford Brown, an alum of *The Rookies* and a member of Aaron's club of repeat performers and creatives, directed several episodes. Could we have done more? Of course. But by the standards of the time, we pushed the envelope in many ways.

And despite the camp, we weren't just fluff. We dealt with hard subject matter. In that first season, we addressed prison reform, alcoholism, sex trafficking, gambling addiction, and the stigma of autism. We went there, in a way that fit the tone of the show.

We were portraying single adult women who were not defined by the men in their lives, who thrived at demanding jobs, enjoyed taking vacations together, had hobbies outside the home, and challenged the male establishment at every turn. Our dialogue reflected a feminist sensibility. I'll grant you, the character of Charles Townsend was a Hugh Hefner lothario type, but he was our boss, not our controller. There was no hostile work environment or harassment, and his antics were, like so much of the show, intentionally over-the-top. On *Charlie's*, everything was dialed up to eleven.

Painting Charlie as a Don Juan also kept the romantic (or at least sexual) focus squarely on him. The Angels' storylines focused on our detective work rather than our love lives. At the start of each assignment, when we convened at the office and Bosley switched on the speaker, we asked, "What's our next case, Charlie?" not "How was your date last night?"

When we read criticism of the show calling it antifeminist, I took it with a grain of salt. I knew that our objective attractiveness was one of the reasons so many people tuned in each week. But our "sexiness," such as it was, was incidental to the movement of the plot and our characters. We used our appeal as part of our investigations in order to catch the men who, most likely, had harmed women and children. The bad guys were undone by their underestimation of us, and we exploited that for the greater good. It was a family show. There was no gratuitous sex, nudity, or violence. Okay, some bikinis, but nothing you wouldn't see at any beach or swimming pool. The one time we thought wearing bathing suits didn't make sense, we said no, and that was that. I never felt like my body was exploited.

I don't think anyone on *Charlie's* set out to raise America's feminist consciousness (except maybe Kate), but we happened to do that anyway. We got on that road and crossed the bridge, not knowing what was on the other side.

As gratifying as it was to have a hit on our hands, our schedule was grueling. Fifteen- and eighteen-hour days were routine. We shared an energy and a work ethic that were so important as a team—we held each other up when the hours got long. At the end of the night, we'd be so exhausted we could barely stand up. Then, as we were finally getting ready to go home, the producers would announce an early morning "forced call," which was as fun as it sounds. The industry had a standard twelve-hour break required between calls. A forced call meant we'd have to report to the set well before our required rest period was over. Kate led a charge to stop forced calls and at one point refused to show up for work. It was a valiant effort, but what could she or any of us really do? The show had to be shot, and we had to be there to shoot it.

We were filming an hour-long drama, week after week, at multiple locations. Nowadays a typical network TV season is about thirteen episodes. For streaming services, it might be as few as six episodes. We were filming twenty-plus. The time pressure didn't let up for six months straight, and forced calls became the norm. Once, when we complained about the hours, a cameraman shook his head and said, "Do you have any idea how lucky you are?"

We all knew how lucky we were. We were thrilled about our success—delirious and absolutely drained. We realized our opportunities were unlimited, but with that came high expectations.

We spent so much time together, it started to feel like we were in a college sorority. We studied lines together, ate in our trailers together, and played with our dogs together. Farrah had an Afghan named Satchel. Kate's was a Siberian husky named Catcher, after her favorite book. Mine was a French poodle named Albert who even appeared in a few episodes of the show.

We did many of our own stunts, including some of the driving and all the running. Then there was the belly dancing, skating, and jumping off ledges. I look at old episodes and think, *My God, we were in great shape!* Kate could really mix it up in fight sequences. I would always stifle a laugh when the Angels—none of us weighed more than 115 pounds—would corner some 250-pound bad guys and yell, "Hold it right there, buster!" and the men would just throw up their hands and say, "Okay, okay, you got us!" Perhaps our reputations preceded us.

One of my favorite episodes was called "The Séance," in which Kelly was hypnotized by con artist manipulator/fake spiritualist René Auberjonois to believe that Jill was actually Kelly's abusive orphanage proctor, Beamish. He instructed Kelly to get her revenge by killing Jill. (At more than twenty episodes per season on such a fast-paced production schedule, the writers had to get pretty creative with some of the plots.) Farrah and I got to do a séance scene with objects flying through the air. But that wasn't the best part.

In the episode, the plan to hypnotize Kelly works. She's put into a trance and relives a childhood trauma of being locked in a dark closet and having her doll, Lilybet, taken away. Acting hypnotized is a hard sell for any actor, but I did my best to seem legitimately dazed. In the climactic scene, Kelly, in a trance, drives her Mustang Ghia at ninety miles per hour down a winding canyon road with Jill in the passenger seat.

"Kelly! Slow down!" Jill yells.

I look at her blankly. "Are you *afraid*, Beamish?"

"I'm Jill!"

"Beamish!"

"You're going to kill us both! I just want you to know that I love you, Sabrina loves you, *and Lilybet loves you*!" That declaration breaks Kelly out of the trance, and the Mustang rolls to a stop, just inches from careening off the cliff.

When that scene was over, Farrah and I broke into hysterical laughter. It was a truly memorable *Charlie's* moment with her and a pulse-racing scene on the show. Honestly, I still laugh just thinking about it. "Beamish!"

I always thought I'd name a pet Lilybet one day.

Some of the dialogue and scenes might have been a bit unrealistic or overwrought, but we managed to carry them off. Our writers made sure we had laughs in every episode while always staying on the right side of camp. A huge part of the humor on the show came from David Doyle, especially when he had romantic subplots, like a lusty lady on a cruise ship or a rich widow in need of a new hubby. All told, Bosley might have had more love interests than the Angels. But for the most part, romance wasn't a big part of the show, and that was purposeful. It would have been too easy to fall into those tropes, and we wanted *Charlie's* to be different.

We sure used every detective show cliché, though. Somehow they became fresh when performed by three women, even if we did them over and over. How many times can you be driving along and suddenly realize your brakes have been tampered with? Cut to a close-up of my espadrille pumping the pedal, then a close-up of my face, distressed. Then cut to a long shot of the Mustang barreling along. My car was blown up with bombs attached to the undercarriage by magnets a few times. I was knocked out by a chloroform-drenched handkerchief at least twice, and also knocked out by a syringe in the neck.

We filmed the episode "Angels at Sea" on the *Queen Mary*, the luxury transatlantic cruise ship. We had the run of the ship for a week, and they gave each of us a royal suite to stay in. Mine had a fireplace, a nanny's room, and gorgeous appointments. The opulence felt on par with that of the *Titanic*.

For the episode, I was back in a black leotard while crawling through air-conditioning ducts. The plot was that someone was killing cruise ship passengers and we had to figure out who was responsible. Was it the lounge singer? The captain? The ship's mentalist entertainer, played by *Batman*'s Frank Gorshin? As it turned out, the psychic was the killer. Gorshin had an incredible five-minute confession monologue that included a dozen impressions. The director just let him riff, and it was so wonderful and weird. Watching the Riddler do this incredible performance, I kept thinking how lucky we were to get to work with so many fine actors, consummate professionals who were immaculate in their preparation.

Our guest stars were actors with distinguished classical careers who could also do comedy with amazing skill. Many could act, dance, and sing better than almost anyone. Some were actors I'd looked up to as a kid. As we got more popular, we attracted even more talented guest stars, including Fernando Lamas, screen legend Ida Lupino, Richard Mulligan, and a pre-mustache Tom Selleck, with whom I shared a romantic scene in front of a burning fire with a steamy kiss. Tom was a triple threat: handsome, kind, and an excellent actor. At the time, he was meant to be a recurring character, playing my boyfriend, which never happened (sadly). It just goes to show you, what might seem like a failure might turn out to be a blessing in disguise. Soon after our *Charlie's* kiss, he was cast on *The*

Rockford Files, and soon after that as the star of *Magnum, P.I.*, a show that ran for nine years.

In one of the last episodes of the first season, "Dancing in the Dark," the villain was an immoral dance instructor who seduced, betrayed, and blackmailed rich, older victims. Kate disguised herself as an eccentric harridan to set a trap for him. Farrah was undercover as a dance instructor. And I acted the part of a crooked freelance PI who was playing both sides off each other. The lady-killer was played by Dennis Cole, a veteran of a dozen TV series, including *Police Story*, *Medical Center*, *Barbary Coast*, and *Barnaby Jones*. In his first *Charlie's Angels* scene, Dennis wore a velvet burgundy jacket with wide lapels, a hot-pink shirt, and jeans that just screamed *gigolo*.

Over the week of shooting, Dennis and I got to know each other a bit. I learned he had a teenage son named Joe from his first marriage, came from Detroit, and had been a journeyman actor, stuntman, and model since he was barely in his twenties. Once his career started to take off, he'd booked one acting role after another until he landed on our set. Dennis was a good actor and, like so many of our guest stars, a real pro. He arrived on set on time, lines memorized and ready to work. Dennis had been judged his whole life on how he looked, but filming together I saw that, beyond his attractive appearance, he had a solid work ethic and strong skills.

When I told Dennis I was from Houston, he said, "I'm going down there for a charity function next weekend."

"What a coincidence!" I said. "I've been invited to the same event. I'm planning to go and stay with my parents."

"Well, if we're both going, let's go together," he replied.

He was friendly enough and seemed nice, so I said, "Why not?"

We had a fine time at the function, running into people we both knew. It was so enjoyable I didn't get back to my parents' house until after two in the morning. While I was out having fun, my father was fretting. As my mother told me, when I didn't show up by one thirty, Daddy got out of his chair, grabbed his coat, and put on his hat.

"Jack, where are you going?" Mom asked.

"I don't know this Dennis person. Ellen said she'd be home by now, and I'm going out to look for her!"

Just as Daddy was about to climb into his car, Dennis and I pulled up. "Daddy, what are you doing?" I asked him.

"I didn't get a call! I was worried!" he said to me. Then he turned to Dennis. "This kind of behavior is unacceptable!"

I was a thirty-one-year-old divorcée, and Daddy was acting like I was a sixteen-year-old debutante who'd dodged her chaperone. Meanwhile, Mom was looking on, trying hard not to laugh.

I said, "Daddy, I'm here. I'm okay."

Taking in the family scene, Dennis was trying hard not to laugh himself. I could tell he enjoyed what he was seeing, especially my father's antics. I already liked Dennis, but that softened me toward him.

As I came to learn, Dennis's father had died when he was young. His mother was an alcoholic and largely absent from his life growing up, and he was mostly raised by his grandmother. From that experience, he'd developed an emotional fortitude that, along with his ambition and square-jawed, Ken-doll good looks, helped him become a successful actor.

Like Farrah's trademark do, Dennis's hair had a life all its own. He was a natural platinum blond, but people always thought it was fake. My mother said, "I think he bleaches it." She simply couldn't believe that it grew out of his head that way.

When Dennis was on *The Young and the Restless*, the powers that be thought he'd look stronger and more masculine with dark hair. (Blond men are judged by their hair color too.) They made him dye it brown, but thanks to the challenges of coloring naturally blond hair, it turned green. Not a good look, even on Dennis. That's saying a lot; the man was stunning, and my attraction to him was undeniable.

In short order, Dennis and I became a celebrity couple. Dennis had been famous for a while and seemed primed and eager to guide me as my star rose. He gave me moral support and advice, as well as attention and affection. At the same time, Kate had recovered from her relationship with Eddie Albert Jr., and was dating actor Andrew Stevens (son of actress Stella Stevens). All three Angels' relationships were daily fodder for gossip columnists, and we were all relentlessly chased by paparazzi. From our first date, the tabloids speculated that Dennis and I were altar-bound. If we were photographed separately, they claimed we'd broken up. Being followed and written about put pressure on our new relationship, but we rode the wave as best we could.

Before long, we fell in love. It was so easy to do! Dennis was thoughtful and sentimental. The first time he sent me flowers, they included red, white, and yellow roses. Yellow meant friendship, white was for passion, and red was for love. He knew I longed for a relationship that included all of that. Another thoughtful gift was a vintage necklace he'd found with a locket that looked like a tiny envelope. The envelope opened up, and inside was a little gold piece of paper with words he'd had engraved on it: "With friendship, passion, and love."

It sure looked good on paper, but all that glittered was not gold.

Chapter Fourteen

At the 1977 People's Choice Awards, *Charlie's Angels* won for Favorite Overall New TV Program, and Farrah for Favorite Female Performer in a New TV Series. Her acceptance speech was as sweet and humble as she was. But soon after that, Farrah stunned us all by announcing that she was leaving the show after only one season. Kate and I were not only sad but confused.

What followed was a legal battle royal between Spelling-Goldberg and their biggest star. They said Farrah couldn't break her five-year contract; she said she'd never signed it. The fighting went on for months and ultimately concluded with an agreement that Farrah could go, but she had to come back as a guest star three times each in seasons three and four.

Why Farrah left remains a question for the ages. When it comes down to it, only she knew her true reasons. I think it was probably the stress. The relentless schedule, everyone wanting a piece of her. Some part of her probably just wanted her life back.

Perhaps it's surprising that Farrah and I never had that conversation, that I never demanded to know why she decided to leave. But I just didn't see the world that way. I wasn't angry. I understood how exhausting it had all become, and so very fast. In my view, she had a right to make the choice that was best for her, or possibly for her marriage, with no explanation required. But the three of us were a team. I adored working with Farrah and I would miss my friend. Still, if someone isn't happy and you care about them, you don't want them to stay in a situation that they don't want to be in. Farrah felt that being an Angel was no longer for her, and that she might be happier doing movies. That was all I needed to know. Sure, I sometimes wonder if she regretted her decision, but if she did, she never said so to me.

Immediately after Farrah made her announcement, the rest of the cast and crew knew that Farrah and Aaron were negotiating terms. We all thought it was still possible that she'd change her mind and come back for season two. When it was time to start shooting, the rest of us reported on schedule to Stage 8. They had us wait around for a while, then finally told us to go home. "We're closing the set," one of the producers announced. It was disappointing and frustrating to be ready to get to work, then be turned away without any idea when we'd start filming or whether Farrah would return. But I didn't reach out to Farrah out of respect for her privacy and whatever process she was in with Aaron.

As we went to leave, I realized I'd left my purse in the makeup room, but when I went to get it, it was locked. Kate said, "I'll get your purse." Like a real superhero, she rammed her foot right through the door, slamming it open. She casually strolled into the room, got my purse, and handed it to me. Even the teamsters were impressed.

Kate was a complex person. She was savvy and skilled, and at times downright silly, but her temper could get the best of her. Once, during season one, she flew into a fury over some slight. She climbed behind the wheel of her motor home, with me by her side, and just drove it in circles around the lot, over and over. It was funny at first, but the teamsters were not happy with us.

While we all had our quirks, there was no denying the unique chemistry the three of us had. If Farrah wasn't coming back, then she'd have to be replaced. But who could possibly fill her Nikes? Farrah's image was emblazoned on millions of lunch boxes, backpacks, and notebook covers. American girlhood worshipped her (and American boyhood did too). Her feathered shag was the most popular Halloween wig of the year by a landslide. Walking down the street of any American city was like joining a parade of Farrah wannabes. It was clear: No one could ever truly replace Farrah. But we'd need to find a new Angel nonetheless.

Farrah might have been gone from my professional life, but she'd never be gone from my personal life. Owing to the demands on our time, we didn't talk or see each other as often as I would have liked in those first years after she left the show, but we stayed in touch.

Around the same time Farrah departed, I met someone else who would become a lifelong friend, more like a member of my family: Alana Voeller.

A Hollywood manager named Ron Samuels was intent on signing me as his client, and he was determined. He would have his assistant, a woman named Alana, call me repeatedly. Each time, I told her, "I don't need a manager." But Ron would not quit. He pulled all kinds of tricks to get near me, or to get Alana near me.

During my years on *Charlie's*, I participated in a popular show called *Battle of the Network Stars*, a prime-time showcase that pitted stars from ABC, NBC, and CBS against each other in races and tests of skill. There was swimming, kayaking, volleyball, tennis, tug-of-war—even a dunk tank! (Imagine getting that many stars to do something like that now. The insurance alone would be too high a hurdle.) Howard Cosell, the host of *Monday Night Football*, narrated the action. In one relay race, Penny Marshall of *Laverne & Shirley* handed off the baton to me, and I ran against stars from NBC and CBS. There's no other way to say it: I left them in the shade, which inspired Cosell to dub me "Jackie the Jet." My proudest moment on television!

Unbeknownst to me, Ron had urged Alana to go to the location where we were filming the show. By that point, I'd spoken to Alana a few times and knew she was a nice person who was just doing what her boss asked of her. I didn't blame her for Ron's persistence. The two of us were chatting while in line at the lunch buffet. When it was our turn, the man serving food said, "I'm sorry, only the stars can eat now. Their guests need to go to the back of the line." It wasn't a matter of hierarchy but of timing. We had to eat quickly so we could get back to filming. But Alana had been keeping me company and I hoped to continue our conversation. I said, "I just have one guest and we'll be quick."

The server was unmoved. "No. It doesn't matter. You have to just go through on your own."

So I said, "Okay. Well, I need two hot dogs. I'm very hungry." I ordered two of everything. The man knew what I was doing, but he wasn't going to tell me that I couldn't have as much food as I asked for.

Laughing about our little rebellion, Alana and I had lunch together that day and chatted more about nothing in particular. We both loved animals and talked about our dogs. And she told me about her current job working for Ron. She wasn't happy in that role. Not to say that Ron was a bad boss; she just felt awkward about the job itself. I offered to take Alana out to dinner to discuss a possible freelance job helping me out with some odds and ends while she looked for a full-time position. I mentioned the idea to Kate, and we decided we *both* needed help and hired Alana to work for us.

When Alana joined our team and started making me her

incredible grilled cheese sandwiches and running lines with me, I knew I'd made the right call. We had so much fun and laughed constantly. Before long, Alana stopped assisting Kate and came to work for me exclusively as my personal assistant, a role she filled expertly for decades. Even though I didn't need a manager, what I got instead was golden. A fifty-plus-year friendship—a real, true friendship—that held adventure and truth, late-night phone calls, crack-of-dawn phone calls, years on location together, often reading lines into the night. We fought, made up, and shared secrets. Through it all, Alana stood back, took the measure of my family and our lives, and saw us clearly. Her devotion to my children was a gift without equal. She knew our goals and understood our values, and she was protective of us. Alana remains in my life today, only now she is family. We have shared so much, and all those memories are safe and sound with her.

I'll be indebted to Ron Samuels forever for bringing her into my life.

Selecting the new Angel was a high-stakes task. The eyes of the television world were on us. Fortunately, because of the show's success, Aaron and Len had their choice of some of the biggest actresses in Hollywood. At times, it seemed like everyone wanted to do a screen test for the part. I remember seeing aspiring Angels filing in and out of Aaron's office. Priscilla Presley, Elvis's ex-wife, was offered the part but turned it down. Kim Basinger tested for the part too. I'm not sure whether she was offered the role and turned it down to pursue her movie career, or whether Aaron and Len didn't see her as a fit. I knew they liked her, though. At the end of the "Angels in Chains" episode, they wrote in a line about hiring her character as a secretary for the Townsend Agency (though she was never seen again that season). It could have been an easy setup to bring her in, but for one reason or another, it didn't work out.

Then there was Cheryl Ladd, a petite blonde from South Dakota. She'd made the rounds as a guest star on some big shows, including *The Partridge Family*, *Switch*, and *The Rookies*. She'd been the voice of Melody on the kids' cartoon *Josie and the Pussycats* and thought of herself as a singer first, an actress second. Cheryl arrived at the production office to audition, but she didn't want to do a screen test. Kate and I were already busy filming season two, so we weren't in the room for any of the tests. However, we did hear that Cheryl didn't want to do one. Eventually, Cheryl did agree to read. I thought she was adorable and would fit the part of Farrah's younger sister, but Kate wasn't convinced she was right for the role.

I met Cheryl briefly and thought she was lovely. When Aaron asked for my opinion, I said she'd be a great addition to the cast and voted in favor of hiring her. They agreed, and Cheryl joined the cast as Kris Munroe. The story was that she hailed from San Francisco and was a frustrated cop who'd decided to go freelance as a private investigator. Cheryl was smart, funny, beautiful, genuine, and full of enjoyment and good cheer. She was enthusiastic, and so was the public's reaction to her.

In the season two opener, Kate and I are in the Townsend Agency office, telling Bosley that no one can ever replace Jill and that we won't stand for anyone else coming in and trying. "We don't want her, and we don't need her!" I proclaim.

Then Cheryl bounces in wearing tight black sateen pants and a matching jacket. "Hi! Well, I'm here!" she announces, beaming from ear to ear. When Kate and I look at her quizzically, she explains, "It's me! Kris Munroe!" Jill's little sister, whom they haven't seen in forever. Apparently, while Jill and everyone else thought Kris was away at college, studying to become a teacher, she was secretly attending the police academy.

"Police academy!" Kate exclaims, putting the pieces together. "Perfect!" The three of us link arms and it's like we're all best friends.

Cheryl was sweet and easy to get along with, and the crew instantly adored her. The cinematographer obviously loved her, given the many long, lingering close-ups of her face and body. And the costume team fell over themselves with excitement because Cheryl was willing to wear the tightest, tiniest bikini they could find. She had no objections to showing acres of skin. In "Angels in Paradise," we filmed in Hawaii (with Don Ho and his ukulele making an appearance). Within twenty minutes of screen time, Cheryl was in a string bikini that made my white one look like a sports bra. She had to do some detecting on a nude beach and did a scene with *Three's Company*'s Norman Fell while hiding her birthday suit with a palm frond.

That wasn't the only memorable event in Hawaii. One day I was hanging out with Kate in her motor home and someone knocked on the door. Kate opened it and we saw a shy little girl with strawberry-blond hair. I noticed that the girl had her own bodyguards and knew instantly who she was. "Hello, Amy!" I said. It was President Jimmy Carter's daughter. Apparently, Amy and her mother, Rosalynn, were on vacation and wanted to drop by the set. Like so many girls her age, Amy was a huge fan of the show. We invited her in and had a lovely chat.

While Cheryl bared it all (or close to it), my own costumes on that episode included purple halter tops, spaghetti-strapped creamy jumpsuits, and white jeans that were flattering but roomy enough for me to give Kate a hula dancing lesson. Our clothes that season were diverse. It was the no-rules decade. The key staples were bell-bottoms, high-waisted pants, and platform shoes. It was a time of bold, earthy colors. Our wardrobe emphasized our natural shapes. In the climactic scene, Cheryl and I both wore teeny-tiny bikinis, but it wasn't gratuitous. We'd just swum across the ocean to sneak onto the bad guy's yacht. The alternative would have been scuba gear, and I know which way the costumers would have voted.

As time went on, Kate and Cheryl did not always see eye to eye. When Cheryl arrived on set each morning, she had a habit of singing "Where the Boys Are," the classic Connie Francis song, at the top of her lungs. The first time it happened, Kate and I looked at each other, then asked Cheryl, "What's going on?"

"I just love to sing!" said Cheryl. It was how she loosened up before a take. Kate cursed, Cheryl sang. We all had our methods to prepare. I broke down the scripts line by line and made notes about the intentions of every character. But Cheryl's singing annoyed Kate.

We definitely had different relationships with the people we worked with. At one point Kate hung a sign on the door of her motor home that read, "Paranoids are chasing me!" It was funny, and yet, given her attitude, there was probably some truth to how Kate saw our shared world.

It was difficult feeling caught between Kate and Cheryl. Kate never fully accepted Cheryl. Maybe it was because she missed Farrah, and in Kate's mind no one could take her place. I got it, but Farrah was gone. We had to move on, and I liked Cheryl.

Even though I disagreed with Kate, I still loved her. She was my friend, and we had a shared history. But I wasn't going to take sides. We had to make this trio work.

The saving grace on set for Cheryl was her close friendship with David Doyle. He was her safety net, a constant supporter. David was wonderful and loved us all, but I think he felt a special need to look out for Cheryl since she was new. David was a leveler and a peacemaker. It was just part of his personality. If there was a fight on set, between Kate and Cheryl or anyone else in the cast, he stepped in to work it out and bring us back together. He used the sharpest tool in his toolbox, his humor, and made us all laugh. When you're laughing, it's hard to stay angry. Only a true pro, a veteran like him, could see the forest for the trees and remind us how privileged we all were to be there.

For season two, the writers upped the ante and put us in exotic settings—and costumes. We went undercover as stewardesses, beauty pageant contestants, singers, magician's assistants, Ice Capades skaters, football players, jewel thieves, Keystone Cops, toy makers, tennis champions, and exotic dancers. For one episode, Kelly pretended to be an unwed pregnant mother to take down a black-market baby ring. We blew the lid off criminal behavior at a couples' retreat, a dude ranch, a movie musical, and a radio station.

A very young Craig T. Nelson, *Gilligan's Island*'s Jim Backus, and *Bilko*'s Phil Silvers made appearances that season, but the biggest guest star of the year was Sammy Davis Jr. He played a dual role, as himself and as a look-alike of himself. The title, "The Sammy Davis Jr. Kidnap Caper," pretty much sums up the entire hour of television. In "The Sandcastle Murders," we saved teen runaways from being killed by a beachcombing psycho, with a climactic carousel scene that some have compared to Hitchcock's *Strangers on a Train*. Barry Bostwick and I flirted shamelessly on the beach in "The Jade Trap," but the romance fizzled when his character was revealed to be a daredevil jewel thief. (Barry and I got another shot at love several years later in the TV miniseries *George Washington*.) My childhood friend Irene guest-starred in the football team episode called "Angels in the Backfield." She played the embattled team coach with a former pro-baller father who constantly belittled her. She had to say lines like "Are you proud of me, Pa?" It was just so needy, we would crack up between takes.

It was during season two that Prince Charles (now King Charles), who was a fan of the show, came to the set. Before his arrival, his security team swept the soundstage—every inch of it, from the bathrooms to the closets. When Prince Charles finally appeared, he arrived with quite an entourage. He was curious about how the show was made and asked a million questions, like "Why is that light there?" and "How long does it take to set up a shot?" He couldn't have been lovelier. I can't remember if he asked to take a picture with us or if we asked him, but we posed for a series of them. (My son, Gaston, has one of the prints hanging in his house.)

My boyfriend, Dennis, returned to *Charlie's* in seasons two and three. In "Unidentified Flying Angels"—our UFO episode, which aired two weeks before the release of Steven Spielberg's *Close Encounters of the Third Kind*—Dennis played an evil former astronaut. He took Kelly up in his airplane and attempted to kill her by flying upside down, having previously cut her seat belt. Kelly noticed in time and quickly rigged a harness out of her own belt (the original MacGyver!). When he turned the plane right side up, Kelly took the gun out of her purse (which somehow hadn't gone flying out of the plane), pointed it at him, and said, "Take it down! Now!" Kelly survived and caught the bad guy, and when the plane landed, not a hair was out of place.

In 1979, the Cold War raged, even on *Charlie's Angels*. Dennis's final role on the show was as an international diplomat who had been targeted for assassination by a cadre of Italian radicals. The assassins had tracked Dennis's character to a five-star ski resort in Vail, and the Angels traveled to Colorado to be his bodyguards. My winter wardrobe was fit for a snow queen: a one-piece royal-blue ski suit trimmed in white mink, snow boots with furry tassels, and a white fur hat. Both Kris and Kelly got a kiss in that two-part episode. Dennis and I had romantic moments sipping hot chocolate at the lodge, watching fireworks over the mountain, and dodging bullets while skiing. In the end, the bad guys were either killed or captured, and the Angels' cheeks were fetchingly windburned. Plus, Dennis and I got a two-week on-location vacation in Vail!

By the time the last episode of season two aired, we were still in the top ten, with a devoted following that embraced Cheryl's arrival. In spite of the on-set friction, we had weathered the storm of Farrah's departure. It was humbling to see how, with the right casting, the show went on.

Chapter Fifteen

Farrah had left the show with the intention to focus on movies, but Kate and I also had opportunities to do feature films, thanks to the exposure we enjoyed on *Charlie's*. According to my contract, I could take on other work as long as it didn't interfere with the show's shooting schedule—and I didn't change my hair.

I was offered the part of Holly Goodhead in *Moonraker*, the 1979 James Bond film that's considered one of the best of the entire series. It would have reunited me with my *Switch* costar Richard Kiel, a.k.a. Jaws. When I asked Aaron and Len about *Moonraker*, they said it conflicted with the *Charlie's* shooting schedule—a schedule they weren't willing to change. So I turned down the part. There's a saying in Texas: Dance with the one who brought you. I felt like I couldn't fight for the part in *Moonraker* because my first commitment was to the show, and to Aaron. There would be more opportunities. Sure, *Moonraker* might have made a big impact on my career, but who knows? I tend to believe that all things happen for a reason, so while I was disappointed, I didn't dwell on it.

Aaron made it up to me, anyway. During the hiatus between seasons two and three, he asked me, "Would you consider doing *The Users*?" It was a TV movie, a Spelling production. The screenplay was cowritten by Dominick Dunne, based on the best-selling novel by *Los Angeles Times* gossip columnist Joyce Haber. The plot was boy-meets-girl *and* fish-out-of-water *and* rags-to-riches, all rolled into one. I would play the part of Elena, a small-town prostitute hired by a movie producer (George Hamilton) to boost the ego of his insecure, faltering star, played by Tony Curtis, while they filmed on location. Tony's character falls for Elena, brings her to Beverly Hills, and introduces her to the wild world of Hollywood.

The Users was the second movie I made during a *Charlie's* hiatus, and I'm glad it was made under Aaron's watchful eye. (The first was a 1977 TV drama called *Escape from Bogen County* that included Mitchell Ryan and Henry Gibson, among others.) I got to join a cast of actors I'd grown up watching, and I was a little nervous. But I didn't want to let Aaron down. Fortunately, the actors were all kind and accepting and I quickly became part of the team.

Tony Curtis and I had several love scenes, and he put me at ease. A generous actor, Tony thought of the person opposite him just as much as his own character. You don't see that a lot, and I appreciated it. He played an A-list star on his way down, and a closeted gay man. The film aired on October 1, 1978, pre-AIDS. It was a real risk at that time for Tony to play a gay man, and he handled it with fragility and sensitivity.

George Hamilton was impressive in every way, from his looks to his acting. He could do any dialect and had an impeccable sense of style. His costumes were always lined up and perfectly crisp—the blazer, the gold rings, the ascot. He was exactly what he looked like, suave and confident. What I loved the most was George's comedic timing. I wish he'd done more comedy in his career. He made us all laugh from the beginning of the day until the end.

Red Buttons played a sleazy agent, and we had a scene in his "casting Jacuzzi." Michelle Phillips, formerly of the Mamas and the

Papas, portrayed Tony's movie-star daughter. I remember her kindness and her natural beauty. Joan Fontaine, the Oscar-winning star of Hitchcock's *Rebecca* and *Suspicion*, played the behind-the-scenes kingmaker, and she was my character's partner in crime. Joan was class incarnate, and devilishly funny too. Working with her was yet another pinch-me moment. In the role of a business magnate, a mysterious millionaire who pulled the strings, John Forsythe was another of my love interests. It was a bit of a wink from Aaron that the voice of Charlie and Kelly Garrett finally met—and fell in love.

Nolan Miller did the costumes, and they were pure glamour. (I'm sure he had a blast, considering how seldom the Angels got to do high style.) One of my gowns was green satin with a brown sable collar and a stole completely trimmed in sable; another was red strapless chiffon topped by a red velvet coat with a brown mink collar. Since one of the characters was the heir to a department store fortune, there were scenes with lots of shopping and trying on dresses. The movie fetishized fashion, which Nolan loved. Even though it was a TV movie, it felt as glamorous as any classic Hollywood film. It wasn't Bond, but it was a delightful experience with some fantastic stars, and it was a ratings hit.

To support that film and *Charlie's* season three, I posed for the cover of *Vogue* and was shot by Richard Avedon. It was a privilege to work with the legendary photographer, who was a lovely man and a brilliant artist. He wanted to capture me as I was on *Charlie's*: fit, strong, and in charge. In one picture, I wore a John Anthony dress. It had a bareness in the wonderful way it revealed the body, with a slit back and a barely-there tulle-and-lace halter. It was a movie-star dress—no ornament needed. My classic hair was slicked back in a low ponytail. During the photo shoot, I kept thinking about my mother, who always subscribed to *Vogue*. There I was, posing for Avedon for the magazine Mom pored over joyfully as soon as it arrived in the mail. I kept picturing the issue arriving at my parents' house, and the thrill Mom would feel seeing her daughter's face on the cover.

Kate was presented with an amazing opportunity of her own that summer. After a courtship with Dustin Hoffman and director Robert Benton, she was offered the part of Joanne in *Kramer vs. Kramer*—an emotionally fraught film about a child custody battle between an estranged husband and wife. Kate asked Aaron if she could do it, but, as with *Moonraker*, he said it interfered with our *Charlie's* shooting schedule. She got the movie producers to change their schedule—then Aaron changed the show's schedule to conflict with it. For Aaron, it was a matter of principle. He didn't want to let her do it because if he made accommodations for Kate, he would have to do it for all of us.

I knew how important that role was to Kate, and I felt horrible for her that Aaron blocked her from taking it. I did my best to support Kate and listened to her vent about it for months. It only got worse when the movie came out. Her part had gone to a lesser-known actress named Meryl Streep who went on to win an Oscar for the role. It was one of five Oscars for the film, in addition to it being the highest-grossing film of 1979.

Again, it's easy to fixate on a missed opportunity, thinking, *If only!* Kate was already angry that she wasn't sharing the *Charlie's Angels* profits, and this was bitterness upon bitterness. In hindsight, it's incredible she stayed with *Charlie's* as long as she did.

As much of our time as *Charlie's Angels* occupied, there was a lot happening in our lives off set as well. In May 1978 I was awarded Advertising Woman of the Year by the Advertising Club of New York. When a big neon sign went up in Times Square, I thought,

Wow, I've made it! My name was finally up in lights. It wasn't Broadway, but I'd take it.

There were goings-on in our personal lives too. Cheryl's husband—*Day of the Locust* actor David Ladd, whom she'd married in 1973—would bring their three-year-old daughter, Jordan, to visit. I loved Jordan. What a beautiful, sweet baby! I was absolutely fascinated with the child. More than anything, I wanted to be a mother and have babies of my own.

Meanwhile, Kate was dating Andrew Stevens. We lived right next door to each other in Coldwater Canyon, and Kate, Andrew, Dennis, and I spent a lot of time together at dinner dates, parties, and events. In August 1978, Kate and Andrew decided to tie the knot. It was a top secret ceremony that took place on Martha's Vineyard at Carly Simon and James Taylor's house.

My own relationship was heading toward the altar too. Dennis and I had been together for a year and a half before we decided to get married. I figured I was making progress by not rushing into things this time around.

We set the date, October 29, 1978, right in the middle of filming season three. It was a much smaller affair than my first wedding, only twenty-five guests, just family and close friends. To keep it a secret from the press, we didn't send out invitations. Instead, we called our guests and told them where to go and when. The service was at Marble Collegiate Church in New York City, home to *The Power of Positive Thinking* author and minister Norman Vincent Peale. We chose New York because we wanted to get away from LA and hopefully evade the paparazzi. But someone leaked our wedding date and location, and suddenly reporters were lighting up the phone lines buying tickets on every United and American Airlines flight out of LA in an attempt to catch us—and they did. Photographers followed me everywhere: to our hotel, to the church, even into the Bergdorf Goodman lingerie department! We'd tried to carve out a private moment, but they refused to let us have it.

Dennis's son, Joe, seventeen at the time, was his best man. His friend Dick Fox was also in attendance. Jill Krask Wagner, a dear friend from Los Angeles, was my matron of honor. My something old: an antique cross my grandfather had given me. My something new: my couture cream silk chiffon dress by Holly's Harp, and my ring, white gold with bands of evergreen leaves, from Tiffany. My something borrowed: a pair of Jill's stockings. My something blue: eye shadow. (It *was* the late seventies.)

Just before our short, ten-minute ceremony, I began to cry. The minister said, "I hope those are tears of joy." I nodded, but they weren't. Honestly, I didn't quite know where the emotion was coming from. Somewhere in my heart of hearts, I had reservations about marrying Dennis. I'd already had one failed marriage, and now I was staring a second in the face—quite literally. I felt overwhelmed. Sometimes physical attraction masquerades as love. It can get you into trouble.

From the church, we taxied to the reception at Tavern on the Green, the famous restaurant off Central Park. We'd booked the space under fake names, so when we came through the door, the maître d' nearly had a heart attack. He wasn't expecting to host two of Charlie's Angels that night, I'm sure. In every picture from that evening, Kate and I are smiling and laughing with our brand-new, handsome husbands.

The night went by in a blur. Despite my secret misgivings, the wedding was a happy occasion, and I got to spend precious time with my parents, along with my brother and sister-in-law. But the respite didn't last long. Dennis and I had a three-day honeymoon at the St. Regis Hotel in New York, then flew back to Los Angeles, where we both went back to work.

Then there was the other man in my life—Charlie. Season three was a high point in terms of guest stars. We opened with Dean Martin in the two-part "Angels in Vegas." Unfortunately, while we were filming that episode I came down with a 102-degree fever. They didn't stop production, though. Their compromise was to put a bed just off set so I could rest between takes. That was one time I definitely leaned on the work ethic Daddy had instilled in me. Still, even Daddy thought they went overboard at times with how much they demanded of us. "This is against labor laws!" he'd say. "You should stand up to them!" He didn't get that it was just how things worked back then. It came with the territory.

In the episode "Winning Is for Losers," a very young, pre-*Halloween* Jamie Lee Curtis played a pro golfer who'd been the target of several murder attempts, including one that had Cheryl wrestle an alligator. (I'm sure that was a fun skill to add to her acting résumé.) In "Angel on My Mind," Jonathan Frakes, a future *Star Trek: The Next Generation* commander, played volleyball on the beach when Kris, stunned by amnesia, wandered by. He gave her a ham sandwich—the universal cure for amnesia. Also in that episode, Billy Barty played a curmudgeonly newspaper salesman. Anne Francis, Honey West herself, appeared on "Pom Pom Angels." Dick Sargent from *Bewitched*, whom I'd appeared with in that pilot that wasn't picked up earlier in my career, made one of his three appearances on the show that season.

For all of season three's star quality, the most highly anticipated guest had already appeared in twenty-two episodes. Farrah made her first of six contractual appearances in "Angel Come Home," although it didn't feel like a homecoming for Kate and me. As tense as it was at times, we'd reinvented the show without Farrah, and bringing her back now, over a year later, felt forced. The chemistry was off. I don't blame Cheryl, though no one on the set was feeling any real connection between sisters Jill and Kris Munroe. That was in part because Farrah didn't love having to come back to fulfill her obligations. The fact was, the magic of the original combination of Farrah, Kate, and me was gone and couldn't be recaptured, though I didn't fault Aaron and Len for trying. But whatever we experienced on set, the audience didn't seem to notice. They were delighted to have their original Angel back.

Our ratings held steady, and by the end of 1979, *Charlie's Angels* was still in the top ten. Yet after three long seasons and lots of friction, Kate was at her wits' end. She felt the scripts had become subpar. At one point, she stopped in the middle of a scene and shouted, "Why do I have to say this garbage?"

Too much resentment had accumulated over the years. Talking to Kate, it seemed that, by that point, she was unhappy with every aspect of *Charlie's* except our friendship.

In the end, Kate's departure was a "You can't fire me—I quit!" situation. And just like that, she left the show.

Of the three original detectives, I was the last Angel left standing.

Chapter Sixteen

After Kate's departure, I felt her absence on set. I might have been alone in wanting her to come back for another year, but I had a sense that, with Kate gone, we'd lose that secret sauce that made the show special. With only one of us left, the spark might go out.

Kate and I no longer worked together, but our friendship went beyond *Charlie's*. In 1979, while filming season four, I remember leaving home at 5 a.m. to get in the limo to go to work. At the bottom of the driveway in Coldwater Canyon, I ran into Kate and Andrew.

"Where are you going this early?" I asked.

"To Paris," she said, grinning.

She didn't have to rub it in. Now that Kate was free of that grueling schedule, she and Andrew could fly to Paris, or anywhere else, on the spur of the moment. Dennis and I hadn't even had time for a decent honeymoon, and the only traveling I'd been able to do was for work, when we were filming on location.

I grumbled just a bit on the way to the lot that day, but I reminded myself that I'd definitely rather be on the show than off. For one thing, I was now the highest-paid Angel. I'd renegotiated my salary, which had gradually gone up from $5,000 per episode to

$70,000. For season five, it would spike to $100,000 per episode, which made me one of the highest-paid women in television.

The money was nice, but it didn't change the fact that by season four I was getting tired of the show myself. And it wasn't just the schedule. The cast changes and tension on the set hadn't been easy on me. I could have gone to Aaron and Len and asked about breaking my contract, but I decided to stay the course. So, while Kate flew off to Paris and got on with her life, I stayed put. And the producers went about finding another replacement Angel. Would our ratings survive yet another major cast change? It remained to be seen.

As before, Aaron and Len had their pick of actresses for the part of the "preppy" Angel, whose name would be Tiffany Welles. Kathie Lee Gifford, Connie Sellecca, Barbara Bach, Cristina Ferrare, and pre-*Scarface* Michelle Pfeiffer were among those in the running. The role eventually went to Shelley Hack. Her claims to fame at that point were a cameo in Woody Allen's *Annie Hall*, a smash hit in 1977, and being the model for Revlon's Charlie perfume ads. Aaron thought it was a cute marketing hook, that the Charlie girl was going to be on *Charlie's Angels*.

Connecticut-born and Smith College–educated, Shelley had a high-fashion pedigree and a New England coolness that would make for an interesting contrast to Cheryl's Western girl-next-door warmth and my Southern roots. I cast my vote for Shelley. I liked her walk, her pop, her affect. And so, she became the Angel from Boston.

Shelley, blond and monotoned, was a master of composure. With her slinky grace, she was like a page in a fashion magazine come to life. She was bookish and cultured, likely at home in any high-society setting.

Despite the challenge of having to on-board a new Angel, season four had some highlights. A particularly memorable episode for me was "Angels on the Street," in which Shelley and I went undercover as streetwalkers. Nolan Miller designed costumes that made us look like French *filles de joie* after the Great War. Shelley walked down the street, swinging her hips and a little purse, saying, "Come and get me, boys!" My friend Irene once again guest-starred, this time as a prostitute. In one scene, she conspired with a pimp to drug me, pouring LSD from a tiny bottle into my cocktail at a party. But then her character had second thoughts. Irene was supposed to yell at me not to drink the concoction, grab my doctored glass, and throw it into the wall. But she just couldn't do it. Irene is no fighter—she doesn't have a vicious or violent bone in her body, even pretending. And she'd never yell. Instead, she put the glass down gently on the bar. The director kept saying, "Yell at her! Throw the glass, *hard*!" It took a few takes, but we finally got her to do it.

In "Avenging Angel," Kelly was unwittingly hopped up on heroin. Cameron Mitchell guest-starred. That episode broke the formula of the show in that it was really a character study about the effects of drug addiction. It was an acting challenge beyond what I normally got to do. And during my brief kidnapping while high, I looked a mess. For that one time only, my hair was allowed to return to its natural curly, frizzy state, and I went without makeup. The fact that it was such a departure made it one of my favorite episodes.

In "Of Ghosts and Angels," we went undercover at an old Victorian house that was, allegedly, haunted by a wheelchair-bound woman who once lived—and died—there. According to our informant (a ghost), the woman's killer would be attending a masquerade party held at the mansion. We put on our costumes and, with the help of a spirit, revealed the killer by taking off his mask, just like in an episode of *Scooby-Doo*. For my Southern belle costume, Nolan Miller designed a Scarlett O'Hara picnic dress for me, and I finally got to swan around like I was in *Gone with the Wind*.

Once again, Farrah made her required guest appearances, including for an episode called "The Prince and the Angel," in which Jill Munroe and an ambiguously European prince fall in love at first sight. At one point, the prince buys a car to impress Jill and pays for it in cash in five-hundred-dollar bills, which have not been printed since 1945. I laughed out loud when I saw that. It was just such a perfect symbol of the unreality of our show. In "Fallen Angel," Jill is in cahoots with a millionaire/playboy/jewel thief played by British actor Timothy Dalton, and he was as dashing as you'd hope a future James Bond would be.

As always, our guest stars were a mix of up-and-coming actors and veteran stars who wanted to be part of the phenomenon. A brunette Kim Cattrall, way before *Sex and the City*, played a bride in "Angels at the Altar." Kelly, as her maid of honor, saves her from being killed by the groom. In "Nips and Tucks," Louis Jourdan was a plastic surgeon, pressed into doing a face-changing operation on wanted man Tab Hunter at the urging of his paramour, Diane McBain. Another *Batman* alum, Cesar "The Joker" Romero, was the leader of a swing band at a dance club in "Dancin' Angels" who kills anyone who calls him a has-been.

The biggest guest star of that season was screen legend Barbara Stanwyck as Toni in "Toni's Boys." She played the boss of a detective agency with three sexy young men in her charge. If the episode did well, Aaron and Len hoped to spin it off into another series with crossover potential with *Charlie's*. The villain of the Barbara Stanwyck episode was Robert Loggia, playing a just-released-from-prison winery owner.

Every week, Nolan begged Aaron to write a scene at a gala or somewhere fancy so he could put us in sequins. "They need evening gowns!" he pleaded. That finally happened in "Toni's Boys." We pretended to be models at a wine auction in gowns that matched the color of the vintage, and Nolan had a blast putting together our high-style looks.

Throughout the season, I thought Shelley did good work as Tiffany in her various duties as an eighteen-wheeler trucker, a classical violinist, a nurse, a real estate broker, and a swing dancer, among other guises. Yet it wasn't smooth sailing. When the directors asked her to make changes or to read a line in a different way, she sometimes seemed to take it as a personal insult instead of constructive criticism.

Toward the end of the shooting season, the Angels were invited to an "upfront," a big network event where the stars were on display for advertisers and press to get them excited for the next year's offerings. Cheryl and I were seated in the front of the room in full view, while Shelley was hidden at a table way in the back. Honestly, it was cruel. Shelley handled it with grace, putting on a brave face. When she approached us, she said in an embarrassed voice, "They seated me in the back of the room." We saw the expectation in her eyes, hoping we might have an answer to why she'd been placed there, but Cheryl and I were at a loss. How I wish we could have simply said, "It must be a mistake. Come sit at our table." But there was no extra seat. Understandably, Shelley felt dismissed, discounted, and hurt.

When we talked about it later, Shelley told me that she had felt crushed and thought the producers had intentionally humiliated her. I don't think they meant to embarrass her as such. It was a brush-off. But everyone who understood such things knew that Shelley's seating could mean only one thing: She wasn't coming back for season five. And she seemed to be the last one to know.

Until that night, neither did I. When I talked to Aaron, he said that they just didn't think she matched their image of her character, so they dropped her flat after one season. Firing her so quickly didn't seem fair to me. I thought they should have given her a little more time to develop the character, but the decision was made.

When it came to casting Shelley's replacement, this time the producers didn't ask for Cheryl's or my input. Aaron and Len came down to Stage 8 and announced, "Shelley Hack isn't coming back next season. We're replacing her with Tanya Roberts." Aaron had asked Tanya, a natural blonde, to dye her hair red. He finally got his blonde, brunette, and redhead. But they'd done it without consulting us, which felt odd because we'd always had a vote before. They'd at least asked our opinions.

Tanya's character, Julie Rogers, would be the "gritty" Angel, up from the street, surviving on her pluck and toughness. The character matched Tanya's personal history. Born in the Bronx, New York, she had left home in her teens, hitchhiked across the country, married at fifteen (the groom's mother later had it annulled), then landed back in New York, where she got modeling work and did random jobs to get by. Meanwhile, her older sister, Barbara, married Timothy Leary, the Harvard psychologist who did LSD experiments in the sixties.

Tanya had met her husband, Barry Roberts, while standing in line for a movie. Soon after, they got engaged during a subway ride. The couple came to Hollywood so Tanya could act and Barry could write screenplays. Getting cast in *Charlie's* was her big break.

By 1980, when season five began, I was thirty-five years old. Cheryl was thirty, and Tanya was twenty-five. She seemed impossibly young, with a worldview that was far more permissive than mine. Tanya and Barry had an open marriage. She wasn't shy about it in the least, or about propositioning people to "swing" with them. I found her honesty about her sexuality to be brave and self-aware. The world is made up of all kinds of people with all kinds of passions, and hooray for that. My own perspective on marriage was traditional, based on the values I grew up with. Her choice seemed complicated to me, with great potential for hurt feelings.

For a few episodes in season five, we returned to Hawaii. On the flight out, Tanya propositioned me to join her and Barry for a threesome. When she got up to go to the bathroom, David Doyle, who was sitting in the row behind me, tapped me on the shoulder and asked, "Do you need some salt?"

I was confused.

He said, "Take it with a grain of salt," and gestured toward the bathroom.

It was typical David: ever the peacemaker, and the one to set people at ease. David's big vice, if you care to call it that, was his sweet tooth. The only drugs he stashed in his pockets were mini Milky Way bars. Whenever he traveled, he filled a suitcase with his favorite candy and soda, just in case he couldn't find chocolate where he was going. I don't know where that would have been, but he really liked his chocolate!

That season, we continued our tradition of spotlighting fantastic guest stars on the show, including Christopher Lee as the menacing boss of a hooker/porn/drug ring. Ronald Reagan's first wife, Jane Wyman, played a psychic who helped the Angels find Kris, who'd been kidnapped. And Hugh Hefner's girlfriend Barbi Benton showed more skin than any of us and helped the Angels uncover a terrorist plot. But one of the show's long-held traditions shifted in season five.

The peaceful, gentle Carter years were behind us. We'd entered the Reagan era, and the mood of the country, along with its fashion, was changing. For years, Aaron had insisted on a timeless look for the show, and that our hair be the same season after season. He didn't want *Charlie's* to look dated by the clothes. In season five, which began airing in 1980, the timeless concept was thrown out the window. Our costume color palette shifted from pastels and creams to fuchsia, magenta, teal blue (which offset Tanya's stunning bright-blue eyes), black, and metallics. Shoulder pads found their way into blouses and blazers. We wore skintight sateen leggings and looked like we'd stepped out of a Blondie video.

Our hair, if it was even possible, got bigger. And our makeup shifted from a fresh, scrubbed, natural look with shimmer and gloss to bronzed skin, irresistible glossy lips, and full brows. I love a smoky eye as much as the next woman, but suddenly we had heavy eye shadow and fake lashes in every scene.

There were other changes around *Charlie's* that I wasn't so fond of—not so much with the show, but with the behavior around it. People were doing drugs—in particular, cocaine. I have never used it and never will. Drugs scare me because I've seen what they can do to people. I've watched that drug, in particular, turn people into the worst versions of themselves, on *Charlie's* and elsewhere. They think they've become funnier, smarter, happier, better—that's the appeal of it, I guess—but actually, cocaine snuffs out their spark. On *Charlie's*, cocaine use became more common, with some people using it constantly. The more drug use I saw on set, the more time I spent in my motor home. I was in there a lot by the end of the series.

I don't judge people for their lifestyle or their choices. It simply wasn't fun, as an actor or otherwise, for me to be surrounded by people who were impaired. We'd all come to do a job, and the users weren't always able to. After a bender, people would call in sick, or they'd suddenly get an illness and have to leave right away. Apart from the annoyances, I found it disheartening to see people I cared about turn into shells of themselves.

We'd come a long way since the first season. There'd been peaks and valleys, but for me, that year, *Charlie's* was definitely on a downward slope. Too many things had shifted. The innocence and camaraderie of the first season were gone.

I knew the fifth season would be my last.

Chapter Seventeen

What would life be like after *Charlie's Angels*? We were all about to find out. The show was canceled due to low ratings before we'd finished filming season five. We weren't having fun, and I think it showed.

I was saying goodbye to something of infinite value—to a job that had opened doors for me and been an education, to friends I loved—leaving for a future that felt not urgent but inevitable. I didn't feel that same urgency about my work anymore. Instead, I was excited and curious to see what would come next.

I spent most of the final episode unconscious, which was a great metaphor for how I felt about the show by that point. "Let Our Angel Live" was a clip job, with Bosley, Kris, and Julie sitting in a hospital waiting room, reminiscing about Kelly, while I had emergency surgery to fix the bullet hole in my head. Cue the wavy-lines fade-out into a scene from a past episode. Surprise! Kelly survives surgery and, miraculously, has no permanent damage. "It's the damnedest thing," the doctor says. Indeed. Kelly regained consciousness, talking so coherently it was like she'd just awoken from a nap (makeup still flawless, of course). All the others were gathered around me, crying tears of joy. I told them that while I was unconscious, I could have sworn I'd heard Charlie's voice in the operating room. Lo and behold, Charlie *had* been in there, watching over his Angel. Bosley had caught a glimpse of him in the chapel as well when the doctors came to find the three of them to tell them the good news. But, of course, Charlie was wearing scrubs and a surgical mask. (The gold chain was the giveaway.) So in the end, the audience, and the Angels, never got their big reveal. Oh well. He was gone before we realized he'd even been there.

The show was not only wrapped but off the air. So much had changed that season, and not just in my professional life.

You might have heard about "the *Charlie's Angels* curse." Supposedly, leaving the show would negatively affect your career, and being on the show would doom your marriage. Well, that idea didn't exactly hold up. Yes, there were plenty of breakups, but that wasn't uncommon in Hollywood. As for departing *Charlie's* dooming your future prospects—far from it. *Charlie's* was like a launchpad.

After Farrah departed, she made millions in endorsements. It took a little time for her film career to pick up; she starred in a few smaller movies, then finally had a bigger hit with the ensemble comedy *Cannonball Run* in 1981. But while her career slowly gained steam, other aspects of Farrah's life floundered. She might have left the show in part to spend more time with her husband, but she and Lee ended up separating in 1979.

Kate's marriage to Andrew unraveled as well. Before they separated, they produced a TV movie together, *Topper*, which was intended as a pilot for a potential show but was never picked up. Kate had a bigger hit with *Making Love*, which costarred Harry Hamlin and Michael Ontkean, about a husband who admits to his wife that he's gay. While Kate was making a movie or two a year,

Andrew's career had hit a bit of a stall, and that was likely part of the problem. It's easy to be in love when life is good and you're jetting off to Paris, but hard times reveal what a relationship is truly made of.

As Kate told the press, she and Andrew didn't have much in common. She also felt that the friction and dissatisfaction she'd experienced on *Charlie's* had negatively impacted her marriage. Whatever the cause, the divorce was the opposite of friendly. Kate once told a reporter, "He pulled up to my bank account with a Brink's truck." But Kate would be okay. *Topper* might have flopped, but a few years later she'd land the lead in another successful show, *Scarecrow and Mrs. King*.

Farrah and Lee split in 1979; Cheryl and David in 1980; Kate and Andrew in 1981. Shelley Hack had been single during her time on the show, so the only marriage left standing was that of Tanya and Barry. Tanya once told me that she and Barry would love each other until the day they died, and she was right. They remained together until Barry passed away in 2006, after thirty-two years of marriage.

So, yes, Tanya's was the *only* marriage that lasted. Dennis and I called it quits in 1981, a little over two and a half years after we tied the knot.

We were ill-suited. As I learned, Dennis had a bit of a savior complex. He loved to be needed and gravitated toward people he could lift up. When we met, he saw himself as someone who could serve as a mentor of sorts, guiding me in my career. But whatever I didn't already know, I wanted to figure out on my own. I didn't need guiding or saving. And while my star was rising, his was falling. Doors were flying open for me and closing for Dennis. He'd gone from a red-hot career to being called Mr. Jaclyn Smith. When that happened, he'd sulk for days.

The final straw for me was finding out that he'd been unfaithful.

In retrospect, I should have suspected that Dennis would start looking for someone else to rescue. One day, I found a note in his pocket. The writer turned out to be a girl I knew. She was his son's girlfriend.

I would not repeat the mistake I'd made with Roger. This time, I wasn't going to overlook what I'd learned, and I was not going to stick around and try to work it out. I didn't rationalize Dennis's actions, and I didn't blame myself. My one and only thought was to get out.

After my breakup with Dennis, I was in a kind of emotional limbo for a time. Dennis and I were not yet divorced, but in every other sense we were over. That year, 1981, I spent many restless nights trying to gain some insight into and perspective on my romantic history.

I was brought up in the 1950s with traditional values. I'd absorbed a lot of my parents' beliefs, and for the most part, that was a good thing. But a child's job is to individuate, to at some point pull back far enough from their parents that they can see the world with their own eyes and make up their own mind about things. Perhaps I didn't do that quite enough. If I could go back in time, I would have given myself a little wiggle room and been a bit more liberal in my view of relationships. I'm not a fling type of girl and never have been. But if I had, it probably would have saved me from two marriages! Live and learn.

Nowadays I don't even think of my relationships with Roger and Dennis as real marriages. If it had been up to me, I'd have left them out of this book entirely. They were mistakes of my youth. I was a romantic who believed in the white picket fence. I now recognize that when the paint starts to peel, it's time to get out!

I resolved that my next important relationship would not be rushed into.

Even before the final episode of *Charlie's* wrapped, I was working on my survival plan: Beyond Kelly Garrett. I really wanted to challenge myself with a feature film that offered me a chance to stretch. I'd gotten a taste of that during the summer of 1980—my last summer hiatus during *Charlie's*—and wanted more. That film, *Nightkill*, was a thriller shot in Scottsdale, Arizona. My character, Katherine, couldn't have been more of a departure from take-charge Kelly Garrett. Katherine was the victim of every man she met. No matter how hard she tried to be the master of her own fate, she couldn't get past the enemy at her door. Sometimes an actor has to trust her old companion: imagination.

Nightkill's noir tone was out of my comfort zone, but I welcomed the change. The change of scenery was appealing too. Spending the summer in Scottsdale would be a nice escape from LA and Dennis.

When I was considering the part, I asked Ted Post, the director, "Who's the cinematographer?"

"Anthony Richmond," he said. I knew Tony's name because my ex-husband Roger had been a big fan of his work. When we saw the 1973 Julie Christie and Donald Sutherland supernatural thriller *Don't Look Now*, directed by Nicolas Roeg and shot by Tony, Roger said, "Write Anthony Richmond's name down. I'm going to have him photograph my first movie. He is a genius." Tony won a British Academy Award (BAFTA) for Best Cinematography for that film.

He collaborated with Roeg again on *The Man Who Fell to Earth*, starring David Bowie. As if that wasn't impressive enough, Tony had worked with David Lean on *Dr. Zhivago* and photographed several classic Hammer Films horror flicks. In the late sixties, Tony shot the rock documentaries *The Rolling Stones Rock and Roll Circus* and the Stones' *Sympathy for the Devil*, and later The Who's *The Kids Are Alright*. And remember that iconic Beatles performance of "Let It

Be" on the roof of their recording studio in London? Tony shot that. He had been at the epicenter of British rock and filmmaking since I was barely out of college. In 1980, our paths brought us both to Scottsdale, Arizona, for a very hot summer.

The first time I met Tony, he came to my house on Lindacrest. The director had said that Tony liked to meet his leading ladies in person before the shoot. He wanted to check the color of my hair and my eyes, as well as my height, so he could pick the right stand-in. He arrived with a production manager. I opened the door, and he reached for my hand.

"I'm Tony Richmond, your cinematographer."

There was something about Tony that took me by surprise. He looked like he'd stepped out of another time. I found myself instantly intrigued by this oddly elegant man standing before me in his sports coat, nice trousers, and dress shoes. His hair was shiny, black, natural, like he hadn't done a thing to it, that was just the way it fell.

The first day on the set in Scottsdale, Tony gave me a big smile. "Hello, darling," he said in his lovely English accent. He caught me off guard the way he looked at me, like he saw more than just a Charlie's Angel.

I took a deep breath. *No, I'm here to work.* Technically I was still married, as my divorce from Dennis hadn't yet been finalized. Then I discovered that Tony was married with three kids. In fact, his wife, a very talented makeup artist named Linda DeVetta, and their children—George, ten; Jonathan, a.k.a. Chunky, eight; and Antonia, just two—had come to Arizona for part of the shoot. In my mind, the line was drawn.

Filming for *Nightkill* went on for two months. I loved Arizona. The heat didn't bother me a bit; after all, I'd grown up in Texas, with its scorching summers and high humidity. The warmth in Arizona was dry. When the sun set, the heat disappeared, leaving a cool, clear night. I loved watching the stars sparkle over the Sonoran Desert.

The beauty of the location helped to balance out the demands of the role. I was in nearly every scene, and in many of them I was crying, screaming, and yelling. A perfect opportunity to exorcise some demons, but it was tiring. The shoot was physically exacting, too, with *Charlie's*-level running, jumping, and fighting.

What made it all fun was the incredible cast and crew. Director Ted Post knew what he was doing, as did Tony, so we didn't have excessive reshoots. I loved watching Tony work; he was obsessed with composition and camera angle. As a fellow aesthete, I appreciated his devotion to the visual composition of a piece. Tony would shoot every scene slightly off-center, sometimes from a side angle rather than straight on. The approach seemed to suit film noir. He used nets and choppers, eye lights, everything to brighten and highlight the face. Sometimes there would be just a sliver of light across the eyes. It was incredible. Tony always said, "Remember, the story is in the eyes."

But it wasn't only Tony who impressed me. My costars included James Franciscus, *Mannix*'s Mike Connors, and one of cinema's greatest villains, Robert Mitchum. Robert's acting was so nuanced; his performance was filled with understatement. He could convey a level of feeling with the subtlest of expressions. When he walked, it was with such ease, like he was on springs.

At one point before we wrapped, Tony mentioned that he'd bought the dramatic rights to a novel by Trevor Meldal-Johnsen called *Always*, and that he intended to direct the movie adaptation himself as soon as he could get financing. "I'd like you to star in it," he said with frank determination in his eyes.

I said, "Well, I'd love to read it."

Although we were talking about film, the subtext was about staying in touch and spending more time together.

Tony told me later that he fell in love with me just looking at me through the lens of his camera. In the final cut of the movie, that sentiment is evident in the many, *many* close-ups of my face.

But I fell in love with Tony's kids before I fell in love with their dad. All three of them were adorable, with their charming accents and impeccable manners. I didn't spend much time with Tony's wife, but I found her to be lovely. Though I'd heard whispers that their marriage wasn't in a good place, to the outside world they were a beautiful family.

The rumor was that Tony had a history of affairs with the women he photographed. I had no intention of falling into that trap. Plus, every move I made was tracked by gossip reporters who were champing at the bit to get the dirt on my first post-Dennis rebound relationship. From every angle, getting involved with Tony seemed like a very bad idea.

Well, perhaps not *every* angle. While my mind was set, my heart held another opinion.

At the wrap party for *Nightkill*, Tony and I gravitated toward each other. After we'd made one circuit around the room, we wandered away from the group. He said, "I'd like to take you to dinner and discuss the film." We spent the rest of the evening together.

Instead of going directly back to London, Tony stayed in LA to get financing for his film *Always*. We continued to see each other, having dinners and lunches, always under the pretext of discussing the film.

Our initial attraction was intense, but as we spent more time together, it began to deepen into something more real. Something that felt like it could be lasting.

We started dating, and after a month or two, Tony asked me to marry him.

So much for not rushing into things.

It was complicated. Technically, we were both married to other people. My divorce was proceeding regardless of Tony, but his apparent separation from his wife had been going on for years, and she wasn't yet ready to let him go. Linda asked Tony to return to London and give their marriage one more try before calling it quits. I hated the idea of losing Tony, but I had to think beyond myself. Tony and Linda's marriage had faltered, but they had a history together that included children. A family was at stake. On the set of *Nightkill*, I'd loved watching Tony interact with his kids—the kind, patient, caring way he talked to them and explained what he was doing. I would not be the reason he left them.

I encouraged Tony to return to London to see if it was possible for them to stay together, if for no other reason than for the sake of the kids. Tony agreed. And if it turned out that our relationship *was* to proceed, we needed clarity and a clean slate. If we were to have a future, Tony had to sort out his feelings.

In the meantime, I went about my life, getting along just fine on my own. I missed Tony, but no matter how things played out, I knew I would be okay.

In the end, Tony did come back.

The last episode of *Charlie's* finally aired on June 24, 1981, and that was that. A glossy, sparkly chapter of my life came to a close, and a new one was just beginning.

I was finally free from forced calls at dawn. I could pick and choose my projects. And I was already truly, madly, deeply in love with Tony Richmond.

I felt I was on a precipice. I could look back on everything that had come before with gratitude, but it had all been like a dress rehearsal for what was to come. The second half of my life would be the real deal, full of excitement, meaning, and purpose, with this incredible man at my side.

Chapter Eighteen

When I first heard that a TV biopic, *Jacqueline Bouvier Kennedy*, was in the works about the former First Lady of the United States, I knew I wanted to play Jackie. The wanting it was undeniable. At the same time I learned of the film, I found out that the part of JFK would be played by James Franciscus, my *Nightkill* costar. It seemed fated. Still, every actress in town wanted the part, and I didn't think I'd actually get it.

Jacqueline Kennedy was the epitome of grace under pressure, and I admired her. She had always seemed to me like a figure suspended between two worlds—the intensely public and the fiercely private. I remembered so clearly her bravery and poise when her husband was assassinated seventeen years earlier. It made an indelible impression on me, and on everyone in the country. Still, the idea of portraying such a singular and beloved figure was daunting. What if viewers saw the movie and thought, *Jaclyn Smith got it all wrong?!* Apparently the producers had similar concerns. They told my agent, "We don't want a *Charlie's Angel* playing Jacqueline Kennedy." The resistance was not unexpected. They didn't doubt my ability; rather, it was a question of whether I could shed one image and convincingly assume another. Jackie had a cultivated restraint, an East Coast polish, and in their minds I represented something less quiet, faster, and more modern. It wasn't about the acting—I'd been on a top-ten TV series for five years, so they'd seen what I could do. It was more about the look. Jackie Kennedy was so distinctive. A far cry from street-smart Kelly Garrett, she was elegant and cultured. I had to convince them that I could pull off playing a northeastern Vassar girl.

I arrived for the screen test determined to show them that I could capture Jackie's look, from college to First Lady. It was nothing short of a transformation. (At least, I hoped so.) I parted my hair on the side and wore it pinned back in a barrette, the way Jackie had in her boarding school days. She'd attended Miss Porter's School in Farmington, Connecticut, before going on to Vassar. I put on a three-quarter wig, changed my makeup, thickened my eyebrows, and donned that iconic pillbox hat.

They must have liked what they saw, because I got the part over dozens of other actresses who tested for it. It helped that I could play the First Lady in both her younger and later years. Initially they thought they'd have to get two different actors to play those parts. I felt that momentary thrill of accomplishment at overcoming the doubts of others. And then, almost immediately, I was flooded with doubts of my own.

Did you ever work really hard to get something and then think, *What did I just do?* With Kelly Garrett and most of the other roles I'd played up to that point, I had given life to fictional characters. This was different. The idea of portraying a historical figure was intimidating, and Jacqueline Kennedy was, at the time, still very much alive and thriving. She was not only real; she was present. There was more pressure playing someone who could watch my performance. She was such a distinctive combination of femininity and strength. An outstanding mother and a supportive wife who was the picture of poise. And although she was a public figure, there was still an air of mystery about her. She was famous, yet famously private. I admired how she was able to create a sanctuary for her children, sheltering them in the eye of the storm of attention directed at her family. She was like royalty, her place in our history entrenched in our nation's collective memory.

My hope was that if Jacqueline were to watch the movie, she would like it. I studied her in film footage, interviews, fleeting glimpses caught between official appearances—anything I could get my hands on that showed the former First Lady. One of the things I noticed was that she truly listened to people. She was fully present and displayed an intense interest in what they were saying. She was also very generous, kindly lending us books she had contributed to about her early family history, such as *The Bouviers: Portrait of an American Family* by John Davis, which helped us research her life. We followed those books closely and based the script on them.

As part of my preparation, I hired a famous dialect coach, Robert Easton, "the Henry Higgins of Hollywood," to help me perfect a Jacqueline Kennedy accent. Though she was an extremely well-known figure, we rarely heard her speak. Her image and her wardrobe were on daily display, but not her words or voice. In the 1960s, political wives were seen more than heard. I studied as many interviews as I could find. The only time I remembered hearing her was when she gave a televised tour of the redecorated White House on Valentine's Day 1962. It was an hour-long special that aired on ABC. I would have studied the video—and marveled at the stunning décor—endlessly, but writer/director Steven Gethers didn't actually want me to try to imitate her real voice with its soft, whispery tones. He wanted my Jackie to speak with clarity and strength. I would have been happy to tackle the challenge, but instead I focused on getting her dialect right. And for that, I had the best of the best to help me.

Bob had worked with everyone in the business: He shaped

Laurence Olivier's Michigan-American accent in *The Betsy* and Gregory Peck's German in *The Boys from Brazil.* He would go on to coach Al Pacino's Cuban in *Scarface* and Arnold Schwarzenegger's Russian in *Red Heat*, among many others. We worked hard on *Jacqueline*, and Bob became my dear friend. In Bob's hands, language became something precise. We dissected Jackie's speech, not to mimic it, but to capture its underlying structure, its rhythm, its restraint. Over the course of my career I became a repeat customer, hiring Bob whenever I had to master new, strange, or unfamiliar dialects. One of my very favorite moments was on our first day of shooting. We were doing a long dolly shot and the camera was right beside me. Also right beside me? Bob. He played the role of David Finley, first director of the National Gallery of Art. He and the First Lady became good friends during her time at the White House, and together they founded the White House Historical Association in 1961.

I loved all the prep work for the film. The routine, working with Lou Antonio and Bob, capturing the character. We knew Jacqueline Kennedy's history, but it was interesting imagining how she felt behind closed doors—the emotions she experienced when she was shielded from the public gaze.

At the very end of the three-hour film, I gave a monologue. It was taken from "An Epilogue," an essay written by Pulitzer Prize–winning journalist Theodore White for *Life* magazine about the JFK assassination. White based the essay on an exclusive interview he did with Jacqueline Kennedy just a week after her husband was killed, and the First Lady helped to shape the piece. She requested that White draw a parallel between the Kennedy presidency and the mythical Camelot. The essay contains some of the most poignant words ever written about that day in Dallas. The first time I read it, I cried.

The following is an excerpt from the original interview, on which we based my speech:

Jacqueline Kennedy: I ask you here, Mr. White, because as a reporter, you're one of the friendlies.

There'd been the biggest motorcade from the airport . . . a hot, wild . . . like Mexico and Vienna . . . The sun was so strong on our faces, I couldn't put on sunglasses.

Then, we saw a tunnel up ahead. I thought it would be cool in a tunnel. I thought if we were on the left, the sun wouldn't get in your eyes.

They were gunning the motorcycles. There were these little, uh, backfires . . . there was noise like that . . . I thought they were backfires. Then, next I saw Connolly grabbing his arm saying, "no, no, no, no" with his fists beating. . . . Then Jack turned, and I turned. All I . . . all I remember was a blue gray building up ahead . . . and Jack turned back so neatly . . . his last expression was so neat. . . . You know, you know that wonderful expression he had when they'd, uh, ask him a question about one of the ten million pieces they have in a rocket . . . and just before he would answer he, he looked puzzled, then he slumped forward. He was holding out his hand, then he slumped into my . . . lap.

Then Clint Hill the Secret Service man, he, he loved us. He made my life so easy. He was the first man in the car, and I, I, I kept saying, "Jack, Jack," and someone was saying, "he's, he's dead, he's dead." . . . All the ride to the hospital, I, I kept bending over him, saying, "Jack, Jack, can you hear me? I love you, Jack." . . . But he was dead. . . . At the hospital, they tried to keep me from him, but I said, "I'm not leaving . . . it's my husband . . . his blood is all over me." . . . History . . . history, is what those bitter old men write about. . . . History belongs to heroes, Mr. White, and heroes must not be forgotten.

Mr. White: What do you want me to write, Mrs. Kennedy?

Jacqueline Kennedy: No one will ever know everything about Jack. This little boy, sick so much of the time, reading the Knights of the Round Table. . . . Jack was full of history. And if it . . . if it . . . made him this way, if it made him see the heroes, then maybe other little boys will see . . . history. . . . Why did I wash the blood off? I should have left it there . . . You let them see what they've done.

Well, I want to say this one thing. It's almost an obsession for me. All I keep thinking about is this line from a musical comedy. At night, before we would go to sleep, we had an old Victrola, and Jack liked to play some records. And the song he loved the most was the last side of Camelot . . . sad Camelot, "Don't let it be forgot, that once there was a spot. One brief shining moment that was known as Camelot." . . . There'll never be another Camelot again.

I practiced this speech over and over—while I was brushing my teeth, when I was driving my car, while I was exercising. I must have gone over it a thousand times. Memorizing the words was no problem, but I needed it to sound organic. With Bob's coaching, I broke it down sentence by sentence, word by word, until it rolled off my tongue. I had to drop my *r*'s—*cah* instead of "car," *mah-age* instead of "marriage."

Once we started filming and scenes were going well, my anxiety over the role faded and I started to feel more confident. Getting through the monologue at the end, being able to say her beautiful words, was one of the most satisfying moments in my decades as an actor. Without question, it was my favorite role.

Jackie's life also gave me much inspiration for my own. She'd suffered a miscarriage, a stillborn daughter, and then, after two healthy babies, she gave birth to another son who lived for only two days. JFK was shot just a few months after this child died. Jackie endured so much loss with quiet strength and dignity.

Not only did I get to play all of that simmering emotion—a wonderful opportunity for an actor—but I also got to play pregnant, which was what I desperately wanted to be.

I'd been married on and off since 1968, and I'd never used birth control because I wanted to be a mother. But in all that time, I hadn't once conceived. I wanted so badly to have a child. While filming the parts where Jackie was pregnant, I left my pregnancy padding on during my lunch break. I did it because it saved time, but I also remember thinking, *God, I wish this were real. Is this ever going to be me?*

The wardrobe people asked me, "Do you need help taking off the pads?"

"No, it's okay," I replied.

Pretending to be pregnant lifted my spirits, and I started to believe that a miracle might actually happen. I was thirty-five, already toward the end of what most doctors at that time considered to be a woman's prime fertility years. There was no logical reason to hope, yet I did.

During the filming, Tony was with me on location to lend his support. On Sundays, my one day off each week, he would have Transportation drive my motor home to the parking lot of the hotel we were staying in. That way he could use the kitchen in the motor home to cook me all my favorite dishes, including these delicious scrambled eggs with tomatoes and cheese, served on an English muffin, that he'd make for breakfast. Throughout the day, Tony would find all kinds of ways to surprise me with things I loved. He made the shoot so much easier for me: cooking, running lines, and shooting a whole photo album for me to help me remember such a special time. He was wonderfully protective of me. A true caretaker.

In June 1981, the night of the *Jacqueline* wrap party, Tony and I were staying at the Hotel Raphael in San Francisco. I was floating on air, having just completed one of the most fulfilling experiences in my career. And I was so delighted that Tony was there with me to share it. He'd brought a feeling of love, purpose, and belonging to my world. It truly felt like I'd stepped into a new life.

Tony and I celebrated by doing one of my favorite things—ordering a sumptuous room service meal. It was the perfect setup for a romantic night. I said to Tony, "Maybe tonight we'll make a baby." What can I say? With so much magic in the air, it felt like the perfect time to wish for a miracle.

Tony and I stayed in San Francisco for another week to do some antiques shopping and spend time with friends. It was a nice vacation, but I wished I felt better physically. The stress of shooting had worn me out. I couldn't shake the exhaustion and the feeling that I just wasn't myself.

We returned to Los Angeles and I went to see my doctor, Elsie Giorgi, concerned that something might be wrong. I asked her to test me for mononucleosis, the virus of the moment. She didn't think my symptoms fit that diagnosis, but I insisted. "Just run the mono test, please," I told her.

A few days later, she called me up and said, "Jackie, it's positive!"

"I have mono?"

"No, it's positive for *pregnancy*! You're pregnant!"

In a daze, I asked, "What do you mean?"

"Listen to me: *You are going to have a baby,*" she said.

Suddenly I understood.

There are moments in life that resist articulation—there are no words big enough, joyful enough. Happiness filled me completely. For the first time, the life I had imagined did not feel distant. Everything I had dreamed about was here.

I couldn't believe how lucky I was! After all this time of wishing and dreaming, I was really pregnant, and I was going to have a baby with the first man I'd ever truly loved who genuinely loved me. I never knew that happiness could be this huge. It was all-encompassing, like every cell in my body was dancing with joy.

It didn't matter that I was sick from morning to night. From months two through five I was plagued with migraines. Tony's two boys were with us that summer, and they were, shall we say, less than sympathetic. They were kids. But it was all okay, because I was having a baby.

Tony was there for me, always helping me and doing what he could to make me comfortable. We would get into bed at night intending to watch *The Winds of War,* the hot new miniseries starring my former costar Robert Mitchum. But I would tune out and instead turn to my copy of *Parents to Be*. Tony had already experienced this happiness, but he took pleasure in my elation. He loved watching me become consumed by my role as a mother-to-be. Even when Tony was busy with work (at the time he was shooting the movie *Slapstick of Another Kind,* starring Jerry Lewis), I was never alone. I hadn't anticipated the private delight of having a baby inside me, right there with me while I made breakfast, ran errands, and lay in bed at night. And, oh, how I adored it every time the baby kicked. It felt like I'd swallowed a butterfly. I was so aware of a presence I had longed for without ever truly believing I would have it, a life—impossibly small, moving within me.

I'd waited so long for a child and prayed that the baby would be healthy and born into a happy, stable marriage. The path seemed clear in that regard. It was July 1981, and Tony and his wife had signed their divorce papers, and my own divorce had just been finalized. I wanted to get married as soon as possible, so we started making plans for an August wedding.

Chapter Nineteen

My first wedding had been big and traditional. My second had been small and sophisticated. For my third, which I hoped would be my last, we went for intimate. It wasn't about anyone else, just us. The ceremony was on the rooftop of our house in Bel Air, out in the fresh, open air. The officiant was a justice of the peace, and the attendants were our three royal poodles. The only people we invited were close friends, including my former matron of honor, Jill Wagner. She designed my bouquet of pastel flowers—peonies, gardenias, roses, ranunculus, sweet peas, and anemones—and it was simply stunning.

Like everything else about the affair, my dress was simple: a white off-the-shoulder by Holly's Harp. I left my hair natural because that was the way Tony liked it best.

My friend and assistant Alana told me later that she and Tony had been talking before the wedding. She said to him, "Gosh, Tony, you look so handsome." He wore an impeccably tailored English suit, navy blue, with a crisp white shirt and a dark tie, navy with touches of burgundy and white. And of course his silky black hair was effortlessly perfect.

"I'm dressed to meet the queen," he replied.

As I climbed those stairs to the rooftop balcony, I knew that I had at long last found the perfect partner, the person I'd been looking for all those years.

We spent our wedding night at the Hotel Bel-Air, where we had dinner with close friends. Jill had decorated our room like something out of *Alice in Wonderland*, with lit candles and garlands of flowers covering the bed. It couldn't have been more romantic. That night, Tony said, "I can't believe I got the most beautiful girl in the world." And that's how he made me feel. It was loving and romantic, and a night I will never forget. In those hours the world shrank to the size of us and our baby. We were all that existed.

The next day, we went home to our dogs and the regular world. Once again, I skipped the honeymoon. But I didn't feel cheated with Tony because we'd traveled together already. And since I no longer had to report for *Charlie's* duty at dawn, I had more time to explore and enjoy my freedom, and now I could do it with Tony. Besides, home was our favorite place to be.

We did have a belated honeymoon of sorts. Not too long after the wedding, we went to London for an appearance for a Max Factor fragrance called Epris, for which I was the face. I loved the commercial we'd done for the fragrance—the look of it, along with the lines I spoke. It was just me in a dark room on a velvet chaise longue, in a black sheer evening gown with diamond earrings, my hair in its natural curly state. After I introduced the fragrance, I concluded with these memorable words: "If Mama never told you, I'll tell you. Part of the art of being a woman is knowing when not to be too much of a lady." I wasn't the only one who loved the ad—it went on to win multiple industry awards.

Since *Charlie's* had wrapped, I'd gotten to play Jackie Kennedy, married Tony, and gone on to do an award-winning commercial. It felt like I was on a roll. But what I loved most about that time was the fact that I was pregnant. I wasn't showing yet, and we hadn't gone public with the news. When you're a celebrity and the media wants to know absolutely everything about you, private moments are something to cherish. In time the public would know, but in those precious months, I held my sweet little secret close.

Jacqueline Bouvier Kennedy aired on ABC in October 1981 opposite the season opener of the wildly popular CBS evening soap *Dallas* (which starred my *Charlie's* paramour Patrick Duffy). *Dallas* was the number one show in the country and nearly impossible to conquer in the ratings. But our three-hour movie came close. While we didn't beat out *Dallas*, we won the night for the other two hours.

The network was ecstatic. The top brass called to thank me personally, telling me, "You did great!"

The role earned me my first Golden Globe nomination. Right away, I got a call from Farrah. "I am so happy for you! You deserve it!" That was one of the things I loved most about Farrah: She always wished her friends well, and she meant it.

What made the event even more special for me was that not only was I pregnant, I was *very* pregnant. My ruffled black velvet Yves Saint Laurent gown made me feel beautiful, but that prominent baby bump made me feel deeply blessed.

It was my first nomination for any major award. James Brown of the *LA Times* wrote about my performance, "Jaclyn Smith is, of course, radiant to look at, has a commanding presence and even a little touch of mystery about her." My "personal triumph," as he wrote, "wash[ed] away the notion that *Charlie's Angels* was the full extent of her acting range." Thank you kindly, Mr. Brown.

I was delighted by the reviews, and the fact that it seemed like we'd done right by such a luminary. It was a spectacular night. I didn't care whether I brought home the statuette. When Jane Seymour won for *East of Eden*, I was genuinely thrilled and happy to cheer for her.

Still riding high from the seismic life changes over the past twelve months, I agreed to let *Time* magazine put me on the cover (again) for a story called "The New Baby Bloom," about late-in-life motherhood. It was a sign of the times. Of course, now it's common for women to start families in their mid-thirties, but back then it was something to talk about.

A team of maybe a dozen people came to my house to photograph me in two different outfits. The first was a Norma Kamali jumpsuit, minus the belt. It was glamorous and sparkly. I preferred that outfit, but the editors wanted something more "relatable" for their readership. Someone suggested that because I could wear a regular-sized, nonmaternity outfit, I didn't look "pregnant enough." (Even while pregnant, women were still judged by others for how they looked.) I'd gained sixty pounds during my pregnancy, and my face was very round, my fingers were swollen . . . What did they want? The second choice was a shapeless chambray maternity frock that, to my eye, held no appeal at all. We went with that one in the end.

The shoot was moving along fine until, out of the corner of my eye, I noticed a small glass vial on the living room carpet. I picked it up and saw that it was full of cocaine. Apparently, it had fallen out of someone's pocket. It could have belonged to anyone: the photographer, the editor, the makeup artist, the hairstylist, the wardrobe person, their assistants.

All this time, I'd managed to keep drugs out of my own life, even when it felt like everyone around me at work was using them. But now the unthinkable had happened. A stranger had brought drugs into our home.

Later that night I told Tony what had happened. "Can you believe that?" I said.

He looked at me for a moment, then said, "It was mine. But I had no intention of using it. A buddy at work gave it to me. Crew members do that sometimes."

"What?" I couldn't believe what I was hearing.

"It was me," he repeated. "I dropped it."

Not for one second had I suspected that my own husband used cocaine, or that he'd brought it into our home and could be *so careless* with it that he'd drop it on the floor where anyone, including a crawling baby, could find it.

I was flooded with a mixture of fury and confusion. I wondered, *If Tony didn't want the cocaine, why didn't he just give it back?*

I was in shock. I let it go without saying anything more.

When the issue came out, the folks from *Time* sent a silver Tiffany dish as a baby present for Gaston, along with a card that read, "To our youngest person to appear on the cover of *Time*." The image of me, beaming with pregnant joy in that chambray dress, was lovely. But the truth behind it, and the associated memory of finding out that Tony was potentially a drug user, haunted me.

For some people, Tony's doing coke in the house might not have been a big deal, especially at that time, when cocaine was treated like candy in some circles. But for me, it felt like a dangerous warning. His substance use wasn't about me, but I feared where it might lead. And I was shaken by the fact that I'd had no idea. I tried to be sympathetic. After all, Tony had lived a rock-and-roll life for a long time. But now he was married to me, and if he was using drugs, I did not approve.

Weight gain, nausea, and all, I loved every moment of being pregnant. But eventually this baby was going to make its entrance.

The week of my due date in March 1982, Tony was filming *Slapstick of Another Kind* with Jerry Lewis. Everyone on set knew that I was going to give birth any day. The film was behind schedule, so they were shooting almost around the clock. I worried that Tony would miss the birth, but Jerry told him, "The minute Jaclyn goes into labor, I'll get a sudden backache that's so bad I can't work, and then you can go." When Tony told me that, I fell in love with Jerry. Forget about "the show must go on"—he was willing to hold up an entire production so his cinematographer could be at his wife's side.

A few days before my due date, my parents came out to LA. As always, they brought with them a full dose of their unwavering support and devotion. I was trying to eat organic during my pregnancy, and they were on their way to the health food store with me when I felt what I thought was Braxton-Hicks—not actual labor, but practice contractions, there to prepare me for opening night when the star would arrive. Up to that point, I'd always recognized them when they'd occurred, so we just went about our shopping. But when I got home, the contractions continued. I called my doctor. "Time them," he said. "When they get to a minute in length and five minutes apart, and the pattern is held for at least an hour, call me."

Tony was on set. I didn't want to give him a false alarm and have Jerry fake an injury for nothing. Mom and Alana were right by my side, timing everything. I did my best to stay relaxed, knowing it would help the baby relax. Every part of me felt my baby: an elbow, a foot poking out. I knew which side the baby preferred. When we hit the doctor's mark, with the future pushing against my rib cage, I picked up the phone and said, "Tony, come home."

Tony rushed home and we went straight to the hospital. We checked in and I was taken right to a room where a young doctor examined me. "You are in labor," he said. (News flash.) "I'm going to call your doctor." Through it all I couldn't believe how calm I was.

The labor progressed, but when my doctor arrived, I was having trouble pushing. He kept saying, "Push! You're not pushing enough." Tony and I had done Lamaze classes, which were still considered controversial at the time. We knew the three stages of labor and I'd practiced the breathing techniques regularly, especially during the last months of pregnancy. But now, in the final stage, I was forgetting everything.

The doctor had Tony and a nurse each put a hand on my stomach to help guide me. "Now push as hard as you can," he directed. "Hold your breath and push. Here we go." Then the most beautiful words I had ever heard: "Go ahead and hold your breath . . . and one more push . . . Here we go!" And with the next joyous heavenly push, at 12:35 a.m., my beautiful blue-eyed son was born. The minute I set eyes on him, he owned me, lock, stock, and barrel. Gaston Anthony Richmond had entered the world.

I looked at my precious baby and was overtaken by a love I'd never felt before. "I'm going to travel the world with you. I'm going to take you wherever I go. I'm not leaving you," I promised. When I married Tony, I felt as if my life was just beginning, but suddenly things shifted in a way I could never have anticipated. Every cell in my body felt irrevocably altered by the arrival of this perfect little boy.

My parents were thrilled, of course. Gaston wasn't their first grandchild—Tommy and Charlotte had three sons by then. But it's special each time one of your babies becomes a parent. Mom and Daddy acted as if Gaston was the light of their life.

As soon as they put Gaston in my arms, I was captivated, taking in every line, every nuance. His perfect face; his hair, which somehow looked immaculately groomed; the innocent gaze from his beautiful blue eyes. I had never seen such tiny limbs, and chuckled at his surprisingly long, delicate fingers wrapped around one of mine. I placed his little head in the crook of my neck and rubbed his warm back. He stretched and yawned, and I laughed with wonder. I felt complete.

After things settled down at the hospital and Tony and I had a moment to ourselves, he told me what I'd missed while I was giving birth. My ob-gyn had to pause at one point to ask some attending nurses to leave the room, and then he brought in a nurse from his own staff. Apparently the initial nurses were too distracted by the thrill of assisting one of Charlie's Angels to focus to the doctor's satisfaction. I was immersed in the world of birth and hadn't thought anything about the staffing switch. I assumed that kind of thing happened all the time. But I did remember the nurses in question.

When I was admitted they'd told us they were *Charlie's* fans and, before my contractions got too intense, I'd posed for pictures with them and signed my autograph. Yes, even in labor people will ask you for an autograph. In fact, I'd signed quite a few of them. Still, I always appreciated the success of the show, and in that moment when I was about to meet my baby, I felt especially blessed. Maybe it would have been nice to be just Jaclyn on that day, just another laboring mother, but they were harmless. And I wanted to share the love and joy with everyone! Unfortunately, not every interaction I had while at the hospital would be so benign.

In those days, you usually stayed in the hospital for about a week after giving birth. During that time, experts would pop into your room to teach you how to swaddle and bathe the baby, change the diapers, and breastfeed. I was doing well with the lessons, and grateful for the guidance. Gaston was thriving and we were on track to leave in another day or two.

At one point when Gaston was four days old, I was alone in the room, resting. The phone rang and I picked it up. "Hello?"

Then, to my horror, a female voice on the other end said something I cannot bear to repeat, but the gist of it was that she intended to take Gaston away from me.

Up to that moment, I thought the idea of one's blood running cold was hyperbole. But when I heard those words, I went numb. "Who is this?" I demanded.

The hateful voice continued with its vicious threats. I slammed down the phone and burst into tears. There I was in my hospital bed, having just given birth. I felt utterly defenseless and vulnerable. Up to that moment, I'd felt safe. The only people who knew I was there were my family and a handful of the staff. Who could do such a horrible thing, and how did they know I was there?

I phoned Tony, crying hysterically. When I told him what had happened, he and my parents rushed to my side. Someone informed the director of the hospital, and he raced to my room as well. "We need to get you out of the hospital immediately," he said. He wasn't convinced their security was up to the task of protecting me and my baby from harm, but they could get us out safely. The next thing I knew, several large guards appeared in the hallway outside my room. My parents quickly packed my things and the guards escorted us all out a secret exit to our car.

When I walked into my house, my baby in my arms and my husband at my side, I finally knew we were safe.

We never did find out who had made that call.

The incident drove home to me another way that life would now be different. In the past few years I'd grown to appreciate the benefits of celebrity and all the doors it had opened for me, but I'd also experienced its drawbacks. How the world can feel entitled to invade your privacy. How fans often think they know you, even though you've never met. And how some of those fans go to extremes and fixate on you. For the most part I'd learned to deal with those downsides, but suddenly the stakes were different. My son hadn't asked to have a famous mom. I would have to do my best not only to give him a normal life but to protect him from the glaring light my career would shine on him.

Chapter Twenty

No surprise, I absolutely adored being a mom. I would steam vegetables, make everything from scratch, then freeze meal-sized portions. I *loved* doing the portions. I am a detail-oriented person, so everything had to be organized and color-coordinated. A little OCD? Maybe. But I was having fun. I loved being able to dedicate so much energy and attention to Gaston. I experienced a sense of completeness I'd never known.

I was at my baby's command, fully available to him. I could lose an hour just watching him breathe, and another watching him sleep. I bathed him, swaddled him, and rocked him until he fell asleep in my arms, his head tucked into the crook of my neck. Motherhood dictated every decision I made. Never had I felt more responsible.

At the same time, motherhood makes you more vulnerable than you ever thought possible. They say it's like having your heart outside your body, and that's true. It takes you to a level of love that is unequaled and unprecedented, but there is nothing safe about it. Nothing routine, and nothing mundane.

The familiar anxiety I'd long felt began to surface again, and this time it had a new target. Periodically I would fret over my son, feeling that familiar urge to invoke my magical thinking, hoping if I did just the right things, Gaston would be protected.

It wasn't all-consuming, though some moments were harder than others. Whenever something seemed like it could be amiss—if Gaston was fussy or had a fever—I'd fall into that familiar pattern: worry, watch, ruminate. I was able to manage it, but it was an ongoing struggle in times of stress.

But while I was totally devoted to my son, my career didn't stop. After the success of *Jacqueline Bouvier Kennedy*, I was much in demand for TV movies and miniseries. I did so many of them in such rapid succession, I became known as the Queen of the Miniseries. All thanks to playing American royalty.

The first and probably most memorable of my many miniseries was *Rage of Angels*, written by the legendary screenwriter and novelist Sidney Sheldon, whom I adored. It was directed by Buzz Kulik, one of my favorite directors. Buzz was an old pro whose career went back to the early days of TV with *Gunsmoke*, *Perry Mason*, and *The Twilight Zone*. His biggest hits were the heartbreaking movie *Brian's Song*, starring a young James Caan, and the miniseries *From Here to Eternity*, starring Natalie Wood and William Devane. Buzz was a charming man, witty and reflective. Underneath that, his insight and intuition changed the way a scene was written. He gave it something more than the words on the page.

Although Sidney Sheldon wanted me in the role he'd created, the stigma of *Charlie's* continued, even after I'd been nominated for a Golden Globe. At first, Buzz didn't think my demeanor was right for the part of Jennifer. In his eyes, I was a Barbie doll in high heels. Buzz wasn't convinced I was tough enough to handle the part, or that I would be able to muster the necessary volatility to project Jennifer's righteous anger. I had to win him over, and I did.

The plot of *Rage,* in a nutshell: Jennifer is an aspiring lawyer in New York. Due to interference from the powers that be in the District Attorney's Office, her chances of serving in City Hall are torpedoed. She has to start her own law office and become a huge success to prove them wrong. Along the way, she has affairs with two men—a married politician played by Ken Howard and a mobster played by Armand Assante. Over a pair of two-hour installments, she faces much adversity—a firing, a betrayal, an unplanned pregnancy, a kidnapping, and the suicide of her closeted gay law partner, played to perfection by John Spencer.

I loved the role. This character had complexities and nuance. We saw her change, losing her innocence, experiencing loss. Later, as she matured, she had a seriousness spiked with charm. As usual, I did piles of research, especially on women with esteemed legal careers. I learned so much about Sandra Day O'Connor and Ruth Bader Ginsburg—fascinating women who inspired me.

For his part, Buzz pushed to see just how much of his trademark authenticity I could handle. He didn't want a stunt double, and neither did I. In one scene, I was running up a set of outdoor steps toward a municipal building where my character was late to start her first job. I was supposed to trip on those steps and fall down. I thought I'd just stumble a bit, but Buzz made me do it again and hit the ground—*hard.* I did, and boy, did it hurt to slam my knee onto that New York City asphalt. I'd done lots of my own stunts on *Charlie's*, and I knew I was physically able to handle whatever I was called upon to do. Ironically, that's where this Barbie doll learned to take a licking. Aaron took good care of us, but he didn't pamper us. He knew his Angels were tough.

Buzz's ideas and demands were viscerally stimulating. He knew how to give us freedom, take from what emerged, and then refine it.

Never once raising his voice, he was among the most talented, most thoughtful, and kindest of men, and a supremely skilled director.

Rage had the potential to be controversial, which would be good for ratings. Jennifer's having a child out of wedlock and refusing to tell the father that he had a son raised moralistic eyebrows. Viewers found the show's two love triangles—one between Jennifer, the politician, and his wife, and the other between Jennifer, the politician, and the mobster—to be scandalous. If I had been Jennifer, I'd have chosen Ken Howard's politician character over Armand's gangster for the long haul. But short-term? I'm not alone in my assessment that Armand Assante is a devastatingly sexy man. He is someone you meet once and never forget.

Ken Howard looked like he had gone to Harvard. He seemed Ivy League—educated and refined. When I was introduced to him at our first read-through, it was so easy and comfortable, it was like we'd been friends for years.

Armand was strikingly gorgeous. I mean it when I say it was hard to take your eyes off him. He was rebellious, but hidden beneath the rebellion was a touching tenderness. He was a person you could quickly lose your heart to.

One of our scenes was filmed in the eighteenth-century castle-like Hôtel de Crillon in Paris. It took place in the Leonard Bernstein suite, a 2,500-square-foot luxury apartment on the sixth floor, complete with a grand piano and a wraparound terrace with incredible views of the Eiffel Tower. On that terrace on a glorious blue-sky day, we shot a very sexy, sensual scene. It was a lot steamier than anything we might have filmed in a bed, and a lot less predictable, thanks to the setup. That was Armand's idea, to take our lovemaking out of the bedroom, as stunning as it was. So we gave in to passion out in the open, and let me tell you, I didn't have to pretend to swoon. At any moment, I thought we might fall off the terrace! Armand was a method actor, so when he came in for the kiss, it was intimate, passionate . . . a *real kiss.* I'd done many on-camera kisses before, but this one was as real as it gets. Yet in Armand's eyes, I didn't respond enough. We cut the tape. Armand went over to Buzz and said, "I don't think I turned her on." (Wrong!) Buzz came to me and said a few words. We tried again, and I let myself go with it. I pushed past my resistance and we got a very memorable take.

I'll always treasure the memory of making *Rage of Angels*. I loved working with Buzz, and he was certainly one of my favorite directors. But the movie also marked the most important shift in my life: my first job as a working mother. When we started shooting, Gaston was a just few months old. Throughout filming in Paris, New York City, and Acapulco, my son was with me. I never went a day without feeding him, changing him, and putting him to bed. We had some long days on that set, but I was able to rally through the exhaustion because I knew that when it was over, I would get to go home to my baby. I took him on every movie. He was my shadow.

Still, traveling around the world with a newborn was exactly the logistical nightmare you'd think it was. Alana, who came with us as my assistant and friend, jokes that we had twenty-three pieces of luggage. She's exaggerating. It was twenty, tops. I even traveled with a portable washer and dryer so I could clean Gaston's clothes myself. Over-the-top? Maybe. Sometimes it was hard to see the line between devotion and compulsion. I just wanted to do the very best I could for my son. That included nursing Gaston whenever I could, and when I couldn't be with him, I pumped. Due to my long hours on set and the stress of juggling work and motherhood, my milk unfortunately dried up and we ended up having to put Gaston on formula. I missed that closeness we had shared when I nursed.

My mother sometimes joined us on location. For our New York stint, Tony and I were planning to rent an apartment for us and

Gaston, but for convenience's sake we booked a long-term stay at the Lombardy Hotel. Our suite was homey and bright, with a kitchen and access to the incredible restaurant downstairs, the Laurent. Tony stayed as long as he could before taking a job in London. His departure hastened my parents' arrival at the Lombardy. When I was with my mom, I was thrilled to be in her presence. At night we would order room service, then sit on our beds, talking about nothing and everything. Moments to treasure. That time I didn't bring the washer/dryer. The only thing I insisted we buy for the hotel was a beautiful rocking chair for feeding and soothing Gaston.

Being back in New York for the summer in 1982 made me nostalgic for my Barbizon days with Irene. And I always loved New York in the summer. The tables were out on the sidewalks, full of people eating in the open air, taking their time over cocktails. Red flowers lined Park Avenue, and every hundred-year-old building entrance had a doorman standing out front in full livery, with the requisite topiary in a planter next to him. So much about me had changed since my first visit to the neighborhood when I was twenty years old. Fashions had changed. The world had changed. But so much about New York had stayed the same.

Either Tony, my parents, or I was with Gaston at all times. But we also decided to hire a nanny, whom we selected based on a recommendation from a friend. The nanny was not what I expected. When I came home from the set, I'd rush to Gaston to start caring for him. The nanny would hover over my shoulder, questioning everything I did. When I took Gaston outside for a walk in his pram, she acted like I was putting his life at risk. The two of us fought constantly about who got to do what, and how. Over and over, I explained to her that I'd hired her to care for my child *when I wasn't there*. When I was around, I was in charge. She just couldn't understand that I wanted to bathe and burp my own baby. She refused to leave our

1

On location for *Nightkill*—my husband Brad's favorite photo of me, 1980

2

Mom and Dad out on the town in Houston, 1942

3

Happy to be here! Houston, 1946

4

Me at age five—an early Goody Two-shoes, Houston, 1950

5

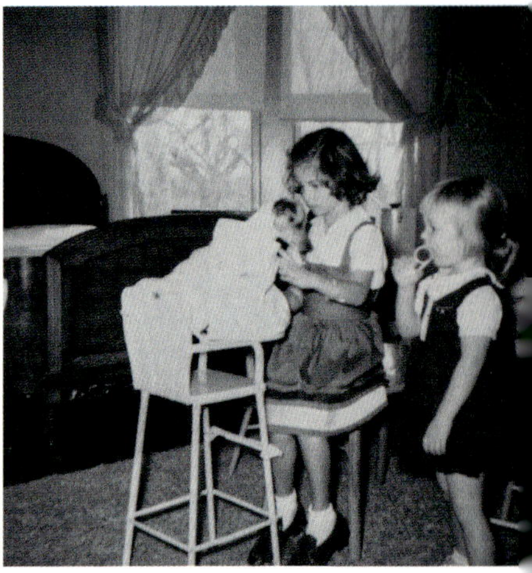

A day at the farm with my cousin Mollie, 1950

6

Tommy—my big brother and protector—and me, Houston, 1948

7

Best friends since seventh grade,
Claire Dishongh and me, 1959

8

My passion—dance recital, 1961

9

Director Lou Antonio—my mentor and the best teacher any actor could have—on the set of *McCloud*, 1972

With my true north—Papa, my grandfather Gaston Hartsfield, 1974

10

11

Charlie's Angels, 1976. As Kelly Garrett (in the famous white bikini), with Kate Jackson as Sabrina Duncan and Farrah Fawcett-Majors as Jill Munroe

12

Sisterhood, season one!

13

Shelley Hack, me, Farrah Fawcett-Majors, David Doyle, and Cheryl Ladd, 1980. Kate Jackson is the only one missing.

14

Prince Charles visiting the *Angels* set at Twentieth Century Fox, October 27, 1977

"Hold it! Freeze!"—our mantra. Cheryl (as Kris Munroe) and I wield our guns on the beach in season three.

16

Everyone's favorite episode from season one, "Angels in Chains," 1976

17

The Angels at the opening night party for *The Users* with Aaron Spelling, 1978

18

The cast of *The Users*, 1978—a truly star-studded ensemble including George Hamilton, Joan Fontaine, John Forsythe, me, Tony Curtis, Michelle Phillips, Red Buttons, Alan Feinstein, Carrie Nye, and John Pleshette

19

Me as Jacqueline Bouvier Kennedy—my favorite role, 1981

20

My passion for period pieces continues—*George Washington*, 1984, with Barry Bostwick and Patty Duke

21

On the set of *Florence Nightingale*, "the Lady with the Lamp," 1985. What an honor!

22

Rage of Angels, 1983—Armand Assante or Ken Howard? A tough choice!

23

Costarring with Angela Lansbury—one of my idols—in *Rage of Angels: The Story Continues*, 1986

4

With my dear friend and favorite costar, Robert "R.J." Wagner, in *Windmills of the Gods*, 1988

25

Richard Chamberlain, the consummate professional, in *The Bourne Identity*, 1988

26

27
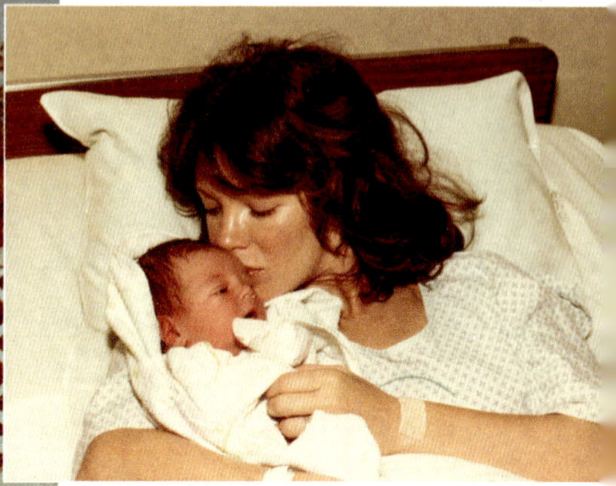

LEFT: My wedding to Tony Richmond on the rooftop of our Bel Air home, August 4, 1981

ABOVE: Gaston was born on March 19, 1982—I couldn't take my eyes off him.

28

Best role I've ever had: mother—here with one-year-old Gaston, 1983

29

Tommy Beville, the world's best uncle

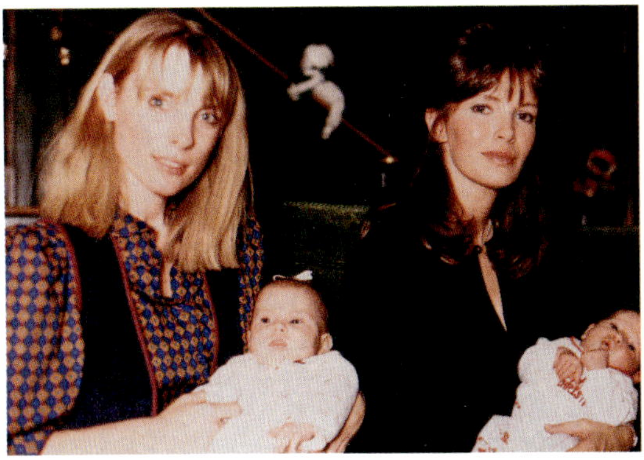

30

A friend for the ages—Irene Fox and me, with our babies, Polly Ellen and Spencer-Margaret, 1984

31

Spencer-Margaret's baptism—with her godmothers, Alana Voeller and Kate, and her godfather, Lou Antonio, and Reverend James Lockwood-Stewart, 1985

32

Kate and I have shared so much. Here, celebrating Spencer-Margaret's first birthday, Los Angeles, 1986

33

My favorite time of day: story time, 1987

34

At a White House state dinner with President Reagan, 1986

Brad Allen and me on our way to a White House state dinner to meet President George H. W. Bush, 1992

35

36

A thrill and an honor to receive a star on the Hollywood Walk of Fame, November 6, 1989

37

38

40

39

CLOCKWISE (FROM TOP LEFT): One of many Max Factor photo shoots over the years, 1991

Epris—the first fragrance I represented for Max Factor, 1981

This Breck ad from 1973 caught Glen Larson's eye and led to my being cast in *McCloud*, in the love story of the season.

A 2004 ad for Kmart. My brand, which went beyond my celebrity, launched in 1985.

41

The apples of my eye, 1988

42

Location day on *Kaleidoscope* with Alana Voeller—whose friendship is golden not only to me but to my children—and the kids, 1990

43

Every kid's dream! Gaston and Spencer-Margaret on the farm in Luling, Texas, 1991

After seventeen years of dating, Brad and I finally said "I do!" Los Angeles, October 11, 1997

44

45

Three generations: Spencer-Margaret, Mom, and me in my backyard, 2001

Our favorite time of year and our favorite tradition—Christmas pajamas. Gaston, Spencer-Margaret, Mom, me, and Brad, 2003

46

47

The Angels' reunion for *People* magazine, 1994

48

The original Angels reunited for the Emmy tribute to Aaron Spelling, 2006

Cheryl Ladd and me, honored at the 8th Annual TV Land Awards, Sony Pictures, April 17, 2010

49

50

Our family at home, Los Angeles, 2005

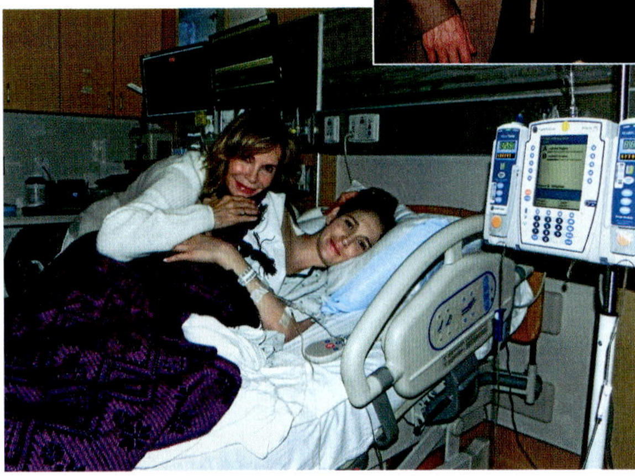

51

Awaiting the birth of my first granddaughter, Bea, September 17, 2015

52

53

ABOVE LEFT: Never too old for an Easter Egg hunt—the celebration goes on. Brad and me with Bea and Olivia, 2024

ABOVE RIGHT: My son-shine, 2024

My reason, 2022

The joys of my life,
my granddaughters—
Bea, Olivia, and Wren

suite, even when we were all there and perfectly capable of handling Gaston ourselves. I had to look her in the eye and say, "It's time for your time off now."

"I can't leave him," she'd say. "You're working eighteen-hour days."

"And for the six hours I'm here, I want to care for my son."

She meant well, but she had to go. When the friend who'd recommended her asked why I'd gotten rid of the nanny, I said, "She wouldn't let me care for my own baby."

She was confused. "Well, what'd you hire her for, then?"

Back then, just like now, different mothers had different ideas of motherhood. I was sorting out what my version would be, but I knew it would entail being hands-on as much as possible, as often as possible.

Taking Gaston for walks in New York was safe, even though I'd gone from an unknown to a recognizable face. I never went alone—Tony or my parents always came along just in case. People recognized me, but in New York, fans give celebrities more space than in Los Angeles or other parts of the country. If anyone did approach us, they were very kind and said nice things about how adorable Gaston was. It was always friendly and never felt threatening. In those days, people didn't walk around with cameras in their pockets, but when someone did ask to take a picture, Tony was careful to block Gaston's face. I didn't want him photographed. The way I saw it, Gaston was ours. He didn't belong to the world.

When *Rage of Angels* aired in February 1983, the competing network, in its wisdom, put up against us another TV movie: *The Grace Kelly Story*, starring none other than Cheryl Ladd. It was an Angels showdown—and *Rage of Angels* won. We got such impressive ratings—part one was the fourth-most-watched show that week and part two the eighth-most-watched—that Sidney and Buzz started talking about doing a sequel, or even turning *Rage* into a series. I was against the idea. Another miniseries was fine; that was a commitment of only a few months. But a series with more than twenty episodes a season would have me back working those insane hours for most of the year. I had a young child now, so that was out of the question.

Buzz and I did collaborate again right away, though, on *George Washington*. I played the part of Sally Fairfax. According to the history books, George was in love with Sally, though both were married to other people (Sally to George's friend, also named George). For the movie I was reunited with my *Charlie's* almost-boyfriend Barry Bostwick in the title role.

I had to jump right into preparing for the film. My preparation was different from when I played a contemporary character. I wanted to avoid modern physical mannerisms and gestures. The clothing of the eighteenth century restricts movement, so your walk, the way you sit, is different.

And of course, there was my usual script preparation. Tony, always supportive, offered to help me with my lines. At one point, I looked up from my copy of the script and noticed that his nose had started to bleed.

"Why is your nose bleeding?" I asked. Right away my thoughts went to the vial of cocaine I'd found on our floor. "Are you on coke?"

"Yeah, a little." He said it with such nonchalance, as if it were no big deal.

I sat there and took a long, appraising look at Tony. He didn't look well. His face was drawn and his eyes seemed weary. I had thought it was the long hours.

"Tony, this is serious. You know how I feel about drugs and alcohol. You need to get help," I said. I demanded that he get treatment. He relented and checked into the Betty Ford Clinic for a thirty-day inpatient program. I prayed that this would be the beginning of his sobriety.

In August 1983, just after Tony returned from rehab, I started filming on *George Washington*. The costumes for that movie were among the finest in my career, Scarlett O'Hara–worthy gowns in gold and royal blue that were authentic all the way down to the undergarments. Gowns were figure-revealing, structured, the waists cinched in. Those costumes were made from scratch—they must have cost a fortune. They were gorgeous, but the corsets made me count the minutes until I could get out of them. (Thank you to Coco Chanel for showing the world that women can be chic and elegant yet still be comfortable!) But what the costumes lacked in comfort they made up for in style, like the red wool, military-inspired riding coat. It had every detail, including gold epaulets and lace coming out of the sleeves, and it was fitted to a T with a peplum that gave a perfect hourglass shape. And, oh, the hats! Everything was exquisitely crafted, from antique Chantilly lace to brocade on the dresses, silk moiré, lace capelets . . . I could go on!

It was a step back in time. More than once while we were shooting, I thought back to that day I'd visited Mount Vernon as a kid. Who would have dreamed that I'd be standing there holding a cup that George Washington had once held, shooting a picnic scene where he and Sally had actually had a picnic, walking on the grounds where they'd strolled. It was heaven to a girl in love with the romance of the past.

The show aired in April 1984, when Gaston was just two years old. The three-part series earned six Emmy nominations, including one for Buzz and one for Patty Duke as Martha Washington. Buzz and I hoped to work together again on *Kane and Abel*, a contemporary business drama, but I had to turn it down because of a conflict. But our paths would cross again before long.

At home, thanks to Alana and less-controlling nannies, we'd figured out a rhythm that worked to care for Gaston, and for Tony and me to take the work we were most interested in doing.

My next project was *Florence Nightingale*, a biopic about "the Lady with the Lamp," the English social reformer and founder of modern nursing. As always, I dove into my research, learning as much about this fascinating figure as I could, about her history and her emotional landscape. I needed not only to understand who she was as a person but to try to embody her physicality, which was a challenge given the constraining undergarments of the time. (Honestly, I don't think historic women get enough credit for overcoming the challenges of their clothing!)

Another hurdle was the accent. The entire cast was English except me. They were all incredibly skilled stage actors. At first, I felt inept with the English dialect, but once again I brought in Bob Easton to work with me. With Bob by my side, I forged ahead. Seldom have I been in the nexus of such elevated and committed artists.

My process with Bob was to go over every line of the script, get the intonation and rhythm just right, then make tapes that I'd listen to over and over. As Bob said, "It's not just an English dialect; every part of the country has a different sound." Florence spoke with what's called Received Pronunciation. Common among the upper class at the time, it included dropping the *r*'s at the ends of words. Her manner was exact, emphatic, and clear, reflecting a high level of education. I had to learn the lines phonetically, word for word, so that I'd have each sentence down the way it should be. I'd prepare a scene all night, then arrive on set ready to go.

In the film I costarred with another *Charlie's* guest star, Timothy Dalton, who'd not yet had a turn as James Bond. Timothy was wonderful, but he didn't hesitate to say what he thought. We'd do a run-through, and then he would stop everything, saying, "No, it's all wrong. We have to rewrite this whole section."

Timothy took the stage with a presence. He was truly impressive. Yet the dialogue changes he was making were hard for me because I'd worked so diligently to prepare the lines as written. Every time he asked for an impromptu rewrite, I groaned inwardly. But, to be fair, his suggestions were insightful, and most of the time what we ended up with was an improvement. Thank goodness Bob Easton was on set with me. We'd all sit down with the director and writer and hash out the new scene until we were satisfied.

Apart from his script tinkering, Timothy was the most fun to hang out with on set, and to dance with. One of our scenes was an elegant party, and Timothy and I waltzed together for hours. My feet barely touched the ground. Filming that movie, I truly felt as if I were in another place and time.

Gaston was with me on set, as always. But he wasn't a baby in a pram anymore. He was a toddler who wanted his mommy's attention. Completely understandable! I wanted to be with Gaston, too, and as soon as I could, I'd rush to his side. I was struggling with Tony a bit during that shoot, though. Like his son, he threw a few tantrums over not getting as much of me as he wanted. I could tell from his behavior that he was overindulging in alcohol, despite my begging him not to.

Somehow I managed to squeeze in one more movie that year, the feature that Tony and I had been talking about making since we first met: *Déjà Vu*, the adaptation of the novel *Always*. The plot was about reincarnation and a love that traveled through time. I played two characters, a ballerina from the 1930s who died in a fire, and the current-day girlfriend of *Excalibur*'s Nigel Terry, who was obsessed with the long-dead ballerina. It got even more complicated than that, with Shelley Winters in the mix as a psychic named Olga. Tony was the director and co-screenwriter. I'd helped him get the financing by introducing him to some people I knew, and we were both excited to have creative control over a feature film. It was what we'd dreamed of.

In the three years since our wedding, I'd fallen even more deeply in love with Tony, which made it all the more difficult when he started drinking heavily. I loved this man so completely. I loved his talent, his intelligence, his charm. I was there for him and he was there for me. It was permanent. We were a team.

I loved the man Tony was when he was fully present—generous, hopeful, funny. But I grew to fear the man he became when alcohol entered the room. I didn't see the seriousness of his addiction at first. It didn't announce itself. He kept it secret for quite a while, then disguised it, saying, "Let's celebrate tonight," or "It's been a long day; I'm gonna have a glass of wine to relax." I learned to read the signs: the shift in his voice, the change in his posture, the subtle loosening of restraint. Tony was never a mean drunk. He wasn't violent or cruel, but he would say things that, if he were sober, wouldn't have crossed his lips.

Before we went to London to shoot *Déjà Vu*, I heard about a drug called Antabuse, which is a medication used in the treatment of chronic alcohol use disorder. Reading the side effects (from fatigue, headache, and skin rashes all the way to neurological and cardiovascular problems), I had second thoughts. When I told Tony, he said, "I want your mind free of worry. I'm not going to drink. So I have no reservations about taking it. It will be a guard-gate." He even made a point to take a pill in front of me every morning and show me the letter *A* on it. With that reassurance, we went on with the filming.

The 1930s costumes of that movie were among my favorites, all vintage, fragile pieces. Marit Allen, future Oscar-nominated costume designer, found some incredible pieces for me, including one beautiful Japanese kimono that had to be forty years old but was in impeccable condition. I treated that robe so gently.

John Frieda was my hairstylist on the film. He did a fantastic job with my long, wavy brunette look and with a platinum-blond pixie cut I wore for part of the contemporary section of the film. Shelley Winters got in a mood one day, turned to me in that wig, and said, "You know what? You look much better that way. You should cut your hair and bleach it." She was larger-than-life, that's for sure. A woman unfettered by convention or boundaries. One day she became frustrated on set and threw a tray of food at Tony.

People have often asked me what it was like doing love scenes with an actor, in this case Nigel Terry, while my husband was directing me. It was easy. I trusted Tony. I felt comfortable with him and knew he'd protect me. At least when it came to the filming.

But as the days wore on, it became clear to me that Tony had somehow started drinking again. I confronted him. "How can you be drunk? I saw you take Antabuse."

He confessed that he'd been substituting aspirin for the Antabuse pills. From that day on, like a parole officer, I administered the Antabuse myself, and we went on to finish the film.

When it came to Tony's addiction, I thought, *This is temporary. He will stop. Love will be enough.* Hope became a habit. So did disappointment. I told myself stories to survive. There were moments of reprieve, promises kept for a time, weeks of sobriety that felt like a beautiful dream I didn't want to wake up from. I prayed constantly for strength, for clarity, for a miracle that would hold our family together. But miracles, I would learn, do not arrive on demand. They arrive when the other person makes a decision to stop.

When Tony was sober, he was the man of my dreams. After *Déjà Vu* wrapped, he was sober for a while, and I felt like we were back on track in our marriage. In early 1985, we went to New York for my appearance in *Night of 100 Stars*, a celebrity roundup televised charity event. Once again, love was in the air. Just like when we'd wrapped the Jacqueline Kennedy movie, we found ourselves in a luxury hotel with room service and lots of romance. Once again, I looked into Tony's eyes and said, "Maybe tonight we'll make a baby."

Sure enough, I became pregnant with our second child. I was thirty-nine, and absolutely over the moon. As I had with my first pregnancy, I decided to scale back on work for a while so I could focus on being healthy, getting rest, and taking care of Gaston, as well as planning for a new baby!

Chapter Twenty-One

The call came in the spring of 1985, without ceremony on a day otherwise unremarkable, which turned out to be a turning point for me. The voice on the other end belonged to a man I had never met, representing a company I had never thought much about: Kmart.

There I was, trying to dial things down so I could make space to welcome the new addition to our family, but Joseph Antonini, Kmart's head of apparel, and his number two, Deborah Grafton, had other plans. I was intrigued by the idea of a partnership and open to hearing whatever they had to say. Right away I found them both to be lovely people, so that was one in the plus column. But I wasn't easily sold.

Joe said, "We'd like to develop a clothing line with you, using your name, with your input."

"Why me?" I asked. And I meant it. Of all the celebrities out there, why on earth had they landed on me out of the blue? At least, it felt like it was out of the blue, but they'd done their research. The answer, delivered calmly and honestly, was that I represented something familiar and reliable to consumers. And now that I'd had Gaston, people didn't think of me only as an Angel or an actor, but as a mother. "You're known as someone women trust," they said.

I sat with that for a moment. Trust is a heavier thing than admiration. It suggests obligation. After we hung up, I thought for quite a while about the conversation. I thought of my childhood, of shopping trips with Mom that felt like small adventures, the pleasure of walking the aisles and looking at everything. Mom always thought beauty should not be withheld like a privilege, that it should be accessible to everyone. That was how Joe and Deborah saw it.

But I wasn't free to simply say yes and jump right in. When I decided I might want to pursue the partnership, one of my first calls was to Max Factor. Not only was I under contract with them; I wanted them to be on board. We'd enjoyed a positive relationship going all the way back to my twenties, and I wanted to keep it that way. Also, I was interested in any insights they might have.

Their answer was swift and decisive: "Don't do it." They told me my audience didn't shop at Kmart. That I'd dilute my brand. To me, it sounded less like advice and more like fear. I listened, nodded, and thanked them.

I was still interested in Kmart, but I remained uncertain. And to me, that lack of certainty said something. Deciding to listen to the advice at hand, I turned Kmart down.

Joe called again. "Please meet with us," he said, politely persistent.

When I finally agreed to go in and talk with them, I couldn't believe what I saw. Order, intention, thoughtful logic behind prices that were unexpectedly low. They explained how scale worked. How volume reduced the cost to something affordable. Because Kmart was able to reach such a large customer base, they could leverage quantity to lower prices.

As they spoke, I began to imagine clean lines, honest fabrics, clothes that did not apologize for their affordability.

There is a moment in every big decision when instinct outpaces reason. I asked myself: *Would I wear this?* If the answer was no, then I knew not to take on the partnership. If yes, then why should anyone else be denied beautiful clothes at an affordable price? Suddenly I had my certainty.

When I told Tony what I'd decided, he was supportive. Honestly, he'd have supported my decision either way. He wanted me to do what I thought was right.

I called Max Factor. "I've changed my mind," I told them. "I know the advice you offered was meant to protect me, but I feel good about this decision." After all, Kmart wanted more than just a licensing deal. They wanted my name, my taste, my participation. Not just my face, but real involvement. It would be a partnership in the truest sense of the word.

The process of getting the line together took months. We started by making sketches of styles that I thought would work for the modern woman. My goal was to share my closet with my customer, the types of pieces that worked for me as a woman with multiple pursuits, including motherhood. The first collection was very much a reflection of how I dressed.

The concept was interchangeable separates: skirts, jackets, pants, blouses. Wardrobe staples. Everything was classic and timeless. The color palette ranged from a soft gray to tan to pale pink, aqua, or blue, all muted pastels. Pleated pants were on trend at the time, so I coupled them with softer blouses with bows. The hallmark of my designs was fit. Each garment had to look good on a range of sizes, from a petite to a plus. I wanted it to be inclusive, appealing to everyone, and multigenerational.

My original collection launched in the fall of 1985. We had an event to announce it at the Pierre Hotel in New York. Every major fashion magazine came to cover it—*Vogue*, *Glamour*, *Elle*, and

Harper's Bazaar, among others. The turnout was huge, and we got a warm reception. Fashion people loved it. But what mattered to me most was what everyday women would think.

When the collection landed in stores, the response was immediate and startling. The clothes flew off the shelves. Women recognized themselves in them. One of the most impactful things I did to promote the brand was store appearances. If I was in a city doing a talk show, afterward I'd go to the local Kmart and do an event to support the line. Store appearances sometimes felt like trying to stay sane and sound amid a hurricane. Well-meaning, enthusiastic strangers reaching for my hands, touching my hair, wanting to hug or kiss me. I was signing autographs and posing for photos. I'd smile, shake hands, and hear their stories while trying to move forward and not look rushed. They were sincere, so yes, I would stay present and listen, attempting to remain balanced in this whirlwind. By the end, my face would be exhausted from smiling. But it was worth it. And I believe those appearances built the rock-solid foundation the brand would stand on for so many years.

With our success, any skepticism about the idea of partnering with Kmart dissolved. Even those who had warned me not to do it found reasons to explain why they had always known it would work!

Perhaps the people most surprised by our success were my partners at Max Factor. At Kmart, we started to gift buyers of Jaclyn Smith Design apparel with a sample of Epris fragrance, and just like that, perfume sales of Max Factor skyrocketed. I had to laugh at how wrong they'd been. We all make mistakes, and I'm glad this one ended up working in their favor.

Within a year of the launch, Joe Antonini was promoted from head of apparel to the company's chief executive officer. He could, and did, attribute his rise to the success of my collection. Deborah Grafton took over for Joe as head of apparel. She was a genius at taking both my collections and my connection to the company to the next level. In 1987, when my book *The American Look* came out, Deborah had me sign a copy for every person in the company, or the "city," as they called it. I signed thousands of them. Deborah was the mastermind behind our launch and our follow-up collections, and I'm forever grateful to her.

As the decades passed, the line evolved, and so did I. What had begun as a risk became a responsibility. I traveled, I listened, I learned the difference between image and intention. We always stuck to that first vision of designing separates, but we ventured into more daring looks too. We shifted to more sophisticated color palettes, including black, khaki, and navy. . . . Since the launch, more than one hundred million women have bought my designs, a number that will never cease to amaze me.

A brand is a promise you make to a customer. We promised quality and value, the ability to look elegant without spending a lot of money. Beauty shouldn't correlate with a price point, be something only accessible by wealth. It is for everyone. I believe we made good on our promise again and again.

When I entered the arena of fashion it wasn't as a vanity project; it was a serious enterprise. I did not set out to make a statement; I wanted only to make something true and useful—something that would enhance ordinary lives—and perhaps that's why it lasted. Because when you do something for the right reasons and when you mean it, people know. They always do.

But it wasn't one-and-done; we had to keep evolving, and that was a challenge I relished. In branding, you embrace what is new and what is different, but you also understand when it's time to change things up without simply chasing the latest thing. I prefer traditions to trends.

Looking back, it all seems obvious now, but when I first heard the pitch for my own fashion line, I truly did wonder, *Why me?* As the partnership unfolded, that question morphed into *Why* not *me?* I think as women, especially, we often question ourselves or the opportunities that come our way, when maybe we'd do well to ask ourselves *Why* not *me?* a little more often.

Kmart gave me a new dream and a new aspect of my career. I was the first celebrity to brand a line of clothing at a major retailer. Today, everyone is in the branding business: doctors, lawyers, businesses, politicians. But back then, we were doing something new. I threw myself into it with all the passion and fondness I'd had as a child making art projects with Mom at the kitchen table. I would go on to have branded lines under my name for clothing, jewelry, home décor, wallpaper, wigs, and fabrics. When the creators of *The Simpsons* asked me to do a cameo as myself selling my own line of axes, I was thrilled. I was in on the joke—that I'd put my name on anything. I *would* put my name on any product I loved and was proud to bring to the marketplace (and there have definitely been some I've declined). As I've often said, you can't fake branding. It has to be genuine. I traveled the country to meet my customers and talk about my products with a genuine passion because I believed in them. You can't pull that off if you're faking it, no matter how good an actor you might be. But it all started with Kmart.

Partnering with Kmart was one of the wisest decisions I made in my career, and our relationship would go on to become one of the most enduring in retail history, all built on intuitive understanding of women's lives and bodies. It's easy to dismiss fashion as fluff, but it's so much more. It's a form of expression. Style should belong to women at every stage of life. Clothes, like storytelling, are an act of intimacy. They tell the truth about who we are and who we hope to become.

Chapter Twenty-Two

When my fashion line launched, I was about six months into my second pregnancy. I hadn't put on nearly as much weight this time, so it was easier to appear in the promotional commercials and ads. After all, we weren't launching a maternity line—I had to be able to wear the clothes!

I had terrible morning sickness this time, though. For the whole launch event, I felt horrible. The perils of being a working mother. I got through it, and then Tony and I took a break in my hotel room, where we had a light dinner. All of a sudden, as many women experience, the nausea I'd endured for five months lifted, just like that.

I said to Tony, "I feel great—let's go out!" We walked all around New York for hours, talking and laughing, arm in arm. I had just launched the line I'd worked so hard to create, I had a precious baby growing inside me, and I was with the man I loved, in the city I adored. My fondest memory of that day was my evening with Tony, strolling the city and making plans for the birth of our new baby. It felt like the conversation between us could go on forever.

In the first week of December 1985, my parents came to LA to be there for the birth. Like clockwork, I went into labor late at night on December 3. Tony was right there, and he began timing the contractions. I could feel things shifting in my body, including the baby! The miracle of birth was happening, and I was so excited. This time, I knew what to expect, so I felt totally in control and much better prepared. I made sure I had everything in my suitcase, ready to go, including family pictures for the hospital room. Because it was late and the contractions were still far apart, I tried to sleep, the way they encourage you to do. After all, labor can last a while, and contractions can stop. I dozed a little, but by morning, they were stronger.

I called to Mom, "I think I'm in labor." I could tell she wanted to step in, but she held herself back. She touched my foot to let me know she was there, but she knew Tony would want to handle everything and didn't want to interfere. I will never forget her loving touch and her way of saying so much without words.

Then I had a contraction so strong that my stomach hardened, and with that, we were off to the hospital. (It was a different hospital this time, but we kept the same doctor.) We were all calm but focused. I had already decided to forgo medication because I felt it would take away my ability to push. I didn't want a forceps delivery, and unlike my first time, I knew what was in store, and I was *ready* to push! And push I did, for eight hours. They say a second birth is often faster, but not mine. At one point, I thought, *How much longer can this go on?* Little did I know that this sweet baby would keep me on my toes and guessing for the rest of my life, in the very best of ways.

At 2:08 p.m., a magic light came into the world. I finally set eyes on my beautiful, unpredictable, funny, bright, surprising little girl. (And at nine pounds, ten ounces, the question of why it had taken so long was answered.) I looked down at her in her perfection and thought of Mom and me, and of the closeness a mother and daughter can share. Of course, we love our sons, but there's something special between mothers and daughters. We travel the same path.

I memorized everything about my baby girl. The shape of her face, the Cupid's-bow lips just like my mom's, her brown hair, and her wide-set green eyes. I talked softly to her as if I were talking to a butterfly. Nothing could have pulled me away from that moment. I was awash in an emotion beyond comprehension. Nothing else mattered because I was with my girl.

We named our daughter Spencer-Margaret. Spencer because Tony chose it, and Margaret for my mother's middle name. As life went on, everyone would just call her Spencer, or Spen, but she'll always be Spencer-Margaret to me.

A new baby at home was certainly cause for celebration, but unfortunately that provided Tony with endless excuses to have a drink. He tried to hide most of his drinking from me, but I could always tell.

When Spencer-Margaret was four months old, we made plans to go to Hawaii together for a vacation with my parents. At the time, Tony was just wrapping *Sunset* for director Blake Edwards. When I visited him on the set a day or two before the trip, I just knew he'd been drinking. He had that affect like he always did, which for me was a dead giveaway.

"I'm canceling the trip!" I said, and I meant it. The last thing I wanted was to go on a vacation with my mom and dad, a four-year-old, a four-month-old, and an inebriated husband. It would have been like taking care of a third child, and it would have embarrassed me in front of my parents.

He said, "Please don't do that. I won't drink. I swear. Please. Please." He begged me to trust him, and he kept his promise. He didn't drink for that whole week. I hoped it would be a turning point, that he'd see that he didn't need to drink and could just enjoy our many blessings. And I prayed for Tony, trying to give him strength so that he, and we, would get through this. That he could stop abusing alcohol. I kept believing that this time he would stop drinking.

It was 1986, and in the five years since *Charlie's* wrapped, I'd divorced Dennis, married Tony, become a stepmother of three and a mother of two, made half a dozen movies and series, most of them ratings winners, and started my branding career. I loved the eighties. Frantic and exhausting, those years were the most gratifying single period of my life thus far. And the best part was that I had finally become a mother.

Everything I'd done before paled in comparison. These two little ones were the portal to the rest of my life—a shining staircase to the next level. As the matriarch of my family, I was part of something bigger than myself and was tasked with a new set of responsibilities. My children were my world, and everything I did was for them. I wanted a work life and a home life, but with some promise that one would never infringe on the other. It was family first in all decisions. So I did movies in LA, or I did them over the summer when the kids could come along.

And I did my best to keep my perfectionism under control. I'll admit, I planned and organized endlessly. Some part of me reasoned that if I could keep things *just right*, it would help to protect my children. It's common for mothers (especially of little ones) to fret; after all, you want so much for them. It's not always easy to know what is a function of OCD and what can just be characterized as highly attentive, but compulsion definitely crept in now and again. "Just please keep my babies healthy," I'd pray. Oh, did I pray. If you want a reason to worry, have a child. They feel so precious and fragile; even when they're no longer little, some part of you will always see them through those same eyes.

Today, my kids are grown and have babies of their own, but I'm still their mom. Sometimes I'll lapse into rumination, but thanks to time, perspective, and a little therapy, I have a better hold on it now.

In the years since we'd left *Charlie's*, I wasn't the only Angel who had big changes in her life. In October 1986, I caught Kate Jackson on *The Tonight Show*, talking about her life post-*Charlie's* with guest host Joan Rivers. *People* magazine had put us on the cover again, the old shot from *Time* magazine, with the headline "Look Homeward Angels: Happy Anniversary! Fun Memories of 10 Years Ago When Jiggle Gave TV a Jolt." It was a "where are they now?" story, despite the fact that Kate, Farrah, Cheryl, and I were all still very much in the public eye.

Kate and I remained close friends—"sisters," as she described our relationship to Joan Rivers. She came to our house every Christmas for many years and is Spencer-Margaret's godmother. Over the years, we've been sounding boards for each other. When I was making *Rage of Angels* and other miniseries, Kate was on *Scarecrow and Mrs. King*, costarring Bruce Boxleitner, a hit series that would run for four seasons. We were both so busy, and I was traveling so much, that the two of us barely saw each other while Gaston was in his early years. But I always knew that if I needed Kate or she needed me, we were just a phone call away.

Cheryl and I were in touch regularly, and I cheered her on in her big- and small-screen roles as well as her singing career. Cheryl never stopped working after *Charlie's*. When she wasn't acting, she was singing duets with Frankie Valli, writing children's books, playing golf, and enjoying her life with her husband, Brian, her daughter, Jordan, and her stepdaughter, Lindsay.

While Kate, Cheryl, and I were focused on television work, Farrah had been making films. Then, during my *George Washington* shoot, she'd taken Broadway by storm in *Extremities*, playing a woman who'd almost been raped, then took her power back by attacking her attacker. It was grueling physical acting, and she performed it night after night. She followed that with 1984's TV movie *The Burning Bed*, about a real-life victim of domestic violence, for which she received her first Emmy nomination. As with Kate, my friendship with Farrah had taken a back seat to our individual lives, but I was always rooting for her and was wildly impressed with her choices and her performances. I thought she was incredible, and critics agreed.

In her personal life, Farrah was in a relationship with *Love Story*'s Ryan O'Neal. The two had actually met while she was still married to Lee Majors. As the story goes, Lee asked Ryan to keep an eye on Farrah while he was away. Farrah and Ryan went to dinner and fell in love. It was an intense relationship—passionate, to be sure—but Farrah loved Ryan, and he worshipped her.

Sometime after Gaston was born, Farrah came to visit me in the hospital. She took one look at me and said, "You look great. Your fingers aren't fat anymore." I always loved her humor.

That day, she confided in me that she wanted to have a baby. I told her, "You'll have one. I know it."

Finally, at forty, she was pregnant. I happily gave Farrah my black YSL Golden Globe Award dress—the one I'd worn while pregnant.

She had a lot of questions about motherhood. "I have no idea about anything," she said. "Let's just start with the basics. What do I need? What do you use for shampoo? What about diaper rash?" We went over all the must-have products and baby gear. Her excitement and nervousness flashed me back to my first pregnancy. It was yet another bond we shared.

After Farrah and Ryan's son, Redmond, was born in January 1985, Kate and I went to dinner at their place. They had a racquetball court at their house and, when we arrived, were just finishing up a game. You never could slow Farrah down! They quickly changed, and then Farrah, a gourmet cook, whipped up a feast of chicken paillard and *pommes frites* served in a cone like they do in Paris bistros. We had a great time enjoying the food and sharing a laugh at how easy Farrah made it all look. I was delighted for my friend because she and Ryan seemed so happy and in love.

For Gaston's third birthday party, Farrah came with newborn Redmond. I remember it clearly: Farrah dressed all in black, walking up our steep driveway with her baby in her arms, wrapped up all warm and cozy—she was so at ease and comfortable with her son. At the party she chatted with my mother, whom she adored because she was so close to her own mom—both women from Texas of the same generation, they had much in common. It was a lovely, peaceful afternoon, and I was thrilled to get to spend so much of it catching up with Farrah.

Kate, Farrah, and I had a connection formed by our shared success during the first season of *Charlie's Angels*. The girls we were on day one of *Charlie's* could not have been further from the women we'd become ten years later, though some things would never change. We would always be bonded by what we'd been through, having built-in compassion based on our shared experience. Fame can separate you from your friends, from reality, from your sense of proportion, from your own anonymity. But in that same fire, something beautiful can also be forged. From the very beginning, we had a kinship that time and celebrity couldn't break.

Now we were far on the other side of that first fateful year together, filled with gratitude and appreciation, and no small amount of relief.

Chapter Twenty-Three

As an actor, I always appreciated when I could have creative control. Tony and I negotiated a network production deal that allowed me to pick and choose my projects and to have part ownership of them. Our company was called Smith Richmond Productions.

Our first endeavor was 1984's *Sentimental Journey*, a remake of a 1946 drama originally directed by Walter Lang. We shot in New York. It was the ideal way for me to work—we all packed up and went together. I had Tony and Gaston with me in my favorite city. This time we stayed at the Essex House. We had a two-bedroom suite overlooking Central Park. It had a small kitchen, so I could prepare all of Gaston's meals. (Spencer-Margaret was born the following year.)

I starred in the film and Tony was the cinematographer. We had to prove our mettle to our financial partners, including Twentieth Century Fox, but with Tony on board, I knew I was in good hands and that we could create something special.

I also thought that with Tony and me on a joint project that we were also producing, things would be all right—Tony would be busy and creative, doing what he loved. He understood light the way other people understood language. I thought he'd be so engaged, he wouldn't feel the need to drink. I thought, *On this movie, with all of us together, we will beat this*. But sometimes love is the enemy of good judgment. I understand now that when it comes to addiction, *we* is not the word to use. This was about Tony and his choices.

This time wasn't different. We started shooting, and Tony started drinking. When he was sober, he was scrupulously prepared. Even inebriated, he could light circles around everyone. He was an award-winning cinematographer. But on cocaine, time meant nothing to him.

In television, you have to make a certain number of pages each day, and we were falling behind. Days are counted like currency. One day the producer came to me and said, "We are losing time; we have to let him go." I was stunned, trying to come up with an answer, an excuse. I couldn't accept failure, so I suggested that Tony get a sober companion, someone to keep a close eye on him. To my surprise, he agreed. I knew it was an imperfect plan, but I wanted to get through the movie. It was worth a try.

We shot through the month of December—in my opinion, the most beautiful month in New York. On my day off, I would take Gaston in his stroller, and off we'd go all over Manhattan. Our first stop would always be the Christmas tree in Rockefeller Center, where we would watch the ice skaters, steam rising from our cups of hot chocolate. Then we'd head to Saks, which always had the most magical holiday windows and light show. Gaston was mesmerized. It was better than Disneyland. We would get ourselves a treat—he usually chose a bag of licorice allsorts—then we'd go from block to block, taking in the beauty of Christmas. I had to stop at my favorite store, Buccellati. Gaston saw me staring at the window, and said, "Mama, let me see." I'd been gazing at a beautiful necklace and bracelet. In his little voice, he said, "I's buys ya da whooole set." With his warm little hand in mine, all was right with the world. Those days with Gaston lifted my spirits and kept me afloat.

Miraculously, we made it through the movie and arrived back in LA just in time for Christmas. My parents were there, waiting. This time of year was when home took center stage. Mom and Alana had decorated the house like the North Pole, and despite everything we'd just been through with the movie, Christmas was like I had dreamed it would be. All those I loved were with me, and Tony cooked his gourmet meals, including a Christmas Day feast.

After Christmas, we'd enjoy the leftovers and Tony would prepare a traditional English dish called bubble and squeak, made from cooked potatoes, cabbage, and leftovers mixed together and fried. (The name comes from the sounds that emanate from the pan while it's cooking.) After the children were asleep, we'd have our dinner on a tray in our bedroom and watch a movie or read in bed. It was the perfect way to reconnect after our trials in New York. Tony was good at absorbing my anxiety, except when he drank. Then the gift vanished.

Another Smith Richmond Production was *The Rape of Doctor Willis*. It's about a surgeon who is assaulted, and then her rapist ends up on her operating table and she saves his life. It was a very dramatic piece written by Steven Gethers, who also wrote *Jacqueline Bouvier Kennedy*. I wanted my friend Lou Antonio to direct, but it wasn't in the budget. So Tony gave up his producer's salary so I could have the director I wanted. Tony wasn't materialistic in any way. What mattered to him was the experience and making a great movie. It was a quality I always admired.

Along with acting in our own productions, I was still in demand for network miniseries. In 1986, I reunited with Sidney Sheldon on the sequel to *Rage of Angels*, called *Rage of Angels: The Story Continues*. This time the cast included Angela Lansbury, who played my mother. I was thrilled to be working with the actress I'd watched as Mama Rose in *Gypsy* so many years before, when I was trying out for every Broadway show I could. It was like something had finally come full circle for me.

Back in 1967, when I had dreams of Broadway, during summer stock I'd auditioned for *Gypsy* and gotten the role of Louise. I was thrilled! But I was having trouble singing. I'd start out fine and then lose my voice. I went to several specialists and it was discovered that I had polyps on my vocal cords. I opted to have them removed, but that prevented me from doing *Gypsy*, which was a heartbreaker. It was one of my favorite shows. My singing voice wasn't quite the same afterward.

Now, here I was, taking the stage with Mama Rose. Then, to put the icing on the cake, or rather the pastry, Angela brought me an apple galette on the first day of shooting. I loved Angela's immediacy and intelligence, and how present she was. She had a warmth and an ability to get along with people from all walks of life. I watched her with the crew, making everyone feel seen and heard. She was quick to laugh, focused, and rooted in the moment. Her sense of reality, her strength, and her enormous gentleness influenced every scene she was in. When the miniseries ran, like the first one, it garnered strong ratings. So, why stop a roll?

My next collaboration with Sidney was *Windmills of the Gods* in 1988. Along with being a brilliant storyteller, Sidney really did his homework. Whether he was writing about Hollywood, the legal system in New York, or communist governments, he knew what he was talking about. In this miniseries, I played an ambassador to Romania who had to face down corrupt politicians in a quest to prevent human rights violations.

As always, I loved the prep work before the movie started. Working with Lou, creating a life around the character, the improvisation . . .

it was all so gratifying. As part of my preparation, I also worked with Nina Foch, an Oscar-nominated actress (*An American in Paris*, *Executive Suite*, *The Ten Commandments*, and *Spartacus*), who, in her later years, had a second career as a script breakdown consultant for actors. I brought her in on *Windmills* and learned a whole new way to read a script. She and I would look at the dialogue and talk about the emotional intention behind it, how each word triggered a feeling. At one point, my character was about to move, which would be the start of a new life in a foreign country. With Nina, I saw how a simple line like "I have to walk through the house before I leave" was more than just a declaration of action; it was about the character honoring her memories. It was about hating to say goodbye but needing to move on. Nina said that dialogue was about not just words but the intention behind them.

We shot the early scenes for the miniseries on Figure Eight Island in North Carolina, which was so beautiful it felt like being on vacation. When my character went to Washington, DC, she encountered her nemesis/love interest, played by Robert Wagner. How lucky can you get? It had been thirteen years since *Switch*, but I'd remained close with him over the years. The only problem was that R.J. was a real cutup, and he kept making me laugh throughout filming, much to the chagrin of the director, Lee Philips. I can't say enough about R.J. I've had the opportunity to work with so many wonderful leading men, but he's at the top of the list. As we all know, he was extraordinarily handsome. He had one of those faces that seemed to hold light. More than just a wonderful colleague, he's still a dear friend to this day. Now in his nineties, he makes a point of calling me regularly and asking, "How are you doing, Jac?" His voice sounds rich and vibrant, as if he were still a young man, and his charm radiates through the phone.

I've been lucky in my life to meet all sorts of extraordinary and accomplished people. Royalty, inventors, ballet dancers, athletes, professors, artists, writers, doctors, researchers, actors, and last but certainly not least, two presidents. Somehow I was invited to not one but two state dinners.

The first was during the Reagan presidency. When I received the invitation in the mail to the state dinner in honor of Germany, I couldn't believe it. I called my mother immediately and said, "I'm invited to the White House for a state dinner!" It was an amazing experience where I got to meet fascinating people and indulge my loves of architecture and décor in a setting rich with so much history!

A state dinner honors visiting dignitaries and heads of government. It's a black-tie affair designed to offer the most glamorous American hospitality. Each president brings their own signature style; they can select their china pattern, crystal, flatware, and linens. It's the height of opulence.

For the dinner, I was lucky enough to be seated at Nancy Reagan's table. She was so personable, asking me about Gaston. She might have been the First Lady, but she was also a mother. I remember her saying, "Little children, little problems. Big children, big problems."

That wasn't my only event with the Reagans. In June 1986, I was honored to cohost an All-Star Salute to Ford's Theatre with Richard Chamberlain, star of *Shogun* and *The Thorn Birds*. The event was part of the Reagans' efforts to raise money for the theater, and it honored the best of the arts from all genres. I was thrilled to meet Martha Graham, the mother of modern dance. At that time she was in her nineties, and even if you didn't know who she was, you'd have known she was a dancer. She was upright and poised, and she walked with such grace. Tommy Tune and Sandy Duncan were performing, both of them friends of mine. (Tommy and I went all the way back to the Drama Shack in high school.)

My second state dinner was during George H. W. Bush's administration, honoring South Korea. That night, I was actually seated at the president's table. The multicourse meal, which highlighted the finest in American cuisine, was heart-healthy yet delicious. I turned to the person next to me and joked, "This is wonderful, but sometimes I just crave a Milky Way." (Okay, maybe I wasn't joking. The food really was delightful, though.) Unbeknownst to me, that comment got around to President Bush. The next thing I knew, a server presented me with a silver tray covered with a silver dome. I lifted it up to find a Milky Way bar. It was a once-in-a-lifetime experience. I was lucky and I knew it.

After *Windmills*, my next miniseries was *The Bourne Identity*, based on the Robert Ludlum novel. I costarred with Richard Chamberlain, whom I'd just seen at the Ford's Theatre event. It was almost preordained: the Queen of the Miniseries meets the King. We'd nearly worked together in *West Side Story* back in New York, but I'd turned down that role. But it often happens in Hollywood that, in time, things come back around. Just like when I got to work with Angela Lansbury.

Richard was a generous actor, nuanced and understated in such a way that he never brought attention to himself. He didn't need to! He made the viewer feel such emotion with only the subtlest of expressions. He would conserve his energy by not overrehearsing at performance level. But when he went for it, it was perfection. There was a touching sense of truth in Richard's style, and when you worked with him the scene never lost its life. His ideas were stimulating, his approach effortless and honest. Beyond his talent as an actor, he was one of the nicest men I'd ever met. Richard's only demand was that he wanted his close-up first, and he'd certainly earned the right.

And of course I'd be remiss if I didn't mention his looks. Richard was incredibly handsome, slim, with a sculpted face and hair that was never out of place. We could be shooting a scene in a driving rainstorm, but female fans would be lined up around the block to catch a glimpse of him. He fed his heartthrob image because it bolstered his career. He believed that if the truth came out that he was gay, it would undermine all he'd worked for. Sadly it was true, and Richard was one of multiple closeted stars I knew in that era.

In the late 1980s, AIDS was a scourge around the world. In Hollywood, it robbed us of so many talented people. Rock Hudson had died in 1985, which sent many actors into a panic about kissing their costars in films. Now we know that HIV is not spread through saliva, but back then, we took every precaution. Richard was asked to test before *The Bourne Identity*, and he said, "Fine. As long as Jaclyn is tested too."

I said, "Absolutely! Let's do it."

He didn't make a big deal about it. He knew this was being asked of him because the producers knew he was gay. He deflected the attention by having the test done on both of us, a small, subtle way to protest the unfair assumptions of the time. I was happy to oblige, and I had no concerns at all about sharing a kiss with Richard.

In *Bourne*, I played a strong woman from a modest background who is thrust into an epic adventure when she crosses paths with a CIA assassin suffering from amnesia. I had to focus on the physicality of the role, which for me actually makes acting easier, thanks to my background in dance. No one studies ballet because it will make them better at stunts, but many action stars were dancers before they were actors. Michelle Yeoh trained in ballet from her early years and went on to attend the Royal Academy of Dance in London, then became one of the biggest martial arts stars of all time (often called "the female Bruce Lee"). Then there's Zoe Saldaña, Charlize Theron,

Jennifer Garner, Summer Glau—all were ballet dancers before they were actors. All I'm saying is, dance can take you places! And it can definitely teach you to take a fall without getting hurt.

We filmed on location in England, France, and Switzerland over a six-month period. In one outdoor scene, it was below zero and I had to run around barefoot in a silk blouse and a skirt. I was shivering like crazy! That scene was probably harder than the stunts.

I loved that miniseries and the opportunity to work with Richard. We had plenty of fun on the French Riviera, in Zurich, and in one of my favorite cities, London. It was also a great adventure for the kids, and they loved every minute of it. But back home, when I took them to the pediatrician for their annual exams, the doctor expressed concern over Gaston's frequent travel. "You can't keep taking Gaston out of school. He should be in first grade and socializing with other children," he declared.

I thought perhaps it was time for me to take a steady job and return to series TV.

Chapter Twenty-Four

My career maintained its momentum, but unfortunately, my marriage wasn't going as smoothly. I'd once thought Tony and I were a match made in heaven, and we were. We were meant to be for each other, not merely by affection but by temperament. And we had two great kids together. But years' worth of chronic suspicion and lies can unravel the tightest of knots.

It was 1989, and I was shooting the crime drama *Christine Cromwell* in Carmel, California. I played the eponymous character, an attorney. The show was part of the *ABC Mystery Movie* wheel, rotating with *Columbo*, *Kojak*, and *B.L. Stryker.*

I'd just returned to our hotel suite on a break to see Tony and the kids. Right away I knew Tony had been drinking.

Then the phone rang. I had just finished shooting and wanted to spend time with Gaston and Spencer-Margaret. I asked Tony to get the phone. Instead, he turned to Gaston. "Tell them your mother's not here," he said.

"Don't ask him to lie!" I said.

Tony shrugged it off as if the truth were a negotiable thing.

I went to the minibar and started counting the little bottles of liquor to see how many he'd drunk while admonishing myself for not having asked that they be taken out. The enabler is always the handmaiden to the alcoholic, tidying up the mess, preserving the illusion.

The nanny with us said, "Don't bother counting. He's been drinking."

I turned to Tony. "Why did you drink?"

"I was thirsty," he replied.

"Why didn't you drink water?"

It was a ridiculous exchange, a circular conversation that led nowhere. I would never understand what made him reach for vodka and scotch in the middle of the day, and he would never allow me my justifiable anger about it. Instead he was flippant, arrogant, and resentful. Meanwhile, I was trying so hard to keep everything together at work and at home. Our eleven years together had included both the highest highs and the lowest lows, but in that moment, I felt like we'd hit our rock bottom.

"I was thirsty. . . ." With those three words, it hit me: I'd had enough. Instead of owning his struggle, he was acting like a petulant teenager. I was done. I couldn't stay with a man who chose drugs and alcohol over his family.

"Pack your bags and go," I said. "If you can get clean, we're here, we will be waiting for you. But as long as you drink and do coke, there's nothing we can do to make this right. It's just not going to work."

In so many ways, Tony was a good husband. I felt his love profoundly, and we had a wonderful life when he was sober. We were well matched. More than that, he was generous. He was a true caretaker. He gave me a family and a sense of belonging. He cooked for me. He'd give me his last bite to see me smile. He didn't care about the superficial trappings of life, like clothes and cars. He was indifferent to status or possessions—he wanted connection and meaning.

He made me laugh and I made him laugh. He made me feel central to his world. But none of that was enough. I needed to do the best I could for my children, to protect them from the ravages I knew could come from substance abuse.

When we separated, it was like I'd lost my anchor. I would miss the easy familiarity that you get with someone you've been with for years. Someone you feel a part of. But when Tony was high, his beautiful qualities disappeared. After eleven years of watching him repeat the same ugly pattern of drinking, repenting, and relapsing, I was done. If not for his substance use, we would have been forever. But I finally made the painful decision to accept what I could no longer deny—my third marriage was over.

When we returned to LA from Carmel, Tony moved into the guesthouse. He hired a cutthroat lawyer and served me with papers, but it was all just stalling tactics. If he served me, he didn't have to vacate the premises, and he could delay the process.

It was a bitter end to a beautiful relationship, a brutal crisis that seemed to unspool in slow motion. During the period of separation, I couldn't stand to see my children disappointed or sad. It always disturbed me to see them upset, but the separation made me sensitive to even the slightest hurts. I did my best to insulate them from my agony and keep my private devastation in check. I learned to brace myself without showing it. As much as possible I wanted their world to remain intact even as mine was unraveling.

Acting was my escape. My work kept me from coming apart.

Christine Cromwell carried me through the early stages of the separation. The show was as much family drama as murder mystery, though we certainly had suspenseful elements, including beloved characters in peril. My character was a lawyer who always seemed to get caught up in murder investigations that, coincidentally, implicated people she knew.

Ralph Bellamy played my mentor, the owner of the law firm, and the incredible Celeste Holm was my scene-stealing divorcée mother. Celeste was feisty, with a salty wit and a light-up-the-room smile. She was an elegant woman from an upper-class family. Ralph Bellamy had a gentle soul. He was humble and appreciative. The most impressive name on the credit sheet, however, wasn't that of an actor. It was that of the show's creator, Dick Wolf.

Dick is a man with 24-karat-gold credentials. He's perhaps best known for creating the *Law & Order* franchises, the first of which premiered in 1990. But before that, and before *Christine*, he got his feet wet on *Miami Vice*, starring a very young Don Johnson. I was fortunate to work with Dick while he was still zeroing in on his signature ripped-from-the-headlines, TV-with-a-twist narrative style. Our scripts were full of complicated plots and subtle character reveals, and I dove in headfirst. Our show wasn't as gritty as his later work set in New York; in her Santa Barbara and San Francisco settings, Christine had healthy doses of glamour and sunshine.

Dick had a deceptive sense of humor that was always right there, waiting to come out. And it was a time when I really needed to laugh. He was polite and attentive, the kind of person who absorbs information, who listens to everything you say, then tucks it all away. But if he needs it, it's there. It always seemed like there wasn't any question he couldn't answer. He was a true friend to me at a very difficult time, and we became close. Not only was he wonderful to work with from a professional standpoint, but he was generous and empathetic to me as a human being when I needed it most.

Dick was the only one on the show who really knew what was going on with me at home. Some of his support was probably to help shore me up so that I'd be able to perform, but most of it came from his deep well of kindness. I came to see him as a trusted confidant, an inspiring leader on the show, and a close friend.

Whenever I had to leave the set a few minutes early to pick up the kids from school or take them to friends' birthday parties, Dick worked around it. On my birthday, he gave me a six-foot-tall card signed by the whole cast and crew. No matter what was happening in my life, Dick made me feel like the set was a safe place where I could leave my troubles behind. Through it all, I could set my grief about my marriage down for a few hours and become someone else. Someone capable. And perhaps that was what carried me forward.

At our daily lunches, Dick and I didn't only hash over my problems. We talked shop, about his goals and the medium of television. I remember at one of our lunches, he said, "Something's coming, Jaclyn. Something that's different and might turn out to be really good." It was the first iteration of *Law & Order*, starring the talented Michael Moriarty, whom I'd worked with on *Rage of Angels*. From that original series, there have been various spin-offs: *Criminal Intent*, *Special Victims Unit (SVU)*, *Trial by Jury*, *True Crime*, and more. It's unbelievable what Dick did with that franchise, how he found a way to use a familiar format in fresh ways while staying current with what was happening in the world.

I got to guest-star on *SVU* in 2010 in an episode called "Bedtime." I played an ex-cop who came on the scene when Olivia Benson, portrayed by the inimitable Mariska Hargitay, was investigating a cold case my character had worked on. Susan Anton and Morgan Fairchild made cameo appearances, but the other major guest star was Ann-Margret as the ex-lover of a local businessman who'd been killed many years ago . . . *or had he?*

Spoiler alert: When they finally uncovered the murderer, it was me! I got to have an unhinged confession scene at the end.

SVU came on the heels of a two-episode stint on *Becker* as Ted Danson's druggy, boozy love interest. I'd done comedy approximately zero times before *Becker*, and I was so anxious before we began filming. But once we got rolling, I wound up having a great time. Ted put me at ease right away. Before we started shooting, he came to my motor home: "This is a such a great departure for you. I'm so glad you decided to do it." Watching Ted work, I marveled at his ease. He never seemed like he was acting. It was so natural. And he could do comedy or drama. It was easy to see how he won two Primetime Emmys and two Golden Globes.

Thank goodness for my work. It gave me ballast in the storm of my breakup with Tony.

Chapter Twenty-Five

When the press got wind that Tony and I had split, my personal heartbreak was suddenly front-page news. It was overwhelm on top of overwhelm. I had to do a great job on set, be a mother to my six-year-old son and two-year-old daughter during what was also a difficult time for them, take calls from divorce lawyers and my management team, design and promote for Kmart, and shoot commercials for my new fragrance, California, for Max Factor. Plus, I had to deal with Tony and his anger, regret, and sadness.

Once again, thank goodness for my parents, who were incredibly supportive. They'd seen Tony at his best, but they'd also seen him at his worst, and that had been as painful for them to watch as it had been for me. I'd been raised by two loving people who adored each other. They'd made the long journey all the way from sweethearts to doting grandparents, and when it came to relationships, I wished my own life looked more like theirs. When you do your best to build a family and keep it together in the long term, but then it doesn't work out, it breaks your heart. And more important to me, it was hurting the two people I loved more than anyone else in the world. I was trapped between the damage that living in a household with substance abuse would do to my children and the damage that divorce would do. There was no good option, so I tried to cushion the blow as best I could.

I was a busy working mom, fully aware that their childhoods would go by in a flash. From the outside my life might have looked elegant, but the reality was, I was struggling to do it all. I couldn't be there every moment, but I tried to ensure that I never missed certain things, like dropping them off at school or tucking them in at bedtime. During summer breaks, I was on hiatus from *Christine* and chose not to take any more miniseries so we'd have a stretch of time where things could be a little more relaxed, and we could enjoy one another. During those periods, home took center stage.

I welcomed normalcy whenever it appeared—those typical childhood moments that leave you weeping happy tears or laughing out loud. One such memorable moment happened with Gaston. He'd been traveling with me to my filming locations since he was a newborn, but he was rarely on set. I also tried to make it a point to refrain from going on about my career around my children because, as much as possible, I wanted to just be a normal mom. At home, I didn't want to be Jaclyn Smith; I wanted to be June Cleaver. As a result, I guess I never really explained what Mommy did for a living. When Gaston was in kindergarten, the teacher asked all the children to say what their parents did for work. The kids sat in a circle on the floor and took turns answering. Then the teacher turned to my son. "And what does your mother do, Gaston?"

He replied, "My mom's a cleaning lady."

The teacher had to stifle a laugh. She could not wait to tell me about it.

Gaston had spent the first years of his life watching me organize and clean—*enthusiastically*, let's say—so, lacking other information, he made a logical assumption. It was a true "kids say the darndest things" moment, and I adored him for it. That was one of the deepest joys I found in Gaston and Spencer-Margaret. To them I was just Mom. It's been the purest, sweetest bond I've ever known.

While I enjoyed a certain kind of anonymity with my children, the rest of the world seemed to feel entitled to know everything about my breakup with Tony. When we separated, our lives were splashed on the front pages of the *National Enquirer* and other tabloids (most of it fiction). That was painful, not so much for me—I knew it came with the territory—but for how it impacted my kids. One day Gaston came home crying from school, saying that one of his friends had told him, "Your parents are divorcing, and your mom is paying your dad four million dollars to stay away from you!" Everything about that statement was false, and while Tony had been throwing up roadblocks to the divorce, he was always honorable and fair where money was concerned.

Through his tears, Gaston asked, "Mom, is this true?"

Cue a long sigh, and a long talk. I had to explain to Gaston as best I could about tabloids, along with the fact that his father and I both loved him very much.

When Tony and I first separated, I took it upon myself to explain to the kids what was happening. I said, "Mommy and Daddy are going to take some time apart. We both love you. It has nothing to do with you. We're trying to work out some problems." I assured them that their lives were not going to change at all in the basic ways. They would live in the same house, go to the same school, have the same friends and toys . . . Still, there was no way to make things okay.

For Gaston, the idea that one of his parents would try to keep the other out of his life hurt him deeply. It was one of many times I asked myself, *What are you doing to your children?* I worried constantly about how our separation was affecting them. My own strength had always come from the love my parents had for me, and their love for each other. What was I giving to my kids if I couldn't give them that same security and stability? What scars would they carry from this? Honestly, sometimes I still think about the mark it must have made on their precious hearts. It's the lot of parents, especially moms, to feel guilty about the times we couldn't protect our kids. I worried about what they absorbed, what they overheard, what people said to them. Wounds that might be forming invisibly beneath the surface.

Gaston was old enough to be fully aware of what was happening. He heard the whispers. There was no doubt he would remember this time. My son, who was very sensitive, carried questions too heavy for his years. When gossip reached him—distorted, cruel, careless—it hurt him in places I could not reach fast enough.

My daughter absorbed the world differently. She possessed an old soul, a freedom of spirit, and I prayed her world would not break. Spencer-Margaret was too young to comprehend everything, but children never escape the fallout from divorce. While Gaston came into the world wearing his heart on his sleeve, Spencer-Margaret arrived with an acute perception that noticed absolutely everything around her. She was tuned in to every nuance and every word, whether spoken or unsaid, and she often had very strong feelings about whatever was going on.

From the time she was young I saw her generosity, how she gave freely of her possessions, her time, and her attention. When she decided to do something, she did it with a sense of purpose and a desire for perfection. She had a merry, unpredictable quality. She was born with enormous individuality and the capacity to entertain herself. Whereas Gaston always wanted to be with me, Spencer-Margaret was more independent. She'd be off singing songs in her room, or she'd just get into her pajamas and put herself to bed. She knew her dad had moved out, of course, but I couldn't tell how it was affecting her, and believe me, I watched her intently for any signs. I hoped the divorce wouldn't take away her innocence and free spirit.

As part of her caring nature, Spencer-Margaret has always had an intense love of animals. As a preschooler, she'd bring home doodlebugs in her lunch box. I'd open it up, find a dozen insects, and shriek. Around this time, she had a blue pet betta fish, Fish Madison, who lived in her room in a glass bowl. She loved that fish. One day, when the kids were at Tony's for the weekend, Alana noticed it floating upside down in the bowl. I was terrified that Spencer-Margaret would be inconsolable—another loss so soon after her father left. Alana and I hopped in the car and sped off to the pet store to get a replacement. The problem was, they didn't have a blue one, so we got a purple one and crossed our fingers.

When Spencer Margaret got home, she went to her room, then came running out moments later. "Mom! My fish!"

I braced myself. "What's going on?" I asked.

"It *changed color*! It's a magic fish!"

Phew! Exhaling, I said, "How lucky are we to have a magic fish?"

We had no idea why the other fish had died, but we weren't going to let that happen again. Alana and I spent *a lot* of time and energy testing water and measuring food. But somehow the second fish died, too, and we got another one in yet another color. I'm not sure how many we went through—as many as five or six. Then the inevitable happened. Spencer-Margaret went into her room and found her fish floating in the bowl. She was inconsolable and insisted on having a funeral for her fish of many colors. We buried it in the backyard, and she gave an earnest eulogy while I struggled not to giggle. But then it struck me how brave this little girl was and how full of heart, to care so deeply for all the beings in her life—animals and people. And fortunately for all of us, that's still very true today.

For his part, Tony was trying everything he could think of to come back home. Despite what the tabloids said, he didn't want money from me; he wanted to save our marriage, and he believed he could. Throughout this whole period, he wrote me love letters begging me to take him back. He called a friend and asked him to go to an AA meeting with him, but having seen him break promise after promise, I didn't put a lot of faith in Tony's newfound sobriety. For his sake I hoped it would last, but I couldn't gamble our family on it.

In his desperation, Tony even tried to enlist Gaston in his attempts to get me back, at one point telling him, "Mommy holds the keys to our family." One night, when I went to kiss him good night and spend some alone time with him, Gaston looked up at me with his big, innocent eyes and said, "Dad said you hold the keys to our family. Bring him back, Mom." To this day I can still hear that plaintive little voice, and it brings me to tears. My heart broke for him, and it does still, remembering. A little boy shouldn't have to have such big worries, and shouldn't be a pawn in a marriage. I know Tony was just desperate and hurting, but I'll never get over that moment.

Around this time, Lois Armstrong of *People* magazine came to my house to interview me about *Christine Cromwell*. We were sitting in the screening room, talking about the show, and I thought it was going well. Then she said, "I'll be honest, Jaclyn, unless you speak about your divorce, I'm not giving you the cover." I got it—the press wanted to have their story—but my private life and my kids' lives weren't fodder for selling magazines.

My response was immediate: "I won't do it."

Then, some relief. After months of acrimony, Tony finally realized the effect his lawyer and the press were having on me and the kids. He fired the cutthroat lawyer, saying, "I can't do this to the mother of my children. She's a good mother. She's been a good wife. She doesn't deserve this." Then he hired a friend of ours who was fair.

We agreed to joint custody, but I would be named the custodial parent, meaning the kids would live with me and visit him at his home a mile away in Westwood. I bought the house for him in trust for our children, and he still lives there today.

Happily, Tony finally got sober, and once he cleaned up his act, everything fell back into place in his career. He was once more in demand and has worked steadily ever since (including on *Legally Blonde*, *The Sweetest Thing*, *Men of Honor*, and many more). In 2024, he was awarded the Lifetime Achievement Award from the British Society of Cinematographers. But perhaps his biggest accomplishment is that he's been sober for nearly three decades.

Chapter Twenty-Six

Mine is a family of celebration. For Gaston's ninth birthday, my parents came from Houston for his party. It was always their favorite present to the kids, and they loved it too. The early bedtime rules would be broken. Mom would bring gifts along with their favorite candies, and they'd always want to sleep on a pallet near their Mimi at night. The kids were always thrilled when my mom was left in charge. It seems my parents took a looser, more relaxed style with Gaston and Spencer-Margaret than they had with Tommy and me!

My mom and dad arrived just in time for the party, which we were having at the Culver City ice skating rink. But while there, Daddy started to feel ill. The parent of one of Gaston's friends was a doctor, and he took a look at Daddy and advised us to see a man at UCLA by the name of Dr. Saleh Salehmoghaddam. He was known as "the doctor's doctor." The following Monday, my parents saw Dr. Saleh, who referred my dad to a cardiologist at UCLA, Dr. Jaime Moriguchi. Dr. Moriguchi ran some tests, then shared Daddy's angiogram with his colleague Dr. Bradley Allen, a pediatric heart surgeon he respected.

I found out later that Brad looked at the scan and said, "He needs a quadruple bypass and a mitral valve repair."

Dr. Moriguchi said, "The patient is Jaclyn Smith's father."

"Okay," said Brad. "He still needs a quadruple bypass and a mitral valve repair."

Dr. Moriguchi agreed and invited Brad to join him at the consultation with my family. If Daddy decided to proceed, he'd be one of the surgeons.

I looked at this young doctor and was reminded of the boys I grew up with: clean-cut, all-American, the boy down the street. I thought, *This doctor is going to hold my precious dad's life in his hands. Does he have enough experience?* Still, Dr. Moriguchi trusted him, which said a lot.

In a perfectly timed waltz Brad went around the room introducing himself and saying hello. When it was my turn, I started to say, "I'm Jac—"

"I know who you are," he said. His tone was businesslike, clear, and efficient, but not unkind. He then calmly explained everything in detail, leaving nothing out. He answered every question we asked as if he had no other plans for the day. I was reassured that this "young" man clearly knew what he was doing.

As Brad spoke, he represented security and straight lines. In spite of his age, he carried the title "doctor" effortlessly. As a pediatric heart surgeon he had to face the highest of stakes, yet he seemed at ease with the weight of responsibility. He was tall and handsome (I couldn't help but notice), with a distinctive mustache. And, okay, not *so* young, in his mid-thirties. The way he spoke, with a rare combination of gravity and excitement, I could tell he was passionate about his work and confident in his knowledge of the heart. We were all impressed by his track record of performing lifesaving surgeries on babies and small children with heart defects. It felt like Daddy was in the right hands.

A few days later, Daddy had surgery at UCLA. His two brothers flew into town to be there for the surgery. As he recovered, I spent as much time at the hospital as I could. One night, I walked into his room and found Brad there, chatting with my parents as if they were longtime friends. He'd gotten to know them on his evening rounds, making a point to stop by Daddy's room last so he wouldn't be rushed.

We talked with Brad for a while, and by the time I was about to head home it was ten thirty. Mom wanted to walk me to my car to make sure I got there safely, but Brad was leaving, too, so he offered to accompany me.

Neither Brad nor I thought for a moment that his walking me to my car had any deeper meaning. It was simply a kind gesture, just the kind of person Brad was. And since Tony was a regular visitor to the hospital, naturally Brad thought that he and I were still together.

On that short walk to my car, we got on the topic of local restaurants, even though restaurants had been the last thing on my mind. Brad was a foodie, and I mentioned a few places I enjoyed, then asked him where he liked to go. He said immediately, "Diaghilev, in the Bel Age Hotel." It seemed his certainty extended beyond the surgical suite.

"I've never been," I said.

He described the old-world-style Franco-Russian restaurant, its caviar and vodka menu, and its charismatic maître d', a man named Dimitri Dimitrov. "It's quiet," Brad said, "a place where 'grandfathers' bring their 'granddaughters' who aren't really their granddaughters. If you know what I mean."

Oh, I did. I'd been an actor for twenty years by then. I said, "It sounds interesting."

"If you want, I'd be happy to take you there sometime," he said.

Was he asking me on a date? I wasn't sure because he was so nonchalant, as if he might say the same thing to anyone. I was noncommittal, but I didn't say no. Then we said good night and I got into my car and drove home.

We didn't make any plans, but I continued to see Brad in Daddy's room. Within the week, my father was discharged from the hospital and returned home to Houston. Brad had heard that Tony and I were separated, and I guess he knew it was now or never. At one point while I was helping my parents leave the hospital, Brad turned to me and said, "I'd love to take you to that restaurant I told you about." He seemed like such a nice man, and I was grateful to him, as he'd been so kind and caring to my parents.

"Sure," I said. "Why not?"

Brad offered to pick me up at my house a few days later. I didn't want him to drive down the driveway because I didn't want the kids to know about him. It felt too soon to expose them to the idea of me going out with someone. I kept an eye out for Brad's car, and as soon as I saw it, I ran up the driveway in my heels and navy Ralph Lauren suit. (I rely on Brad's memory for the recollection about my wardrobe—he never forgot what I was wearing.) If he found it strange that I'd rather jog up a hill than let him pick me up at my door, he didn't mention it.

We arrived at the restaurant, which was small, with only about twenty seats. The ambience was romantic, opulent, a blend of tsarist Russia and Belle Epoque Paris. A pianist and a harpist played softly in one corner. But something was odd: the place was empty. We were the only customers.

Dimitri, the maître d', rushed over and couldn't have been more charming. To every question he answered, "With pleasure!" (Dimitri would go on to become an LA institution, Hollywood's favorite maître d', the subject of a documentary, and the longtime majordomo at Sunset Tower.) It was like a scene in a movie. In my mind, this was not supposed to be some big romantic night. And I wasn't even sure I wanted to be there. It wasn't about Brad; I was just so nervous to leave the kids and couldn't help wondering if everything was okay at home.

To my relief, Brad seemed genuinely surprised too. As Dimitri explained, there had been two large parties that were supposed to show up and, coincidentally, both had canceled. The restaurant had prepared tons of food they no longer knew what to do with and had twelve waiters standing around, twiddling their thumbs. They showered us, their only customers, with attention, piling extra plates of food on our table. It just kept coming, and it was all delicious.

At dinner, our conversation was surprisingly refreshing. Up to that point, I'd been involved almost exclusively with men in the film industry. Brad was nothing like them. He was earnest, eager, and more enthusiastic than most Hollywood types would ever let show. And he was interesting. He could dredge up facts on a huge variety of subjects and do it with ease and enjoyment.

When the meal was over and Brad drove me home, our easy conversation continued. I enjoyed it enough to want to prolong it, so I invited him in. It was way past the children's bedtime, so there was very little chance that they'd come into the living room and see him. On my couch, I found a man who was unfettered and pure. He talked about his childhood in New York City and New Jersey, how much he loved his parents, and how their divorce after thirty-four years of marriage had deeply upset him. It was a subject that interested me, since I had two young children and I worried about how my own divorce was affecting them. We ended up talking until five in the morning, and over that time my attitude about him changed. When Brad left, he didn't try to kiss me good night. This was a man who was not in a rush. He was a surgeon, after all, so I shouldn't have been surprised by his patience, but I found it very appealing.

For our second date, we went to a movie, *The Hunt for Red October*, starring Sean Connery and Alec Baldwin. I'd had a long workday and wound up falling asleep in the theater. Instead of taking it personally, Brad was amused. As someone who'd worked many long shifts himself, he understood.

Before we had a chance to build up any real momentum, Brad decided to take a position in the training program at Toronto's Hospital for Sick Children. It was a great opportunity and I fully supported his decision. But by pure coincidence (or perhaps fate), I was going to be in Toronto, too, for six weeks. I'd be filming a movie called *Kaleidoscope*.

The film had a complicated plot about sisters who were separated when their parents were tragically killed in the aftermath of World War II. I played a lawyer (again) with a dark past. Perry King was the leading man. I enjoyed working with him and the whole cast. But I walked away from that movie with a lifelong friend who didn't appear on-screen at all.

Danielle Steel, the best-selling American author of all time, had written the novel on which the film was based. Some people think of her as a romance novelist, but she is so much more than that. Similarly to Sidney Sheldon, she does extensive research for each book, whether it's about diamond mines or war zones. And she still uses the same 1973 typewriter on which she wrote her first book. She has pounded out nearly two hundred novels on those keys! I'd go on to appear in one more movie based on a novel she'd written: 1994's *Family Album*.

For the six weeks I was in Toronto, Brad and I saw each other almost every day. When his birthday rolled around, we decided to go to Niagara Falls, just a two-hour drive from Toronto. My children had just arrived in Canada to be with me, having spent part of their summer on vacation with Tony in Mexico. They were a bit under the weather from traveling, but I didn't think it would be a problem. The day of our road trip, Brad met us at my hotel. I introduced him to Gaston and Spencer-Margaret as "a friend"—an accurate description, since I didn't consider Brad to be my boyfriend. I was still healing and not ready to commit to anyone.

The four of us climbed into a rental car and headed to Niagara Falls. Not ten minutes into the drive, both kids said they felt queasy. About twenty minutes later, they both threw up in the car. Brad calmly pulled over, leaned into the back seat, and cleaned up while I comforted the kids.

I had to admit, he was good with the kids. Throwing up seemed to get the sickness out of their systems, so we continued on to the falls. Once there, Brad put Spencer-Margaret on his shoulders to give her a better look. She liked him from the start. Gaston seemed to tolerate him, which was fair enough. Even though Tony and I had been separated for a year at that point, he was loyal to his father and suspicious of who this man really was.

Never ones to forgo a celebration, though, the kids and I made Brad a birthday cake with an "operating table" made of Lego as the base. Brad had officially become part of our fancy-cake tradition, which he embraced. In years to come, he'd make me cakes that looked like a Kelly bag and a white poodle. When Brad commits to something, he gives it his all!

When the film wrapped, I went home to LA, and Brad started flying cross-country every month to see me.

The more time we spent together, the more I came to love, respect, and appreciate Brad. He's such a knowledgeable person, fascinating to listen to about so many subjects. With a brain capable of sorting through any problem and solving it, he relishes complexity. I always say that Brad owns one of the world's most intact psyches. Ever an optimist, he believes in magic and lives in a sort of mental Disneyland where he sees the best in people and situations. He never holds a grudge. Brad has a deep self-awareness and an earnest, innocent demeanor, despite a career where he holds people's lives in his hands. It helps that he's impervious to anxiety! From the start, he's been a great foil for my worry and has always encouraged me toward the blissful state in which he lives.

After about six months of flying back and forth every few weeks, Brad decided to move back to Los Angeles. It was a big sacrifice because he was leaving a job in pediatric heart surgery, the specialty he'd trained twenty years for. Back in LA, there were no job openings in his field at his level, so he had to take part-time jobs in different hospital emergency departments. Everyone in Brad's life—his father, his mentors at UCLA—asked him, "What are you doing in emergency departments? You're a surgeon!"

I hadn't asked him to come back to LA; that was his choice. He made it because our relationship was more important to him than being a heart surgeon, and he reasoned that at some point he'd find another position more suited to his skills and experience. But I felt terrible about it. The guilt was compounded because whenever the subject of marriage came up, I shot it down immediately. I'd been there, done that. And it wasn't an option for Brad to simply move into my house. On the nights we spent together, he would get up at three in the morning and go back to his place so my kids would never see him leave. The next time I married, it would be a decision made by all three of us.

Finally, in November 1992, after two years back in LA, Brad got an offer to return to heart surgery . . . at the University of Illinois in Chicago. I was flooded with relief that he could once again do what he loved, and I encouraged him to take the position. Of course I would miss him, but I knew I wasn't ready for marriage, and I didn't want him staying in LA just for me. But Brad and I weren't done with each other just yet. With his trademark optimism he held out hope that he'd be able to find a position in LA again soon, and we agreed to keep seeing each other and see how things played out.

And so we began our lives of being together and living apart, which we did for the next seventeen years.

Chapter Twenty-Seven

I'd learned during my *Charlie's* years that critics had their own agendas and that they often intentionally ignored reality to suit their own purposes. Like calling *Charlie's* "sexually exploitative" simply because the main characters were attractive women. We were judged relentlessly. Praised for our beauty and dismissed for the same reason. So I got used to being misunderstood and typecast.

Still, I was taken aback by a long article in the *Los Angeles Times* in January 1992 by media critic Howard Rosenberg. The title was "Consistency to a Fault: Jaclyn Smith Never Lost Her 'Angelic' Character." I'd just appeared in a TV movie called *In the Arms of a Killer*, costarring my *Rage of Angels* friend Michael Nouri and future *West Wing* star John Spencer. It was shot by Tony, our last collaboration.

Ever since I'd first started to dance, I'd been taking criticism. It's simply part and parcel of trying to do anything meaningful or well. If you can't handle criticism, don't go into the arts! But critique is one thing—embedded within it is guidance and feedback you can learn from. Negative criticism is another—it's simply mean-spirited and offers nothing of value. Unfortunately, the *Times* article was an example of the latter. Among other insults, it implied that my face and body were the only reasons anyone ever watched me on TV. Beauty, I came to understand, was a currency that could be spent against you as easily as for you. Alongside the article ran twenty-plus publicity photos from my films and series over the years—I suppose as evidence of the author's claims? It felt hostile, like a hit piece.

In the wake of the article, I was grateful to receive an outpouring of supportive letters from colleagues and friends—Mary Tyler Moore; her husband, Grant Tinker; and Aaron Spelling, to name a few—that made me feel better. And one letter I received was so special, I've kept it all these years:

> *Dear Jaclyn,*
>
> *You don't know me, but I've been able to watch you from afar. I've always enjoyed your choices and efforts and movies, and was completely taken aback by Howard Rosenberg's assessment of your career and work. It's a sign of the times that we have become so careless with people that we've become familiar with them. The revelation alone can give you little comfort when someone so mean spirited has access to a medium where they choose to embarrass and insult. He obviously has no character himself so I'm not surprised at his inability to describe it in writing.*
>
> *You should be proud that every time you said "yes" to a project, hundreds of people work and feed their families. Be proud that you are an actress and that you try every time out. And know that those of us who have also suffered the slings and arrows that we are proud of you.*
>
> —*Kevin Costner*

Kevin had just won a raft of Oscars for directing, producing, and starring in *Dances with Wolves*. That this man, at the first of many peaks in his long career, took the time to write that letter meant the world to me. It still does.

Kevin understood what the price of fame is, and what it is not. Criticism, a certain lack of privacy . . . some amount of that comes with the territory, and you learn to deal with it. But when someone attacks you solely based on the desire to sell papers, they've crossed a line. Kevin's letter made me realize that kindness restores balance. It reminded me that decency is still there beneath the noise.

In those years, I found myself moving through a succession of projects, each with its own individual atmosphere. In 1991, I starred in *Lies Before Kisses* with Ben Gazzara. The plot was twisty, about a couple whose marriage blows up when the wife (me) overhears her husband talking to his twenty-year-old girlfriend (played with trashy zeal by Lisa Rinna). I had a very sexy scene with virile young Canadian actor Nick Mancuso. My dear friend Lou Antonio directed the film, and he suggested we try our lovemaking a certain way. I said, "I don't see it. Will you demonstrate?" Bless Lou. Pretending to be me, he acted out the scene with Nick to the snickers of the crew. But when I stepped in to do the scene, they all got serious. Lou would bend over backward to take care of me, and he just had!

The following year, Corbin Bernsen and I worked together on the movie *Love Can Be Murder*. It had a different tone—a lightness that carried through the script. Corbin was taking a break in the middle of his long series run in *L.A. Law*. During his hiatus, he signed on to play the ghost of a gumshoe who'd been murdered in the office currently being used by my character, also a private detective. (Did you follow that? Corbin and I were both amused by the premise.) At one point I mentioned to Corbin in passing that, after I'd worked with his *L.A. Law* castmate John Spencer on *In the*

Arms of a Killer, John had given me a homemade peach pie when we wrapped. When we finished *Love Can Be Murder*, Corbin sent me flowers with a note reading, "It ain't peach pie, but it'll have to do."

Then Christopher Reeve and I did emotional battle in 1992's *Nightmare in the Daylight*. He played a San Francisco man obsessed with the wife he'd lost in an earthquake. He saw my character on vacation with her family and became convinced that I was his long-lost wife. Like his character, Christopher was serious and a bit moody on set. He often questioned the director—once again it was Lou Antonio—about his choices and wasn't shy about demanding that a scene be reblocked or rewritten. Christopher was intense, always questioning the boundaries of the material in ways that suggested a restless dissatisfaction. The one time I saw his hard shell crack was when his wife, Dana, sent him roses for his birthday. When they arrived, he was clearly touched by the gift, saying wistfully, "I'm very lucky to have her." Everyone has their soft spots.

In *Cries Unheard: The Donna Yaklich Story*, my stepdaughter was played by a teenage Hilary Swank. I believe it was only her second film, but even then, her talent was undeniable. It was such a treat to get to work with such a promising young actress who had such a delightful personality. To know Hilary is to love her. She was comfortable in her skin, authentic, and truly a warm and kind human being. I next heard from her when she called me to say that she was auditioning for Drew Barrymore's first *Charlie's Angels* reboot and asked me for any tips that might give her an edge. She didn't get the part, but later she was cast to play Brandon Teena in *Boys Don't Cry*. She was stunning in that role and embodied it with courage and depth. I wasn't at all surprised when it garnered her an Oscar. At that point in my own career I'd gone from being the new kid on the block to a Hollywood staple, and it thrilled me to see such talent and integrity in the future generation of actors.

But the tide comes in, and then it goes out again. I'd been enjoying my life at work, but in my private world, things were about to take another difficult turn.

Chapter Twenty-Eight

"Your father is losing ground." I'll never forget those words. Mom never wanted to worry me, but she knew that if something was happening with my dad, I'd want to know as soon as possible. I flew home immediately.

Even though the heart surgery he'd had a few years before had bought him time, he had another problem that had gone undetected. Being a dentist of a certain era, he'd worked with asbestos on gold inlays. Over time this took a toll on his lungs. While I was there, his doctors admitted him to the hospital for a minimally invasive procedure called a sympathectomy, which interrupts some of the signaling in the sympathetic nervous system. But instead of helping him, the surgery weakened him even more. I could tell that we were losing him.

Mom and I kept vigil at the hospital. On July 19, 1993, with Mom, Tommy, and me by his side, Daddy passed away at age eighty-four.

Walking back into my childhood home after that, everything seemed different. This man who had been my tower of strength, my totem for morals and ethics, and since the day I was born one of my biggest fans . . . he was gone. Daddy loved music—Sinatra, Tony

Bennett, and Nat King Cole were his favorites. But when I walked through that door there were no familiar songs to greet me. Only a void. The house seemed suspended in a peculiar half-light, as if time had lost its ordinary sequence. It echoed with his absence.

In our family, Mom was the free spirit, while Daddy was the watcher. He was the man with the plan. The worrier. With him gone, we'd lost our protector. When he died, I took over that role. It was now on me to stay watchful, with a special eye toward not just our family's safety, but our happiness. Our cohesion. Daddy always seemed to be made of something sturdier than other men. That's one of the ways I have carried my father forward in me. He is also in my posture, my decisions, my refusal to cut corners. Parents do not ever leave us. They settle into us. They become the architecture of our conscience. Even now, I hear his voice when I am tempted to compromise on what matters.

Brad understood better than anyone how much my father meant to me and how much I missed him. But he was far away in Chicago while I was grieving in Los Angeles.

A few years into our relationship, we briefly discussed my moving east, but that was a nonstarter. Gaston and Spencer-Margaret were happy in their respective schools with their friends and their lives. Tony and I had established a workable rhythm of co-parenting, and understandably, he'd never have been okay with me taking the kids so far away from him. We agreed that the most important thing was to, as much as possible, keep our children grounded.

Brad understood that my life was about my children. Even if he and I got married one day, they would still be my top priority. At eleven and eight, they were at ages when they needed to be near their friends on weekends. They had their own social lives, activities, and classes. It seemed like we had a birthday party to attend every weekend, so it wasn't all that simple for me to fly to Chicago to see Brad. The burden of commuting fell on him, and, God bless him, it was a burden he was willing to bear (he freely reminds me of this to this day if he suspects that I'm questioning his devotedness—which I never am). He'd leave Chicago as soon as he got off work on Fridays and be in Los Angeles in time for dinner. On Sundays, he'd catch the red-eye back to Chicago. All told, he was jet-lagged for half of every month! But we were happy and made the best of the situation.

During all those years, Brad got to know the kids in small doses, on weekends and vacations to Aspen and Hawaii. We always got two rooms: one for Brad and Gaston, and one for Spencer-Margaret and me. I wanted the kids to grow up with respect for the institution of marriage and see it as something special.

The years went by like this, and before we knew it, Brad was a constant in all our lives. He was there for the milestones—birthdays, holidays, recitals, camp visiting days. It was hard having a long-distance relationship, but it afforded us the time to all grow close naturally, and for the kids to get to know Brad on their own terms, something I think we're all grateful for today. As is Brad's way, he moved easily into the perilous and sacred role of stepfather. Love was not proven in grand gestures, but in daily acts: a ride to school, a question answered, a silence respected. My children, fierce in their loyalties to me, studied him closely, watching to see if he would hold. And he did. They found him steady and true. It was one of the most precious and important gifts Brad gave me.

While my family life took on a new shape, Kate was undergoing similar reconfigurations. She and her third husband, Tom Hart, an Aspen resort owner she'd met on a ski vacation, had divorced in

1993 after two years of marriage. Kate and Tom had talked about having a child, but the marriage hadn't held up long enough.

A short while after Tom and Kate split, she made a decision that surprised me. Single at forty-seven, she decided to adopt a baby.

She was paired with an expectant mother, and when the birth mom went into labor, Kate called me. "I'm going to the hospital now. I want you to come with me! I'm nervous."

Well, what's a friend to do? Of course I went right over. Not wanting to draw attention to ourselves, we put on hats and big sunglasses like we were going incognito on the Riviera. It was like *Charlie's* all over again, with our flimsy disguises that anyone could see through. It seemed some part of us would always be Kelly and Sabrina.

I was honored that Kate trusted me to come with her, and the entire experience, including its moment of comedy, was lovely. It was happier still when Kate asked me to be her baby's godmother.

Then, two years after we added a new member to the *Charlie's* family, we lost one.

In 1997, David Doyle died too young of a heart attack. He was sixty-seven. David was the humor on the show, and the only other cast member besides me who went the distance. For five years, he kept us balanced and on course, and I would miss him.

Like so much of life, those were years with both blessings and sadness. I'd endured some difficult losses, especially the heartbreaking passing of my father.

Brad had been with me through my father's illness, and when 1997 rolled around, our cross-country romance was somehow in its seventh year. I liked the world Brad and I were creating. There had been so many hellos and goodbyes, owing to our work and other commitments, but when we came together there was so much to share and so many stories to tell. There was nothing impulsive about our relationship! But that was Brad—loyal, steady, faithful. He'd taken on the burden of commuting in the hopes that someday we'd move forward to marriage. And I was finally (yes, finally!) ready.

But it wasn't just up to me. If I officially agreed to marry Brad, it would have to be a three-way decision, with Gaston and Spencer-Margaret having votes equal to mine. When we sat down and discussed it, Spencer-Margaret was all for it. They'd both become fond of Brad, but Gaston accepted Brad into our family a little differently. As the older one, he'd been more aware when Tony and I divorced, and though I'd tried to shield him from it, he'd had a front-row seat to the hurt I had experienced. He was protective of his mother. But he liked Brad, and he couldn't deny that Brad loved me well. "He'd never do anything to hurt you," Gaston said. That was true. And with that, the last vote was cast.

On October 11, 1997, at 5 p.m., Brad and I stood at the front of Westwood United Methodist Church along with our minister, Sharon Rhodes-Wickett, and were married. The simple ceremony included Reverend Sharon reading a beautiful passage from the book of Ruth, chapter one, verses 16 and 17. It was about unwavering commitment, symbolizing unity and a permanent bond. "Where you go, I will go, where you stay, I will stay." It was lovely, if ironic, given that Brad and I would continue to be long-distance for many years to come. But after seven years, we already knew the sentiment—that our lives would be inextricably linked, no matter where we were—to be very true.

I wore a pale-lavender silk charmeuse gown by Richard Tyler. Gaston, fifteen, gave me away. Spencer-Margaret, eleven, served as my maid of honor. All those we loved most in the world were there to share in this moment, whether in person or, in the case of Papa and Daddy, in spirit. We were surrounded by love. When we both said "I do," I felt the power of what we were doing, our future still unwritten. Whatever was out there, I had faith we would do it together.

Chapter Twenty-Nine

I was essentially a single mother throughout my children's early lives, trying my best to raise them on my own. But as challenging as it was, I wanted to do it all. To be able to pull everything together. I didn't want a nanny in there doing all the day-to-day basics with my kids—the little things that, over the span of years, are actually the big things. I wanted to be involved in their homework, what happened at school. I wanted to give them all of me. When I became a mother, I arranged my life around them.

I assumed my kids and I would stay close as they got older, like I had with my parents. But as they approached adolescence, I began to feel like I needed a passport to visit them. I didn't understand their breaking away because I had never done it with my own mother.

It was unsettling, feeling mystified by my children. I could no longer figure them out. They started to have their own lives, which in retrospect was very normal. For a period of about seven years, I remember asking "Why?" constantly, just hoping they'd allow me to enter into a discussion. But they were doing what kids naturally do, learning who they were, figuring things out.

I already tended to obsess about their well-being, so accepting this was a tall order. I felt at a loss at times. Over the years I began to understand that I could maintain my motherly vigilance, but I'd have to mix in healthy doses of surrender so I didn't suffocate them. I'll always want to know what's going on with my kids, and I'll always be there for them if they want me (and sometimes when they don't), but I accept that they need to live their own lives. And I'll keep saying that until I start to believe it.

In spite of what they might tell you, I'm much more open-minded and accepting than I used to be. Once, when Gaston was sixteen, we were driving somewhere or other when he let it be known that he'd gotten a tattoo—a small wave on his ankle to represent the ocean. But to me it looked huge. A tattoo! At sixteen! I stopped the car. "Gaston, get out of the car," I said.

"Mom!" he protested. "It's winter. I'm in flip-flops!"

"I mean it!" I said. "I can't drive with you with a tattoo!"

When I told my mom about it, she took it in stride, which was absolutely *not* the reaction she would have had if I'd done that at sixteen. Or ever. I got over Gaston's tattoo. I couldn't stay too mad at him. It turned out to be good practice for when he got the next one, and the next one . . .

Gaston's heart is arranged similarly to mine. I see so much of myself in him, with his loyalty and attachment to family. Like me, he wasn't always an engaged student. He took a gap year after high school. At the end of it we did a family cruise with my mother, and he shocked me by saying he wanted to go to college. Then he found his way to USC. It was a big day when he graduated—we couldn't have been prouder. You never know what path your kids' lives will take.

At so many times and in so many ways, I had to step back and tell myself: *These kids are not me.* If I could get another take on some of my responses in certain moments—a parenting do-over—I like to think that I'd play those scenes with a little more curiosity and less judgment.

But kids will also find a way to get annoyed with their parents no matter what. Again, it's their job. Regardless, I'm so proud of my kids, and I always have been. We've had our moments. The worst thing for me still is seeing either of them in pain. But even when things get messy and the world seems upside down, we know who wins the race: family.

When the kids were young, managing life as a mother was hard enough, but co-parenting had its own challenges. It's difficult to be on the same page with someone you don't live with. When all is said and done, Tony and I did as well as we could. Like many divorced men of that generation, who often preferred to let their ex-wives be the disciplinarians, Tony left most of the difficult parts of parenting to me. All I know is that I'd gone into parenthood romanticizing the idea of building a family and making choices alongside a supportive partner. That was not how things worked out.

For instance, Tony gave Gaston more freedom than I did, and when I tried to insist on some basic rules, it caused friction. Having two sets of rules can be confusing. Gaston and I had more than one argument about his father's more lenient rules. That's when I got to hear myself say, "Well, in this house, we do it my way!" May we all be so lucky that we live long enough to become our own mothers.

In sixth or seventh grade, Spencer-Margaret started going to Harvard-Westlake School, and around the same time, her natural spiritedness and independence were at an all-time high. She always had a point of view, and it didn't necessarily line up with mine. She needed to figure out how life worked on her own. She was stubbornly original. I found her personality complex, but in the best ways. She was the person who asked the questions no one else asked, keeping me on my toes. I had to step up my game to keep up with her. But while she put me through my paces, I never worried about her. Her personal compass of right and wrong was always on point. And she could always read me without me saying a thing; she knew what I was thinking before I even said it.

My daughter and I had our awkward years, as she reminds me often. Times when we were out of step with each other. She absolutely hated it when I took her and her friends to the mall in Century City. The other mothers would drop off the kids, let them hang out by themselves for a few hours, and then pick them up at a designated spot at the appointed time. That wasn't my style. I brought them to the mall and I stayed with them the whole time. Spencer-Margaret's eye rolls and groans did not dissuade me from my mission of being an involved parent.

Compared to her friends' moms, I was definitely more overprotective. It's possible I hovered. Spencer-Margaret would yell, "Why can't you be like the other mothers?" She favored the carefree parents who let things slide, who dropped off and picked up, who didn't ask annoying questions like "Where were you?" "Who were you with?" "What were you doing?" I cramped her style. I admit it! Unlike most of her friends' moms, I worked. I had responsibilities outside the home that took me away from my family. Maybe that was why I stayed at the mall, because I wanted as much time as possible with my daughter.

Spencer-Margaret has a way of expressing herself that's all her own. I think she describes her experience of me as a mother better than I can. After high school, she enrolled in the Tisch School of the Arts at NYU. She was in her first year there, and sent me this Mother's Day letter:

Dear Mom,

Ironically, the act of writing to you or even telling you, for that matter, the countless reasons that make you a truly exceptional mother is a very difficult task, being that it is not the first Mother's Day card that you have received. I worry that my words might suffer the sting of redundancy and hence lose the sincerity with which they are felt.

Over the course of my life, particularly in the volatile years of my adolescence, your love has been illuminated both in times of joy and in times of disappointment. The awkward years of junior high brought us the unknown lands of Century City, and being that you wouldn't let me wear a bikini until the age of 15, it was clear that you weren't going to settle for mere drop-offs in the valet without a fight. Hence, at fourteen, I began to fight for my cause . . . freedom. (A cause that would remain at the center of our mother-daughter struggle for subsequent years to come.) I must say, we both put up a good fight. Obviously, yours far more honorable and responsible than mine. But nonetheless, full of emotion and bizarre behavior on both sides. Harvard-Westlake brought a colorful buffet of Mothers. The introduction of such adult characters revealed to me the numerous ways in which a mother raises her daughter, and of course, I favored the ones who exercised a more carefree ideology. The utilization of such ideology, as we both know, was something that was never and will never be utilized in the vicinity and the surrounding areas of our home. Looking back to these times and thinking how you probably wish the subject of our fighting was that of Century City, I can't help but think how much easier it would have been for you to have abandoned your rules and simply dropped me off in the parking lot and let another mother pick me up and bring me home. However tired or unappreciated you felt, you never did this. Just as I fought for my cause of freedom, you fought for a cause of love, and that makes you the best and most unique mother in the world. It's hard to label something as perfect, but it's not hard to see that your intentions as a mother are. You know I am a staunch disbeliever in comparisons, but in this letter, I think their use is appropriate. When thinking about my friends' mothers, it is not a deep, dark secret that none of them work. These mothers' actions are not evil, but they are selfish by their nature. You, on the other hand, have never experienced such a day in your life; a moment does not pass without your intervention as a mother. And although this is at times annoying, it is something to be praised. In truth, I think you are a bit cuckoo, but if you weren't, your love would lose the authenticity that makes it what it is. You have always been authentic, even though it made you the uncool mother.

You never stop at trying to help and give knowledge to your children. If you didn't hold the answers to such questions, you would explore the world until finding them. And in this respect, you are the only person I have ever encountered that is ready to willingly give. The downside to this, is that because you are so generous by nature, it is easy to forget that such qualities in man are a rarity. You don't give because you think it's right. You give because it's embedded in your soul.

My definition of love is not one of eternal words, it is defined by those I love and those who love me back; thus, I define love with two simple words . . . my mother. In remaining faithful to my close companion late, I wish you a happy belated Mother's Day. And anyway, you should have a Mother's Day all to your-

self because you are unlike all the rest of them. . . . Don't eva forget it lady.

Spencer-Marg your procrastinating and loving daughter.

Twenty years later, now a mother herself, Spencer-Margaret gets it too. She is now just as loving and protective with her daughter, Bea, as I ever was with her. In my eyes, Bea is the luckiest little girl in the world. She gives Bea a safe and magical place where she is able to live up to her full potential. Spencer-Margaret's love is pure, sensational, and life-giving.

Chapter Thirty

In spring 2002, Spencer-Margaret was accepted into a highly selective four-week summer intensive course for dance at the Ailey School in Harlem. It was quite an accomplishment, and I was so proud of her. My daughter had a quality you couldn't teach—an innate talent as a dancer. I recognized in her something that did not belong to instruction. She moved like a cat with thrilling quickness, lightness, and grace, and with more assurance than most girls her age. Of course, I was thrilled that she loved dance as much as I did—and she was brilliant at it! But she was too young to live in New York for a month by herself, so we thought it would be fun for all of us to go with her and spend the summer in the city. The idea of stepping back into New York's unique energy made me nostalgic for my twenties.

We started planning the trip right away. I had so much to do before we left, and I made a long list. One task was to get my annual mammogram. On June 11, I went in for a routine scan, like I'd done dozens of times before. The procedure was identical to the previous years, but this time, my doctor didn't just send me home afterward. "I see a few little things," he said. "I'd like you come back tomorrow for some further tests. I don't think it's anything, but we have to look."

I knew and respected my doctor, Dr. Armando Giuliano. Brad had trained with him, and he was a close friend and an amazing doctor, having pioneered the sentinel node biopsy. I thought, *Okay, no big deal. This happens all the time.* If he wasn't alarmed, I wouldn't be either. I was glad he was being thorough. My family didn't have a history of breast cancer, or any cancer. I scheduled an appointment for the next day and got on with my to-do list.

On June 12, I showed up at the imaging center and was told that I'd be having a "core biopsy." I had no idea what that was, but if it would rule out breast cancer, I was all for it. I was eager to get it over with. For the procedure, I was face down on a table, one arm over my head, the other pinned to my side, with my breast in a hole—a posture that was both clinical and strangely vulnerable (and exactly as comfortable as it sounds). For an hour, they sliced into my breast and took photographs. They didn't give me any anesthesia because I had to be alert enough to stay very still. It was excruciating. While biting my lip so as not to cry, I took cold comfort in hearing the technician say, "This isn't cancer." Part of me thought, *Great!* while another groaned, *Then why are you putting me through this trauma?!*

It didn't end there. The next day I had to get a needle biopsy guided by ultrasound (less invasive but still painful). When that was over, they told me I wouldn't need any further testing. Thank God. I had things to do! I'd have to return the following day, though, to get the results.

The next day I arrived as scheduled and was taken aback when Dr. Giuliano's assistant asked me, "Did you come alone today?"

"Yes . . ." I should have realized her question was an indication of something, but I didn't. She said nothing further.

In his office, Dr. Giuliano said, "I have some good news and some bad news. What do you want first?"

I was at a loss for words. How do you answer a question like that?

"Well, you have breast cancer," he said. "The good news is that it's a small tumor. We caught it early."

In a heartbeat my entire world shifted. Hearing the word *cancer* makes you unable to see anything clearly. It's a short word, just two syllables, nothing more. Yet it opened into something unmanageable—fear. It was as if meaning had been temporarily suspended. I didn't know what to think.

Right away I asked, "Am I going to be here for my kids?"

He nodded. "Yes."

But that word bounced right off me. I was in the dark, squinting into the glare of possibility and sensing its enormity. If that day had unfolded as planned, it would have been just like any other, but now, so many years later, it is clearer than the present. What I remember most vividly is the fear. Anxiety over unfamiliar words like *core biopsy*, *sentinel nodes*, *margins*, and *radiation*. Apprehension over admitting to my family that I was terrified. Panic that I would never see my children grow up. That day, June 14, taught me a lesson that I have incorporated into my life ever since: Never get screening results by yourself. Always have someone with you—a friend, spouse, mother, sister, anyone. A person who can think clearly and take notes, because at some point, you might lose the ability to process or remember the words coming out of your doctor's mouth. A few phrases penetrated my mental fog—*estrogen-positive* and *caught early*. But that was about it. After he said "cancer," my mind was devoid of anything but fear.

Life is a sudden thing, for better or worse. I never dreamed I was going to have breast cancer. I looked fine. I was fifty-six, in great shape, full of energy. It couldn't be real. But the images and printouts on his desk said otherwise.

I looked at him. "Well, I'm taking my daughter to New York for the summer and I need to get this done right away, so . . . just take my breast off."

"Hold on, that might not be—"

"No, I'd like to meet the surgeon today. I want my breast off. I don't care. It doesn't matter to me. I want to be there for my children."

Dr. Giuliano was calm. I'm sure he'd become accustomed to all kinds of reactions. "Well, let's think that out," he said. "Are you sure you want me to choose your surgeon?"

"Absolutely. I just want this over." I was still fixated on my pre–New York checklist. In my mind I'd already added "get mastectomy" to it. I just wanted the cancer gone so I could move on. I know it's not the most rational response, but again, that's what hearing the word *cancer* can do to you.

The doctor urged me to slow down and talk it through. If I was going to have a mastectomy and reconstruction, I needed a plastic surgeon. But for a lumpectomy, Dr. Giuliano could do the procedure himself. These things had to be considered carefully. I couldn't just pick a name out of a hat. Interviewing multiple surgeons? How in the world would I have time for that? I lurched out of the office feeling numb and overwhelmed.

As soon as I got in my car, I called Brad in Chicago.

"Hi!" he said. "It's—"

"I have breast cancer," I blurted.

"No, you don't," he said with his typical certainty.

"Yes, I do. And I'm getting a mastectomy."

"Wait a second, you might not need to do that! The studies show a lumpectomy with radiation . . ." He wasn't listening to me. Brad is impervious to anxiety, and he's a problem-solver to his core.

I said, "It's easy for you to say that I don't need a mastectomy. But I don't want it to come back. I'll do whatever I have to do to get rid of this for good. Call Dr. Giuliano if you don't believe me."

"Okay, I'm calling Armando. I'll call you back. I love you."

As I sat in the car, reality hit me. You are a mother with a marriage, a career, and you hear that word and right away you're a little kid again, wanting someone to make it all better. I dialed my mom, and when I heard her warm "Hello?" I thought, *Thank heavens I am still someone's daughter*. There was something about hearing my mother's voice in such moments that took me to a simpler self. I believed that she could make everything okay.

"I have breast cancer," I told her.

"Honey, you must be mistaken," she replied.

Why did no one believe me? "Yes, I do, Mom."

Somehow I broke through her denial. "Honey, I'm on my way," she said. Mom hung up with me and immediately called Tommy, who lived nearby. "We're going to LA," she said. "We're leaving right now."

"Mom, I can't leave this instant. It'll be okay if we go tomorrow," he said.

"You either come now or I'm getting on the plane without you," she said. Seems I have a bit of my mom in me.

Mom was eighty-eight at the time and no one wanted her to travel alone, so my brother dropped everything and went to pick her up to go to the airport. Within two hours they were on their way to me, and within ten they were on my doorstep.

The funny thing is, all these years later—twenty-five, to be exact—I have never known anyone who could take away my fears like my mom. In her company, everything had an answer. She had a force all her own. She reassured me that I was going to be fine, and that we'd get through it together.

The next day, Saturday, I gathered the kids to tell them what was going on. Gaston was twenty and Spencer-Margaret was sixteen.

The look on their faces was like the earth had suddenly stopped spinning. Gaston always thought I could make the world bend to my will and dance to my whistle. He kept waiting for me to say the words he so desperately wanted to hear: "I'm going to be fine." I had the power with him that my mom had with me—the ability to make his worry go away. He needed to believe that I was going to be okay.

Spencer-Margaret burst into tears. She was pure emotion. Her reaction was immediate and unguarded. I'd been warned by my doctor that this diagnosis was often hard for teenage daughters to hear. Through her tears, she said, "I'm not going to New York."

I said, "No, no. I'll have surgery before we leave, and then I'll do any other treatment there. Whatever I have to do, you're going to New York."

"No, no, no," she insisted. "You need to be with your doctor."

"Nope, we're going to New York." I was convinced that I could do both. She could go to Alvin Ailey and I could go with her. She was sobbing hysterically, but she had more good sense in that moment than I did. Seeking a distraction and a compromise, I said, "Look, let's go shopping. We'll get some leotards for New York."

"I don't want to go to New York. I don't want to shop!"

My daughter wasn't taking the news well. That day, I learned another thing I have never forgotten: Cancer is a family disease.

Eventually Spencer-Margaret agreed to go shopping. As we made our way along Rodeo Drive, I moved with a heaviness that felt like I was walking underwater. She looked over at me and saw it right away. She hugged me and wouldn't let go. Another mother passed by and saw us. "Wow," she said. "My daughter doesn't want to walk down the street like that with me. You are a lucky lady!"

I smiled. "Thank you," I said. Little did she know.

When we got home, Spencer-Margaret once again declared, "I don't want to go to Alvin Ailey."

I said, "You need to; this is a wonderful opportunity. You got selected out of so many people."

"I'm not leaving you or making you get treatment away from home," she said. The look in her eyes told me she was set on this; she wasn't going to change her mind. In her resistance was clarity. There was no working around it. I felt crushed that my daughter was going to lose this incredible opportunity because of me. In time, I'd come to realize that she didn't cancel that internship only to support me. She needed to be as close to me as possible for her own sake, and her own sense of security. We will always be dedicated ships sailing together, weather be damned.

When I was first diagnosed, I had never heard about the different types of biopsies, or the rationale for choosing between a lumpectomy and a mastectomy. I didn't know anything about radiation or chemotherapy. I had to learn it all and get up to speed quickly to understand what was happening to me and what I was facing. Fortunately, as someone who needs to feel prepared, I had always been a researcher. My history of studying scripts and learning about my characters helped me research my diagnosis and treatment options. And I had a secret weapon: my husband.

If I'm a researcher, Brad is the same times one hundred. And as a doctor, he could explain it all to me in detail. Fear can be a bigger beast than cancer. I remember how much better it felt to gather the facts and understand my diagnosis. To go toward the fear. To understand what I was facing instead of it being something undefined that left me in the dark. Brad explaining everything to me was like turning a light on.

Years later, when I traveled the country speaking about my experience with breast cancer, I told women not to act impulsively like I had when I was first diagnosed and demanded a mastectomy. I was shocked and afraid, but being informed made me feel better. I tried to underscore for them that knowledge is empowering—it leads you out of the dark.

Another great source of information and support was my close friend Jan Perlow. She'd been where I was and I couldn't wait to talk to her. When I called Jan and said "breast cancer," she came running. Our boys had been best friends, but then they went to different schools and we lost touch for a while. Friends can come and go, and sometimes if you're lucky, they'll reenter your life and you'll remember why you loved each other. Jan insisted I get second opinions, lots of rest, and the best surgeon, which I had in Dr. Giuliano.

I also had two other close girlfriends I leaned on: Alana and Jill Wagner. Together with Jan we formed a club called the Ya-Yas. I had read the book *Divine Secrets of the Ya-Ya Sisterhood*, by Rebecca Wells, and I loved it. The friendship those girls shared really was unbreakable.

I would have never found the courage I needed without my girlfriends. Their support got me through it. Their phone calls, their concern, their insistence on taking me to lunch after every treatment . . . I never went to radiation by myself. When I was told I needed a certain kind of bra, they took me shopping. Oprah Winfrey once said, "You want a friend who takes the bus with you when the limousine breaks down." For me, those friends were the Ya-Yas.

Four days after my diagnosis, I had a lumpectomy. Spencer-Margaret taped a heart-shaped note on my sleeve, and they let me keep it on my arm during the surgery. Dr. Giuliano performed the procedure, as well as a second surgery two days later because they hadn't gotten clear margins the first time around. My lymph nodes were negative, which put my cancer at Stage 1. During this time my husband, children, mother, brother, and closest friends were ever at my side.

My three-inch scar would fade quickly and become barely noticeable. The mark that cancer left on my mind would stay. The memory of breast cancer is a peculiar creature. An eccentric curator, I still look back on that day, although not as often as I once did. I don't want to live looking over my shoulder.

Since we weren't going to New York, we decided to take a family trip to Paris and London after my surgery. When we got back, I'd start radiation treatment. (I didn't need chemo, and I thank God every day for that.) We had a lovely time, and I could not stop smiling. The cliché was true: Having the life scared out of you makes you appreciate your many blessings even more.

On the flight there, a little girl who was just a toddler had a seizure, and the flight attendant called out, "Is there a doctor on the plane?" Brad sprang out of his seat and rushed to help, and thank goodness. He continued to care for the child for the rest of the flight, holding her in his lap until we landed. His fast action drew the attention of everyone on the flight, including a woman who recognized me. I recognized her too. It was Denise Di Novi, a film and TV producer who'd worked on classics including *Heathers*, *Practical Magic*, and several Tim Burton movies, among them *Edward Scissorhands*, *Batman Returns*, and *Ed Wood*.

Denise came over to me and we chatted briefly. Out of nowhere, she said, "I'm producing a new TV series called *The District*. I'd like you to join the cast—would you think about it?" The show was a prime-time crime drama about a police chief in Washington, DC.

I hadn't worked on series TV for a while, but I said, "Yes, absolutely. I would love to read the script."

She sent me the script and I loved it. I became a semiregular for two seasons, playing District Attorney Vanessa Cavanaugh, a love interest for Craig T. Nelson as Chief Jack Mannion. Craig was skilled and enthusiastic, and his presence on the set elevated the scene. He had a sense of when something worked, and if it didn't, we would stop, go to the table, sit down, rewrite, and try it another way.

Working on the show was a godsend. Having to show up for work forced me to pick up my pace. It reminded me that I didn't have time to feel sorry for myself. *The District* was my chance to get back into the game.

I worked on that show throughout my radiation treatments. Everyone was incredibly kind and patient with me. When I had to leave early, they let me go, no questions asked. *The District* turned out to be a wonderful, positive thing in my life that mitigated the big, scary thing I was dealing with.

My radiation schedule was demanding. I received treatments with Dr. Leslie Botnick in the Valley, a thirty-to-forty-minute drive each way from my home. I made that drive Monday through Friday for six weeks, followed by a weeklong boost a few months later. Before they zapped me, first they had to get a mold of the breast. Then they mapped out where to aim the radiation and gave me a tiny tattoo for guidance. (There's got to be a bit of dark humor in that, considering I once tried to kick my son out of the car for the trespass of a tattoo.)

Before my first treatment, the doctor warned me: "You're going to be very tired." But I flew through it. I was excited about *The District* and had a new lease on life. The treatments had purpose. I understood what was going on and why it was a good thing. I never said, "Why me?" I said, "Thank you!" I knew I was lucky to be there, lucky for everything.

The secret sauce for me was staying busy. Doing a lot kept my energy up, so I decided to get even busier. I launched a furniture line. I know it sounds crazy to pile on the work, but I felt really good. It helped me. Onward and upward, as Papa always said!

So when another wonderful opportunity arose, I didn't hesitate to say yes.

Chapter Thirty-One

In 2000, Drew Barrymore, Cameron Diaz, and Lucy Liu captured the tone of the original *Charlie's Angels* series in their reboot film. I liked the movie and its message—how it understood that, at its heart, *Charlie's* was about the bond of friendship—and I loved Drew.

Two years later, Drew and company were making a sequel called *Charlie's Angels: Full Throttle.* She approached me about doing a cameo. I readily agreed, radiation be damned! I had one scene with Drew in a bar. Her character was feeling down about her contributions to the Angels team. I appeared as a backlit vision, a hallucination, the spirit of Kelly Garrett, to motivate her to buck up and get back on the horse, essentially. The entire scene was no more than two minutes, but it took a whole day to shoot. (That was night and day from the *Charlie's* of old, where we shot several scenes per day.) I loved how the scene turned out. It was beautifully photographed, and it was perfect for my character. Gaston, Spencer-Margaret, and I went to the *Full Throttle* premiere and had a blast.

Staying so engaged with life through my treatment was an enormous help. It underscored the fact that life would go on. It already was!

At first, I didn't want to go public with my diagnosis. I thought it was a private matter between me and my family. But an article came out in the *Star* that outed what I'd been going through, citing an anonymous source. The source could have been connected to the radiation center, the doctor's office, the hospital, or someone else in my orbit.

It was hard to keep news like this under wraps. But I was so incensed at having my privacy violated that I was willing to pay to find out what had happened. My agent put me in touch with a private detective named Anthony Pellicano, a well-known, rather shady character on the periphery of Hollywood. I said, "I really need to know who did this because I've told no one. And if I were going to put it out, I would have wanted to do it in a certain way."

He said he'd be in touch and called me back soon after. He said, "I hate to tell you this. It was your assistant, Alana." With a Brad-sized level of certainty, I declared, "That's ridiculous. I know it's not Alana."

He said, "Okay, I know people at the *Star*. I'll call them."

A day later, he got back in touch and said, "The source is Tony Richmond."

Also not true. In the end, I never found out who leaked the information, but soon after this whole debacle, Pellicano was arrested for a host of offenses.

Regardless of the source, it was my story to tell, not someone else's. I decided to take control of the narrative and opened up about my cancer journey in the January 18, 2003, issue of *TV Guide*. When I publicly joined this club—one you never want to be a member of—I found an enormous community of love waiting for me. When the news came out, people I knew reached out to say "Me too." Strangers on the street came up to me and said, "I've had breast cancer"—or their mothers, sisters, daughters, or friends—and suddenly, we became friends. That made such an impression on me, how much it helps women to talk about what they've been through, even to a stranger.

The more women I spoke to, the more I emphasized the importance of educating yourself about your options. I was inspired to become an advocate for survivors through a few organizations, namely Susan G. Komen for the Cure, the John Wayne Cancer Foundation, and the Strength in Knowing: The Facts and Fiction of Breast Cancer Risk campaign, a collaboration between the National Association of Nurse Practitioners in Women's Health and Eli Lilly.

With Strength in Knowing, I traveled the country for two years, speaking to women about breast cancer. One of the risk factors for many women is that they put themselves on the back burner, thinking, *I don't need to worry about this, I don't need my mammogram.* Early detection is the best way to survive breast cancer. With each passing decade, your chances of getting breast cancer go up. Even if you don't have a family history, you are still at risk simply by being female, and your chances increase as you age.

One thing that will always stay with me, ironically, goes back to those early days of *Charlie's*: The power of girlfriends can save your life. My family was absolutely there for me, but they were dealing with it too. Sometimes I felt the need to take care of my daughter and my mother and their emotions when I was sick. My mother actually fell into a depression over my illness and consulted a doctor about it. When he asked her what was wrong, she said, "I just don't know why it was her and not me." I get it. But that's why you need people outside your immediate circle to help lift you up.

Gratitude helps too. From day one, I just kept saying, "Thank you, God. I'm still here. I'm going to watch my children grow up. I'm lucky." Twenty-five years later, I'm still saying it. And I even say thank you for that initial fear, because it propelled me to learn.

Chapter Thirty-Two

In June 2006, at age eighty-three, Aaron Spelling suffered a catastrophic stroke. Five days later, he died peacefully at his 56,000-square-foot Holmby Hills château.

I learned of Aaron's passing like the rest of the world, on TV, but I'd had a sense that it was coming for a while. Even before the stroke, he'd become reclusive. Aaron had given the world so much, I think at that point maybe he just wanted peace and privacy.

No question, Aaron lived and died a legend. He'd produced more than five thousand hours of television across more than seventy shows. We always joked that ABC stood for Aaron Broadcasting Company. Aaron was a true friend and the most generous producer I had ever worked with. He helped me and my family personally as well. When I was applying to grade schools for Gaston, I loved the idea of John Thomas Dye, but they had a reputation for not admitting the children of actors and celebrities. Aaron's children went there, though. He called the headmaster on my behalf and told him, "Jaclyn Smith is somebody you should take seriously. She's going to be an active participant in your school." I was thrilled that both my children were admitted, and I certainly lived up to Aaron's promise that I would be an enthusiastic presence in every aspect of school life (much to the chagrin of my children, at times). Aaron always went beyond the call of duty for me. I was going to miss him.

Kate, Farrah, and I were invited to do a special tribute to Aaron at the 58th Emmy Awards on August 27, 2006, two months after his passing. The tribute would have two parts. First, Joan Collins (*Dynasty*), Stephen Collins (*7th Heaven*), and Heather Locklear (*T. J. Hooker, Dynasty, Melrose Place*, and the TV movie *Rich Men, Single Women*) would talk about working with him. Then, as a big surprise, the original Angels would walk out onto the stage together. The Emmys would be the first time we'd appeared on television as a threesome since the late 1970s.

Naturally, the producers wanted us to come in early the day of the show for a rehearsal. But Kate was against it. "We don't need it!" she said.

I called her right up. "Are you kidding? We're going to be on live TV in front of millions of viewers. I want a rehearsal," I said.

"I'm telling you, we don't need one," she said. "We're professionals."

"Kate, you're being ridiculous," I told her, but she wouldn't budge.

I hung up and called Farrah. "Kate isn't going to rehearsal. You can do whatever you want," I said, "but I'm going."

While I was still talking to Farrah, the buzzer at my front gate rang. I answered it and it was Kate and her son, Taylor.

"Oh, fuck, I can't believe this," I said, still holding the phone.

Farrah gasped. "*What* did you just say?"

"Kate's here and she's not going to let this go."

"Jackie," Farrah said, "you said 'fuck.' I've *never* heard you say that before." She couldn't contain her laughter. "You know what? I love you. I have such respect for you right now. Ryan is going to love this!"

I had to laugh at Farrah's excitement over hearing me curse. But she was right, I never did back then. I guess that's what a few divorces will do to you! But Kate was driving me crazy. On top of it, I had a full evening planned and didn't have time to debate her.

I let her in. "Kate," I said before she could speak, "I don't have time to talk to you about this right now. I'm going to the rehearsal whether you are or not."

Farrah was still on the phone. "I'm going too," she chimed in.

Kate had no choice. "Fine," she sighed. "I'll go."

She showed up to the theater on time, but then she didn't want to rehearse her speech. It wasn't because she didn't think she needed to rehearse (though that was probably still true) but because she wasn't done writing it.

In the meantime, the poor director explained the setup, including the lighting, how we'd enter the stage, and the moment we'd come out. It sounded fine by me. But Kate had some thoughts. "We're not doing it that way," she said. "The houselights are going to go to black, and then there's going to be a spotlight behind the curtain. We're going to pose to re-create the Angels silhouette." She meant the iconic silhouette that was part of the show's opening sequence. Our appearance was top secret, a big surprise for the audience in the theater and at home. We weren't even allowed to walk the red carpet so that we wouldn't spoil the big reveal. Kate's idea was a great one—as so many of her creative notions were—in that it would have made quite a visual impact. The problem was, to make a spotlight silhouette work, you needed a total blackout in the theater, which would be confusing for the TV audience. They'd wonder, *Why did the screen suddenly go black? Is it broken?* Plus, a blackout wasn't really possible in that particular theater.

We kept going back and forth about it, which ate up our rehearsal time. With only a few minutes left, I quickly rehearsed my speech, then Farrah did hers. Kate just walked away, as she still hadn't finished hers.

On the night of the Emmys, the director and some of the production staff came to me. "We're taking Kate off," they said. On top of her throwing up roadblocks, Kate's speech, which she'd finally finished, didn't pass muster with them. It was obvious she still held a grudge against Aaron, and the event was meant to be a tribute. Instead, they wanted me to go on with Joan, Stephen, and Heather. But that meant Farrah would be left out too. Apparently they'd mistakenly thought she had taken up Kate's cause.

Finally Kate relented. "I'll rewrite it and you can approve it," she told them.

Backstage, Kate was still tinkering with her speech when the Emmy broadcast began, and she continued to make adjustments as awards were presented and accepted. I was starting to get anxious that she wouldn't finish in time to get her remarks loaded onto the teleprompter before we went onstage. At the very last minute, she stood there feeding her speech to the teleprompter operator as he typed it into the system. Brad had come backstage to check on me and noticed that my speech had not yet been entered. He took the liberty to alert the director. "Don't worry," the director said, "it'll be in on time."

The moment of our appearance was fast approaching. Then it was time.

As the original *Charlie's Angels* theme song played, clips of the first season splashed across the huge screens set up for the theater audience. Then a spotlight picked up the three of us walking hand in hand from downstage to the center-stage microphones.

More than thirty years later, we were no longer those three little girls who went to the police academy. We had watched each other get married, usher our children into the world, and endure divorce, loss, and health crises. We'd crossed the bridge from aspiration to celebrity under the unflinching gaze of the media. We had been through many things together, and the person who'd brought us together in the first place was Aaron.

"Once upon a time, there were three little girls . . ." Kate began, and then she went on to talk about Aaron's uncanny ability to recognize the hard-to-define quality that makes an actor a star. "That magical thing called chemistry," she said. Or as Aaron called it, "stardust." She'd first met Aaron when she was twenty-two. "I can still smell his pipe and the cologne that he wore every day. I can feel his arm around my shoulders and the thrill I first felt when he looked at me and said, 'Katie, you have stardust in your eyes.'" She praised what he gave to us all, "the gift of sixty minutes free from every care and woe."

Farrah went next. She said, "The three of us didn't experience the *Charlie's Angels* phenomenon like the rest of the world did. We experienced it from the inside, the eye of that televised storm, together. Fortunately, our friend and leader Aaron Spelling stood there alongside us, a much-needed calming influence. . . ." True words, indeed.

After Farrah finished, it was my turn. The teleprompter screen was blank. I turned to Farrah and said, "Oh boy, they don't have my speech up." I'm sure the front row could hear me, along with the sixteen million people watching from home.

Farrah said quietly, "We're on live television, Jackie."

Thank God for decades of acting experience. Thank God, too, that I had my speech memorized. After a quick beat I shook it off and jumped right in. "Miracles do happen, Aaron," I started. "I'm sure that he's looking down and smiling on us right now, knowing that he brought us together again as only he could."

Kate interrupted suddenly, saying, "We're reclaiming the brand, man." It was a not-too-subtle dig over the fact that she hadn't been compensated for her creative contributions.

I laughed it off and got on with my tribute: "Aaron loved actors, and we all loved him right back. He gave us breaks that changed our careers, and he did the same for so many others in our business. But in the end, it was Aaron's friendship that I'll treasure most. He was on my side without conditions. And Aaron was a true Texas gentleman who somehow found the time to call or write when it mattered the most. Whether it was a birthday, an anniversary, or you just really needed him by your side, Aaron Spelling always remembered. And let there be no doubt, Aaron Spelling will be remembered."

I think the mishap with the teleprompter worked out for the best. When you read from a teleprompter, you have to keep looking at it. It feels stilted, less heartfelt. Since I was speaking from memory, I could be more natural and connect with the audience. I truly felt the words as I looked out at everyone in the theater.

It was a bittersweet moment, and I was grateful for the opportunity to join so many in honoring such a remarkable man. I was grateful, too, for the warm response from the audience, even after all those years. And it wasn't just the theater audience who received us warmly. Our Emmy moment put us back in the public eye in a big way, including a front-page photo of the three of us on the cover of the *Los Angeles Times*. We may have lost Aaron, but apparently Spelling magic never fades.

Chapter Thirty-Three

Among the millions who tuned in to the Emmy broadcast and saw the Aaron Spelling tribute was Andy Cohen, then the executive vice president of development and talent at the Bravo network. He'd been involved in the creation of the *Real Housewives* franchises, the cooking show *Top Chef*, and the fashion design show *Project Runway*.

The formula for *Top Chef* and *Project Runway* was simple and irresistible: Talented people were given creative challenges and competed against one another for prizes and, they hoped, a boost in their careers. The hosts (Padma Lakshmi for *Top Chef* and Heidi Klum for *Project Runway*) interacted with the contestants and were part of the panel of expert judges who ranked the contestants' work. One contestant was named the winner of the episode, while another was eliminated, always with a catchphrase—for Padma, "Please pack your knives and go," and for Heidi, "Auf Wiedersehen."

A few weeks after the award show, Andy called me out of blue. "We saw you on the Emmys," he said. "We're creating a new show for Bravo called *Shear Genius*. It's a competition for hairstylists, and we want you to host it."

I had to admit that I didn't watch reality TV, though I respected *Project Runway* as a unique way to celebrate creativity while entertaining an audience. The way Andy framed it, the concept for *Shear Genius* was straightforward and had a lot of appeal.

My career had started with hair—with Breck ads. From all the time I'd spent getting my hair done for different films, miniseries, commercials, photo shoots, you name it, I understood the power of a good cut and color. Your hair frames it all. It matters. Even in acting, hair can help create a character. Our hair was a key aspect of our look on *Charlie's*. We each had our own do and it matched our characters' personalities, and girls and women all over America sought to emulate those styles. The way I saw it, the new show's real potential was in its ability to tap into this truth—that hair is important. It is a woman's crowning glory.

I also liked the idea that *Shear Genius* could be a launchpad for young stylists at the beginning of their careers. Who would be the next José Eber, John Frieda, or John Sahag? I'd worked with all of those legends, and I had nothing but respect for stylists and the skill involved in what they do. I liked the idea of celebrating and promoting the next generation.

I took a meeting with Andy in LA, and I liked him right away. What was not to love? He was warm and friendly, with a boyish eagerness about his work. He was smart, with a contagious enthusiasm that I found fun. But while Andy himself made a great impression, I wanted to be clear on what I might be getting into. My main concern was having to judge the contestants. Andy assured me that the competitors would be talented hairstylists who knew what they were doing. Plus, I wouldn't be the only judge on the panel. But as I'd learned early on, sometimes fear is a neon sign pointing toward opportunity. It could be fun to stretch myself.

I asked Andy if I might cohost with José Eber, my dear friend whom I'd worked with for so many years and who was undoubtedly one of the biggest names in the business. He would've been great on the show because of his delightful French accent and his out-there, funny personality. He was always warm, relaxed, with an element of delight in his manner. But José always took his work very seriously. I knew that, as a judge, he would be piercingly honest.

Andy told me that they had already begun talks with New York stylist and salon owner Sally Hershberger, creator of the Meg Ryan shag. Despite the price, she had months-long waiting lists at her salons. With those credentials, it made sense that they'd pursue her. I looked forward to seeing how the show would come together and what we could make of it.

On season one of *Shear Genius*, I believe we achieved what we set out to do. I got to deliver the good news to the winner each week ("Your look was shear genius!") and the bad news to the loser ("This was your final cut"). Did I ever get used to delivering the bad news? Not really, but I knew it was an essential element of the show.

We taped shows back-to-back-to-back, so the days were very long. *Charlie's* long! Fortunately, Sally and I had a great rapport, which really helped. She could take anyone's hair—curly, straight, what have you—blow it out, and make magic. We understood each other and had a good time together. On-screen, you could tell that we were genuinely enjoying ourselves.

When season one wrapped, I was happy to sign on for another go.

In season two, our taping schedule was more controlled, which was a relief. But there was also a surprise—Sally wouldn't be returning. I wasn't told why, but apparently she had some other opportunities. She was replaced by color expert Kim Vo. As I'd learned long ago, when you change the cast, you change the chemistry, and not necessarily for the better. While Kim certainly knew his way around color, he was not a hands-on stylist. He had a different skill set that shaped his focus and how he was able to mentor the stylists. Kim was very talented and a nice person, but I missed Sally. Once again, I had that feeling that I wished I could have gone the distance with the people I'd started with.

There were other challenges too. One episode of season two was called "Hair from Heaven," and contestants were asked to update the classic 1970s *Charlie's Angels* looks for the modern era. They seemed really excited about the challenge, and so was I! I couldn't wait to see what they'd come up with. Sadly, the stylists got it all wrong. Even now, I hate saying that, but it's true. Everything was sprayed and done. The poor models looked like they were wearing bad wigs. We brought in Kate Jackson as the surprise guest judge. (I wanted to bring in Farrah, too, but she was just too ill to do it.) At the end of the episode, I made a surprise announcement: "There are no winners this week."

Season two dragged for me. The show wasn't as enjoyable as it had been. It wasn't just the casting changes; the tone had shifted. The producers seemed to be putting their fingers on the scale, giving more airtime to the contestants they wanted to stay in the competition, regardless of their performance or talent. Winners and losers were manipulated, which just wasn't fair. The challenges were also unnecessarily hard, if not impossible. You can't cut and color hair and design an outfit to go with it all in an hour. To me, stressing out the contestants just to get them to have a meltdown on-camera was not the showcase of talent that I'd signed on for. There was little reality in the television show we were producing, and I thought that was a disservice to the contestants and the audience.

My choice was clear: The last episode of season two would be *my* final cut.

Chapter Thirty-Four

While *Shear Genius* didn't make the cut after two seasons, I had plenty of other opportunities to focus on. Around the same time as I was filming the show, Kmart expanded my clothing line to include bed and bath collections—towels, sheets, accessories—all coordinated and cheerful. When they approached me about the idea, I was all in. I'd always had such a love of décor, and it seemed like a natural extension of a successful brand.

It seemed natural to *me*, at least. At first, there was some hesitation in the C-suite about whether my brand would translate into the bedroom and bathroom. So they did some testing. Then, in a throwback to our *Charlie's Angels* pilot, they didn't believe the results, so they ran the tests again! What is it with decision-makers on my projects not believing the data? Maybe it was because, just like with the pilot, the testing came back through the roof. Not only did the products test well among women *and* men, but the recognition and reviews my brand got were on par with those for some of the biggest brands in the world, like Disney and Ralph Lauren. If that sounds like a brag, rest assured, I was as surprised as anyone. But with that assurance, the powers that be decided to move forward.

I'm delighted to say the new lines were received wonderfully, and they sold extremely well. Our first year alone, we reached $32 million in sales. Then we more than doubled that in the second year, and doubled it again the third! Incredibly, by our fourth year—at which point the lines included dishware and, to my utter delight, a Christmas collection—we had $236 million in sales. From zero to nearly a quarter of a billion dollars in just four years . . . that's a lot of towels and soap dishes! Going in, I had confidence in the products, along with my partners, but those numbers were nothing short of shocking.

What was also nice for me was that my brand had transcended just being a "celebrity brand"; it had become a beloved fixture at one of America's oldest and most reliable stores. In my mind, you just couldn't do better than that.

Yet not everyone shared my way of thinking.

When you're young, you think that one day your life will settle down and be predictable. It always seems to be just around the corner, but as I've found, that last corner never seems to come. Just when things are rolling along, all of a sudden something shifts. Relationships that you thought were as solid as cement can crumble and fade. Your needs change; your desires evolve. New things appear in your life that bring unexpected joy, just as old ones fall away.

My partnership with Kmart began in 1985. Beyond our shared financial success, I appreciated the relationship we'd created. From those early days with Joe and Deborah, we'd built my brand on a foundation of trust and a shared vision, and that meant a lot to me. Then we'd managed to keep it all going those many years, carrying it into new places and product lines. Along the way I'd met a lot of wonderful people and learned *a lot* about merchandising, production, design—you name it.

In 2013, Kmart/Sears (Kmart had purchased Sears in 2005) had a change in leadership. They brought in Eddie Lampert as the new CEO. I took it in stride—I'd been through five or six CEOs before Lampert. My first, Joe Antonini, had been a dream, and he was followed by a succession of other men who, even if I didn't agree with every aspect of their approaches, I generally respected. Through it all, my business and my relationship with Kmart stayed steady, and our numbers continued along a positive trajectory.

Imagine my astonishment, then, when at our first meeting, Lampert said to me, "You've made enough money, and now it's our turn." I was taken aback. Obviously, the company had made millions upon millions selling my product lines, or they wouldn't have kept doing it for nearly thirty years. But Lampert wasn't a retailer; he was an investment banker. While my lines were doing well, the Kmart he'd inherited was hurting due to changes in consumers' shopping habits. The way he saw it, belts needed to be tightened—including my stylish-yet-affordable ones.

Instead of taking a measured approach, he decided to cancel entire lines of products. He fired my whole team and announced that the company was going to go elsewhere for design and supply while continuing to use my name. I still bristle thinking about that. More than the slight to me, which was bad enough, my heart hurt for the many people who'd been callously let go, some of whom I'd grown very close to.

In my opinion, this is why you don't let the numbers people call all the shots. Lampert's lack of experience in retail showed in decisions that only served to make things worse. For instance, Kmart, like many retailers, had often relied on cross-promotions to entice customers to purchase products in different departments. (*Got a big night out? You'll want a cute pair of shoes to go with that delightful new dress!* Or, *Redecorating your bedroom? Don't stop with the bedding.*

Some practical yet elegant storage containers would help you organize that closet!) Lampert put a stop to cross-promotion and instead siloed each department, effectively placing them in competition with one another. Each brand had to fight for survival. If you wanted to help a lagging brand with a cross-promotion, you wound up hurting the successful product line in the process. The energy went from cooperative to cutthroat, and it was just a shame.

Within two years, Kmart's annual sales from my home collection alone dropped from a quarter of a billion dollars to around $70 million. Over the next five years, what had once been one of America's greatest affordable, wide-reaching stores was effectively destroyed.

I thought it might help if the company put some of my product lines in Sears as well as Kmart. Initially, management rejected the idea because it didn't fit with their plan (or maybe it was just that they hadn't come up with it themselves). Finally, and after much persuading, they agreed, and I sold very well at Sears. Over the years I have learned to trust my instincts, about products and people. I'm no longer that naïve little girl who left Houston so many decades ago—I've learned a lot. I don't mind saying, I'm someone who's developed a lot of business acumen. Of course, I still have lots more learning to do—that will always be true—but when you're spearheading a successful brand with such diverse product lines in multiple markets, you're going to pick up a thing or two.

And I didn't just stick with Kmart, or fashion and homewares. I've launched a fabric line for Trend, a skin-care line (with my wonderful and wonderfully detail-oriented husband, Brad), and a wig line for Paula Young, with my dear friend José Eber. My favorite thing about that collaboration is how it gave me an opportunity to give back. Once a year, José and I would go to City of Hope and put wigs, donated by my line, on cancer patients there.

José would bring stylists with him—all of whom donated their time—and we'd give the patients a day of beauty, with new hair and makeup.

My longest-running charitable partnership is with AbilityFirst, an organization that supports children and adults with disabilities. I first got involved with them back in my *Charlie's* days; it all started with a little girl named Julie, who I fell in love with. Her mother had abandoned her, leaving her devoted father with all the responsibilities of care. That child could not have been sweeter or more optimistic. I took her under my wing, spending time with her and bringing her to family events. I've served as a celebrity ambassador for the organization ever since, now for more than forty years.

I was successful in getting Kmart to see the wisdom of selling my products at Sears, but that wasn't the end of my battle with leadership—the conflict continued. Something that especially upset me was how they changed my fashion brand. One of the hallmarks of my clothing line had always been meeting the needs of *all* sizes and shapes of women, and being consistent with sizing. That was very important to me. The new executives decided that my brand should cater to women of a smaller silhouette. They got rid of my plus-size options and only put sizes 4 through 12 in stores. Fashion is a passing thing, but style and elegance are forever. Simple lines allow a woman to move easily and can adapt to many sizes and shapes. My strength is to analyze the market and to respond by offering a collection that fills those needs. We were no longer doing that. No surprise: Sales fell off a cliff.

In 2018, Kmart/Sears filed for bankruptcy. Like a slow-motion train wreck, I watched the company that had been a huge part of my professional life and success, and that had taken up space in my heart, crash and burn. I stayed with Kmart/Sears until my contract ended in 2021, and not a moment too soon.

It was extraordinary, what Kmart and I had created—to take what started out as a celebrity brand and transform it into a real brand that would perform well for thirty-five years. I was lucky that Kmart had seen something in me those many years ago (just like Harry Abrams back in Central Park), but I worked hard to extend that luck.

I would miss Kmart, but I didn't mind the idea of dialing things back a bit. And that's what I *thought* I was about to do.

In 2022, freshly released from my contract with Sears, I was approached by the Home Shopping Network about a new partnership. I was at a point in my life where I didn't need to relaunch my design career. I had nothing to prove to myself or anyone. I was busy with my family and charitable work, with other product lines, and with entertainment projects here and there. But when I heard from HSN, I couldn't help it. I had such a love of design, it was like *The Godfather*—they kept pulling me back in!

And the need still existed: Women would never stop wanting comfortable, inexpensive, fashionable separates. So once again I found myself asking familiar questions, like "Where should the buttons go on this blouse?" and "How do we make this jacket ethically but at an affordable price point?" Puzzling over these issues—which in some ways have gotten even more complex as the years have gone on—and finding solutions gave me the same thrill as before, and I realized how much I'd missed the creative process and working with a talented team.

"Something totally different from Kmart" is how we promote the products. Instead of shooting ads or filming commercials, a big part of the marketing involves me going live on HSN to talk about the collections. That has been an eye-opening experience, to be sure. When I was with Kmart, I made store appearances. I shook hands. I loved the conversations and hearing about how customers used my designs in their real lives. At HSN, the televised conversation is between me and a host. To fill the time, I offer up anecdotes about things I wore in movies, how the past informs the present yet we constantly evolve, how the garments are designed and constructed, or how I wear them myself. It's hard work, talking about a white shirt for an hour straight. (Though I'll be honest, I do *love* a white shirt—so classic! I guess that means I'm in the right job.) I'll reach a point someday when I've exhausted my ability to wax poetic about cuts and fits, but not quite yet.

After a day of doing two or three hour-long segments back-to-back, I do have to wonder what keeps me pushing ahead. There's something in me that doesn't stop. My dad always told me to think ahead and have a Plan B. My branding work started out as my backup plan, and I'm grateful for it. It keeps me involved in life, puts me in a room with new faces and new ideas. HSN gave me a new challenge. I'm not a natural self-promoter, so I was more nervous than I'd ever been going on HSN the first time, on January 20, 2023. But I like going toward the fear and taking big swings, and I'm sure I'll keep doing it, whatever shape that takes in the coming years.

Chapter Thirty-Five

Shortly after the 2006 Emmys, when we'd honored Aaron Spelling, Farrah and I met up for dinner. I noticed she didn't look well. Her skin was pale and her famous hair was lifeless. But no matter how she looked or felt, she never lost her sunny disposition and her innate humor. Still, I was concerned.

I heard from Farrah again when she called me in September. This time, she had horrible news. She'd gone to a doctor, which led to testing and a diagnosis of anal cancer. She came to see me one night soon after and we sat together in my living room. Her initial reaction to hearing that word was the same as mine: "I don't have cancer. It's got to be a mistake," she said. Denial comes first.

But after she accepted the diagnosis, she was determined to fight. I knew that feeling too. You have a child and you're terrified to leave them behind. I also knew from my own experience that Farrah would have another battle. She'd have to fight for privacy while fighting to survive her illness.

Farrah and Ryan had been separated, but they reunited soon after her diagnosis. He'd had his own cancer battle years before, with leukemia. During Farrah's illness, he kept saying, "I would take it for you."

She would say, "Okay. Then give up your leukemia drug and let it come back." Humor even then. I knew she loved Ryan and I was grateful he was by her side. I recalled how once, back in the late seventies, Farrah and I were chatting on the phone and she said, "Oh, I have to go. My honey's here!" She said it in that cute little voice—pure coquette—and it was like I could see her legendary smile through the phone. Ryan *was* her honey. They'd been the love of each other's lives. As volatile as their relationship had been at times, she adored him, as he did her. He was at her side throughout her fight.

On October 8, 2006, exactly what I feared came to pass. The *National Enquirer* broke the news of Farrah's condition. What they printed was essentially just made up. One headline from December screamed, "Farrah Begs: 'Let Me Die.'" That never happened. Farrah's chemo was rough, but she never said that or felt defeated.

Her first course of treatment *was* aggressive—four months of chemo and radiation at UCLA Medical Center with a doctor named Gary Gitnick. And it seemed to work. On her sixtieth birthday, February 2, 2007, Farrah announced to the world that the treatments had been effective and that she was cancer-free. Her statement read: "In the face of excruciating pain and uncertainty, I never lost hope. I hope that my news might offer some level of inspiration to others who unfortunately must continue to fight the disease." Dr. Gitnick was also quoted in the press release, saying, "[She] has had a full and complete response to treatment."

I can't tell you how relieved I was to hear that she was doing well and that her prognosis was excellent. But Brad said, "I don't believe it." He wasn't sold on her being cured just yet. In his view, it was too early to tell.

Sure enough, four months later, Farrah's cancer was back. On a scan, her doctors found a malignant polyp. The news leaked again, and her doctors informed her that they suspected that a UCLA hospital employee had gained access to her medical records and might have sold the information to the *Enquirer*. The same hospital had fired over a dozen employees around that time for selling details of Britney Spears's hospitalization to the tabloids.

Farrah plotted her own sting operation, not telling her friends and family. With her doctor's help, she planted false information in her medical chart. Within days, the information appeared in the *Enquirer*, and a suspect was named. Frustratingly, the hospital didn't fire the alleged culprit right away, but she later quit and pled guilty to felony charges. Farrah wanted the tabloid to be charged with a crime, but that didn't go far. She went public with how violated she felt by her UCLA experience. Partially because of that, the then governor of California, Arnold Schwarzenegger, signed a law that would hold institutions responsible for securing their patients' privacy. If they failed to do so, they'd face hefty penalties.

I think Farrah's sense of betrayal by and disappointment with UCLA was one of the reasons she discontinued her treatment there after her recurrence. She called my house to talk to Brad about what he thought she should do next. He wasn't an oncologist, but he knew many of them. They talked for a while, and after they hung up, Brad started doing his own research, going through medical literature and speaking with experts.

The specialists in Houston he spoke with thought she'd need surgery that would have her wearing a colostomy bag for the rest of her life. He found a doctor in London who'd had success with medical and surgical treatment that wasn't as radical, and he left a message with Farrah urging her to get in touch with him. At that point, as memory serves, her cancer had not yet spread.

A few days later, she called to thank Brad for all he'd done but said she'd decided to go in a different direction. She was heading to Germany. Through friends, Farrah had found a doctor named Ursula Jacob based in a town called Bad Wiessee. Dr. Jacob had made a name for herself treating celebrities with supplements and ozone therapy. Over the coming months, Farrah would go to Dr. Jacob's clinic and to other German clinics—one in the Bavarian Alps, one in Munich. She also worked with Dr. Thomas Vogl, a medical doctor in Frankfurt, who gave her radiofrequency ablation to blast her new liver metastases. My husband was skeptical of her course of treatment, especially the clinics that offered her untested "cures." But I knew what the word *cancer* did to someone. I knew how devastating it was for her or anyone to be told that radical surgery was her only chance. She thought she had time to try something else first.

Farrah ultimately came back to Los Angeles, where her condition rapidly declined. I questioned whether she would have lived longer or even been cured if she'd chosen a different treatment path after her recurrence. But we'll never know. As I understand it, her chances of beating it were slim from the start.

When she was back in LA for what turned out to be the last six months of her life, I got to see Farrah and spend more time with her. She had been video-recording all her doctors' appointments for a future documentary about her cancer fight. She believed that documenting her experience might help others. As she weakened, Ryan and our friend Alana Stewart took over the filming for her.

One evening, Farrah and Alana came over and they wanted to record my conversation with Farrah. I didn't understand why it was necessary. "I don't want to be filmed," I said. I was emotional.

But Farrah insisted. "Film her."

I didn't get it then. But now, I see that those recordings—what ultimately became a documentary called *Farrah's Story*—opened people's eyes to the brutal truth of what she went through and showed her strength throughout the ordeal.

Farrah said to me, "You know what, I never thought I'd get this. Maybe heart disease, maybe breast cancer like you. Never this." When she broke down and cried, I cried too.

She became increasingly tired and sick. I would visit her and bring her a Pinkberry frozen yogurt, which she loved. When she was in pain, I'd rub her feet.

One day I picked her up for acupuncture, hoping it would lessen her pain and decrease the swelling in her legs. Farrah was running a little late and I had to drive faster than usual to get there on time. She braced in her seat. "Is my driving scaring you?" I asked.

"Not at all." After a pause, she said, "I have to tell you, Jackie, I wouldn't have missed this time with you for anything. It's the best thing for me. Thank you for being here."

Once the session was over, Farrah told me the acupuncturist had said to her, "You're going to get well, I know it." Farrah seized on hopeful words from anyone and took them to heart. When she left the session, her mood was light, and it turned out to be a joyful day.

I wanted to keep the good feelings going, so I said, "Come home with me for dinner."

"Okay," she said, "but I want to go home first."

"I don't want you driving by yourself. I'll take you home, wait for you, then drive you."

"No, no," she insisted. "I'm fine. It's just down the street."

A short time later, when she came over for dinner, she brought a German chocolate cake that she'd just whipped up!

We had a wonderful dinner, with her delicious chocolate cake for dessert. Then she said, "I want to go to your closet. I want to try on the shoes you were wearing the other day."

"Let's do it!" I said.

But her legs and feet were so swollen, she couldn't get her feet into the shoes. She struggled with them for a minute, then just gave up and offered a smile and a joke about Cinderella. Even with what she was going through, she was still a bright light.

"I'm going to get them for you," I said. "Better yet, take these and I'll buy myself a new pair." Nothing can match the treasures of common memories. Two girls trying on shoes, just like we did on *Charlie's* so many years ago.

Farrah was so depleted. She'd been so sick and weak, in and out of the hospital, losing her hair, nauseated. It made me sad to see her so diminished, but I was determined not to show it. She didn't want to dwell on her illness, and I made it a point to be positive. I did my best to hide how I truly felt. It was hard watching my dear friend struggle for her life.

I saw Farrah again on an early summer afternoon in 2009. I brought a Pinkberry to her house, then sat on her bed and rubbed her feet for hours. I told her I was flying to Houston because my mother wasn't doing well. Farrah understood that I had to be with my mom. "Don't worry about me," she said. "I'm going to get well."

When we said goodbye, we held each other close. I felt an energy pass between us.

That was the last time I ever saw her.

Farrah died on the morning of June 25, 2009.

As much as I loved Farrah when we first got to know each other, I realized the importance of being there and holding each other up at the end of her life. We were closest then, and I got to see a different side of her. We all saw the true depth of her beauty when she bared her soul and used her struggle with cancer to help other patients in their fight. She pushed beyond her personal pain to bring hope, enlightenment, and healing to the world.

I miss her to this day.

Before her passing, Farrah formed the Farrah Fawcett Foundation, which continues to raise awareness about HPV-related cancer, fund scientific research, and provide financial support for patients. Our good friend Alana Stewart runs it, and runs it beautifully. Years after her death, my friend is still fighting cancer and saving lives.

I will always be grateful that Farrah and I stayed present with each other in the last years of her life. I always admired how she engaged with life as a free spirit. She wasn't afraid. She wasn't locked in by convention. Her choices were always surprising, unexpected, and provocative. Heroic and generous to the end, in one of her final acts she opened a window into her last days through her documentary.

Soon after Farrah's death, ABC aired a special celebrating her life. In that tribute I spoke to Barbara Walters about my friend and read part of a letter Farrah had written to me. When I first received the letter, it made me cry.

It was Farrah's last Christmas. She sent me a gorgeous bronze sculpture of a woman's torso, perhaps hers. It has a very special place in our home.

Accompanying the sculpture was this letter:

> *First of all, I want to wish you, Brad, Gaston, and Spencer-Margaret, a new year filled with love, good health, and happiness. And to thank you for my beautiful Christmas scarf wrap. I love the color and it is so comfy soft. But most of all, I want to thank you, my dearest friend, and Brad for helping me take*

this ambiguous journey I have found myself on. I can't begin to express my deepest gratitude for your support, compassion, encouragement, love and understanding. And Brad, your never-ending search for knowledge and progressive out-of-the-box statistics. It has given me strength, hope, and helped me fight the fear. Fear of everything seems just around the corner every day. And it's my biggest test because I was never bothered by fear. I always felt that if I succeeded, that was great. And if something failed, my attitude was, What's the worst that could happen? A failure. So you just move on. But this fear doesn't work that way. So, dear ones, thank you with love and deep appreciation.

—*Farrah*

Talking about Farrah in that interview and thinking about our long friendship brought up so many memories. A favorite was when Farrah and I were interviewed about what we learned during the first season of *Charlie's*. At the same time, we both said, "We learned a lot about cursing!" It was thanks to Kate's pre-filming prep. Memories . . .

Of course my mind went back to the beginning, when Kate, Farrah, and I had a sisterhood that was felt by millions. On- and off-camera, the three of us were a team, and we were so proud of one another. Although our paths diverged, we were always part of one another's lives, a kinship that lasted. That's a gift. At the end of Farrah's life, we recaptured the spirit we'd had in our first year as friends. It felt special then, as it does now.

Chapter Thirty-Six

Life often goes in cycles. There are times (or perhaps just fleeting moments) when you're flying high, and those when you struggle to comprehend the grand plan, perhaps wondering if there even is one.

At the same time as my dear friend Farrah was making her own graceful exit from the world, I faced another unfathomable loss. My mother had been in excellent health until she was ninety. Even in those advanced years she was still the keystone that held our family together. Then she fell and broke her neck. Thank goodness she wasn't paralyzed. She had arthritis, and her cervical vertebrae had fused—perhaps that served as some measure of protection—but the doctors made her wear a neck brace nonetheless. It slowed her down and robbed her of her usual energetic pace.

From there, we noticed small problems—high blood pressure, some GI issues . . . Because I was ever vigilant when it came to my mom's wellness, I insisted on her seeing specialists, and that led to her being hospitalized. The more time she spent in a hospital, the worse she got. The cluster of little problems just got bigger, and her hospitalizations grew longer, with each new intervention weakening her even more. I tortured myself thinking that if we'd kept her home and hadn't overreacted, the problems might have resolved on their own.

Still, her spirit remained strong and she somehow maintained her kind, gracious disposition. At one point, when she was introducing me to her doctor, she said, "This is my daughter. I got the best daughter there is."

During a stretch when she was at home, I got her into her portable wheelchair and took her shopping. She continued to look amazing and was, as always, so beautifully put together. A woman came up to us and said to me, "I know you've been known as a beauty, but you do not compare to your mother."

That just made my heart light up. I thanked the woman and wheeled on. "Mom, did you hear that?" I asked.

She said, "That lady's crazy." We both laughed. We each wanted the other to have the compliment. Mom never liked comparing, but I knew that the lady was right. Even in a wheelchair at ninety-four years old, she was the most stunning woman in any room.

I was in Houston at my mother's hospital bedside when I learned that Farrah had passed. Mom was okay at the time, and she insisted that I go to Farrah's funeral. She asked her doctor to assure me it was fine for me to go, and he did.

I headed for the airport to fly to LA for my friend's funeral. Once the flight landed, I checked my messages. I'd received a call from Mom's doctor that she'd taken a turn for the worse. Immediately I turned around and flew right back to Houston.

When I arrived at the hospital, I was shocked to find my mother on a respirator. I'd left her just hours before and she was fine. Suddenly she had a tube in her throat and was in obvious discomfort.

Her doctor, Ronnie Sheena, walked me through their decision to intubate and showed me an X-ray of her chest. I pointed at the image and asked, "Why is that little white spot there?"

Dr. Sheena said, "They didn't tell you? They pierced your mother's lung when they put in a feeding tube. She couldn't breathe, and that's why she had to be intubated." I was furious that this had been kept from me, that the hospital had failed to reveal such a grievous error.

The respirator cost my mother her voice, so I took it on myself to speak, and speak up, for her. Her medical team suggested moving her out of the hospital and into a rehabilitation facility unless she showed immediate signs of improvement. I wasn't having it. I said, "You're not moving her. You pierced her lung. There will be a lawsuit. She is staying right here."

They didn't move her.

Once again, as in past times of fear and stress, I engaged my magical thinking, also known as OCD. I tried to send her healing energy and I sacrificed whatever I could think of, hoping that if I gave up those things, my mother might receive the reward. When someone you love is at their most vulnerable, you'll do anything you can think of to try to save them. I believed foolishly that my sacrifice could bargain for her life. Desperation and fear speak to you in the same way sometimes.

Weeks went by with Mom on the respirator. I held out hope that she'd recover enough to have the breathing tube removed so I could hear her lovely voice again.

During this time, Brad was a force of life for Mom. The word *defeat* never entered his mind. Like me, he refused to give up on her. We were at her bedside night and day.

She stayed on the respirator for two months. The whole time, the ICU team told us that she wouldn't come off the respirator, but Brad and her own team of doctors felt she could. So we waited for her to recover. I tried to make her as comfortable as possible. I rubbed her feet and legs, did her hair, and talked to her around the clock. She loved books, so I would read to her. I never left her for a minute. Did we do the right thing keeping her on the respirator? It's impossible to know. We were just trying to do our best for her, and so I went on praying while Brad and the rest of her medical team continued to search for options.

With no warning, Mom started to bleed around the incision site on her trachea. When you witness something like that, it eclipses the imaginable. I pressed the call button. They were there in a split second. Everything froze; time was suspended.

Then the doctors turned to me and said, "You have to let her go."

When the doctors removed her breathing tube, I was at her side, holding her hand. She knew I was there; I'm certain of that. And then it was over. She slipped away.

A nurse said quietly, "Your mom is gone."

I began to cry, and then that cry grew like a tidal wave inside me until I was crying at the top of my lungs. The nurse reached over to put a wet cloth on me and I didn't know what was happening. I took the cloth and threw it across the room, then ran out. And I kept running.

I ran because standing still was impossible.

Then something stopped me. *What am I doing?* I thought. *I need to be with Mom.*

I went back to her room, where Brad was waiting.

I was in shock. That my mother was gone was inconceivable. It felt out of line with the natural order of things. The world had gone suddenly and irrevocably wrong.

My mother's death, on August 17, 2009, was the most traumatic experience of my life.

For a long time afterward, I couldn't tolerate the dark. I had to leave the light on, or the TV. In darkness, I experienced the loss again.

Mom's passing left a fissure in my psyche. Even when I was grown and on my own with a productive career, anytime something bothered me, I looked for that familiar and safe place that was my mother. For the times that were simple. Mom's opinion was so important, it affected my own. So much of what happened to me in my career belongs to her. People often say, "I wouldn't be here without my parents," but that's true for me regarding my mother in a way that's difficult to fully articulate. She is part of everything I do.

Mom would join me on location when I was shooting a movie and we'd go back to the hotel and order room service, sitting on our beds, talking about the day and everything else under the sun. After every interview, I'd call her, wanting to know what she thought. In my younger years she was at every recital, watching me perform, along with the countless rehearsals I staged in our living room. She would see every school play multiple times, and when I performed at Theater Inc., a small theater in Houston, she'd come not once but through the entire run of the show. I would always look out into that audience, searching for her smile of approval.

Nothing will carry me away from her. Death cannot possibly make me forget her voice on the other end of the line: "Hi, honey, when are you coming home?"

When you lose someone you love, your foundation breaks apart. There's no level ground to walk on. You are blasted into emptiness. It hurts to be alive. The simplest things seem impossible, like going into a restaurant you had gone to many times. You feel something grip you, and all you want to do is run. Getting up, brushing your teeth, picking an outfit for the day, starting your car. *Where am I going?* Nothing seems to make sense. Food loses its taste. Colors are flat. All the beautiful memories deepen your loss.

At Mom's funeral, I lost my voice. It was hard to deliver my eulogy about how giving Mom was throughout her whole life, especially to Tommy and me. Because of her, my life was filled with a sense of place, of belonging and permanence. From the time I was a little girl, I realized the immensity of her gift to me. I couldn't bear to be anyone but her daughter.

I talked about how the example of her life taught me that it might be possible for a woman to follow her own path and carve out her own life. Even though she was a wife and mother first, she was an independent woman who was forthright and opinionated and followed her own beliefs. The only thing she wasn't objective about was Tommy and me.

When we made a few mistakes along the way, she would talk to us privately. And I never once heard her say, "I told you so." What she gave to me is what I want to give to my children. A safe place. Arms to hold them. Stories to hear, a history in progress.

After the funeral, I tried to put order to things, but nothing made sense. The only thing I do know is she is never more than a breath below my consciousness.

In time, loss becomes memory. It's not about strength but about endurance. Learning to live with it. It doesn't get better with time. There are losses you don't recover from; that's just the bottom line. Grief is not something you conquer but something you carry. It is nonnegotiable.

But in my grief, I still had to deal with practical matters. First and most importantly, Mom had a three-year-old poodle, Honeybun, who needed a home.

I then found out that before Mom passed she'd said, "I want Ellen to have Honeybun."

I thought she would have wanted her to go to Tommy, because Honeybun might be frightened of my royal poodle, Elizabeth. But that little dog knew her own mind. The minute my mom passed away, Honeybun glued herself to my side, and she was with me every day after. Anytime I was upset, she climbed into my lap or pressed her body against my side. I think she was the bravest, most courageous dog I have ever met in my whole life.

She was my soul sister. After all, we loved the same lady.

After Mom passed away, Brad started looking seriously for a job in Los Angeles. He was offered a research position at USC, which he took. In 2009, Brad packed his things and moved into the house.

For the first time in seventeen years, Brad and I were living in the same city, and for the first time ever, the same house. In a difficult year, there was finally cause for celebration.

The kids were grown and living on their own, and I was so happy to have Brad home. It was such a treat seeing each other every day—and, for Brad, to no longer have to commute! Finally, we could experience the joy of sharing everyday life.

As I've learned, drama may be fun on-screen, but in a relationship it's highly overrated. It was so nice to settle into the life we'd built together.

Chapter Thirty-Seven

As a kid, I always thought, *I don't want a boring life*. Mission accomplished.

The day I accepted *Charlie's Angels*, I had no idea how that one decision would drastically alter my life. I didn't realize I would be part of something people would still be talking about fifty years later. It's a rare gift for any actor to have an enormous hit. But there was no review, no response, that could tell us that the show would stand the test of time. And nothing to tell me how those friendships forged under hot lights and long days would form bonds that would outlast the applause.

An actor's life can be prescribed and demanding. Also privileged and fascinating. That journey you take as a celebrity can bring unknowns into your life you never dreamed about. The attention was disorienting, especially because it was hard to understand at first. I get why many around me turned to drugs and alcohol. When life becomes overwhelming—whether it's on set or off—you want to turn down those feelings, or simply feel nothing at all. Believe me, there were times when I wished I could have numbed out, but to me it wasn't worth the cost. So I had to learn how to hang in and be present with whatever was happening.

For so many, *Charlie's* is tucked into memory like a photograph that never yellows. The *Charlie's* chapters in this book are a love letter to those who walked with me, and to those who found themselves reflected in whatever story I was telling at the time. They are a remembrance of a beginning, and a reckoning with endurance. And they are an acknowledgment of every Angel who came after, wings beating against the limits the world tried to put on her.

But as you've now seen, there was life for me before that, and there has been much since. Through it all, my constant has been family. The people who know me have always mattered more than the people who know my name. Family has been the source of the greatest joy in my life—and the greatest sorrow. When you lose them, you are irrevocably altered. The entire world changes.

Life has rolled on. I'll start by talking about my children and grandchildren, because what proud grandmother wouldn't? In 2016, Spencer-Margaret gave birth to my first grandchild, Bea, followed a few years later by Gaston's daughters: Olivia in 2019 and Wren Jaclyn in 2023.

The experience of being a grandmother is unequaled. It's a whole other universe of caring. You'd die for your children. You'd give them your arms, your legs. You'd run in front of a train. But nothing quite compares to how you feel when a grandchild arrives, turning your own child into a parent. Not only is there a wonderful new being in the world, but that little person also holds the strings to your child's heart. You love them for who they are as individuals, and you also cherish them as your baby's babies. To make room for all that love, your heart has to grow and grow. It's like you get another chamber in your heart.

I've often said that perfection is an illusion, but I'll amend that now. Perfection is an illusion, except when it comes to my grandchildren. They call me Mimi. It was what Gaston and Spencer-Margaret called my mom, and now it's mine. Hearing it from those divine little beings makes my day.

Spencer-Margaret lives a stone's throw away in Santa Monica, so I get to see her and Bea all the time (though I'd still like some more!). Olivia also lives locally, with her mother, Julia. Gaston was lucky to inherit four stepchildren, and he, his wife, Bonnie, and Wren Jaclyn now live in Roundhill, Virginia. He opened a restaurant in Purcellville called the Local Cut and is in the process of opening a second. I am so proud of him.

A marriage ends, but treasures are left behind. A bonus from my marriage to Tony is my stepdaughter, Antonia, who is very much still a part of my life.

Brad and I have now been together for nearly three decades. I guess the fourth time's the charm. Honestly, in my mind he's really only my second husband. Those earlier relationships were so short and belong to a past so distant, I don't count them the same. In fact, I don't really count them at all. They say that we enter into the same relationships over and over. I didn't. Each of my marriages was very different. Tony was my first real connection, but sadly our relationship also gave me a front-row seat to how addiction can take from you what you love most.

Brad missed clinical medicine, so he took a consulting position at USC/LA General Medical Center in trauma and critical care and is a clinical professor of surgery there. He also still plays doctor-on-call for our family, friends, and pretty much anyone in need. He's always been generous with his knowledge.

I'm glad to say, I found my happily ever after.

It is a curious cruelty of the mind, the way it recalls certain moments with unnerving precision. I remember the call from my sister-in-law,

Charlotte. Her voice was low, hesitant, carrying the weight of something it did not want to say.

Then, without warning, she said, "Tommy died." I couldn't breathe; air was suddenly out of reach. It was as if my body refused the fact before my mind could grasp it. Tommy had been in rehabilitation after a fall, to help him build muscle tone. But he was improving and expected home soon.

Denial was a reflex. I asked Charlotte to repeat herself as if her words might change on a second hearing. But they remained. He had fallen and hit his head. Most likely he had tried to get up on his own without calling for help. He was always independent and never wanted to give that up.

Tommy was my first understanding of loyalty. We shared a unique territory, the same rooms, the same holidays; we loved the same beautiful people, and we grieved the same losses. When one of us forgot something, the other supplied the missing detail. He was the witness to my beginnings.

On February 15, 2023, I lost my brother. The keeper of our shared past.

Years ago, when Brad and I were in Texas, we went back to my old neighborhood, to my first house. Brad encouraged me to knock on the door and see if I might peek inside. Reluctantly and after much persuasion, I walked up to that front door. The current owners graciously let us take a look around, and while I was delighted to show Brad the house I'd so often talked about, I was also taken aback. It was much smaller than I'd remembered.

But I guess it's not the precision of our memories that matters; it's how we hold them. In my mind's heart that house is still huge, and everyone who once put their feet under that dining table is still alive. And they are, inside me.

I talk about remembering my childhood, but in many ways, I am still very much there. Texas gave me a way of perceiving the world. Its imprint is subtle but permanent, like an accent you think you've lost until emotion brings it rushing back. A simple *y'all* takes me home quicker than an airplane. Texas is my true geography. Its voices, its manners, its gentleness and resolve. Its coordinates by which I navigate, which make my world safe. Thanks to Texas, I grew up believing that people were, for the most part, good. The world was intelligible and, at its core, kind. I know I sound like that Goody Two-shoes again, but trust me, if that were true, I wouldn't have survived what I've survived.

When people talk about where they're from, it speaks of their past. For me to say my roots are in Texas is a present-day thing. Like the roots of a tree, that's where I draw my nourishment, my wisdom, my guidance.

Every day my entire history still animates me. I'm still the mother, the wife, the dancer who dreamed. Still that same girl who stood in front of the Warwick, crying when my parents left. I don't think those things ever leave you.

Celebrity has brought its gifts, but my true wealth is my family. My parents taught me that my worth is not measured by my success. My children taught me that love is the only legacy that matters. And life taught me that there is no such thing as a safe heart, only a willing one.

Through it all I have tried to be the best mother, wife, and daughter I could. And looking forward, I will continue as I always have.

Onward and upward!

Acknowledgments

There is absolutely no way that I would have completed this book without the patience and encouragement of Aimée Bell. She has a rare gift of listening in a way that makes you feel truly seen. Thanks also to her colleagues at Gallery: Jennifer Bergstrom, Jill Siegel, Caroline Pallotta, and Abby Knudsen.

Kelly Madrone, who helped breathe life into these pages. She understood not just the story but the heart behind it. She is talented and scrupulously prepared; plus, she has a genuine generosity of spirit.

Val Frankel, whose careful eye and relentless pursuit of truth brought clarity and precision where it was most needed.

Dennis Brown doesn't just research; he hunts for the truth with intention, peeling back layers others don't realize are there. What he found was a part of my past that was even unknown to me, and brought such joy. It is the kind of insight that shifts how you see the whole picture.

Janell Martin for running my day-to-day life without a whisper of complaint. Your enthusiasm, energy, and passion kept me on track throughout an emotional journey. With your unwavering support and laughter, we formed an unbreakable bond.

Jay Schwartz, his perseverance should be rewarded. A tender heart he keeps hidden, but I see it.

Alana Voeller, who probably knows my story better than I do. She understands loyalty as a calling. A bond that would outlast decades. Thank you for helping me select the photographs for the book and for photographing so many of them over the years.

I would not be able to function successfully in this world as a mother, wife, friend, and in my profession without my team at home. Peach, also known as my sister, Aleina, for her delicious meals, and Gaudy for curbing my OCD and keeping our home immaculate.

My parents, who formed the axis of my world, whose profound love and devotion have been my compass throughout my life. I miss them every single day.

Papa, whose selfless, gentle spirit is woven into every chapter of my story.

My brother, Tommy, my first co-conspirator in life's adventures, my partner in discovery, and a constant thread throughout my life.

Brad, thank you for loving me, Gaston, and Spencer-Margaret so fiercely. You are my partner in all things, my companion in quiet moments and loud ones alike, and a stepfather whose goodness sets a standard few could ever meet. You're my heart.

Gaston and Spencer, you are my reason.

And finally, to my granddaughters, Bea, Olivia, and Wren, you arrive like light through an open door, you are joy made visible, and every time you enter a room, you are so unaware of the magic you make.

And to the long-distance runners Charlotte and Mollie, a true connection to my past.

Illustration Credits

All illustrations are courtesy of the author unless otherwise noted.

Ben Martin: 1
Getty / ABC Photo Archives: 11
Charlie's Angels. Courtesy of Sony Pictures Entertainment: 12–14
Cinematic Collection / Columbia Pictures Television / Alamy: 15
Getty / ABC Photo Archives: 16
Getty / Bettmann: 17
Getty / Walt Disney Television Photo Archives: 19
Courtesy of MGM Media Licensing: 20
Ronald Reagan Presidential Library and Museum: 34
George H. W. Bush Presidential Library and Museum: 35
Getty / Ron Galella: 36
Coty Inc.: 37–38
Herb Ritts / Trunk Archive: 47
Getty / Jason Merritt: 48
Getty / Michael Kovac: 49